News as Entertainment

News as Entertainment

The Rise of Global Infotainment

Daya Kishan Thussu

SAGE
Los Angeles • London • New Delhi • Singapore

First published 2007
Reprinted 2008 (twice)

SAGE Publications Ltd
1 Oliver's Yard
55 City Road
London EC1Y 1SP

SAGE Publications Inc.
2455 Teller Road
Thousand Oaks, California 91320

SAGE Publications India Pvt Ltd
B 1/I 1 Mohan Cooperative Industrial Area
Mathura Road, New Delhi 110 044

SAGE Publications Asia-Pacific Pte Ltd
33 Pekin Street #02-01
Far East Square
Singapore 048763

Library of Congress Control Number: Available

British Library Cataloguing in Publication data

A catalogue record for this book is available
from the British Library

ISBN 978-0-7619-6878-8
ISBN 978-0-7619-6879-5

Typeset by C&M Digitals (P) Ltd, Chennai, India
Printed in Great Britain by Biddles Ltd, King's Lynn
Printed on paper from sustainable resources

To my wife Elizabeth, for all her love and unstinting support

CONTENTS

LIST OF TABLES AND FIGURES

ABOUT THE AUTHOR

Daya Kishan Thussu is Professor of International Communication at the University of Westminster in London and Founder and Managing Editor of the Sage journal *Global Media and Communication*. He is the author of *International Communication – Continuity and Change* (second edition, Hodder Arnold, 2006); co-author, with Oliver Boyd-Barrett, of *Contra-Flow in Global News* (John Libbey/UNESCO, 1992); editor of *Electronic Empires – Global Media and Local Resistance* (Arnold, 1998) and *Media on the Move: Global Flow and Contra-flow* (Routledge, 2007), and co-editor, with Des Freedman, of *War and the Media – Reporting Conflict 24/7* (Sage, 2003) and, with Katherine Sarikakis, of *Ideologies of the Internet* (Hampton Press, 2006).

INTRODUCTION

At a talk I gave to a group of journalists from around the world attending a seminar at Oxford University's Reuters Institute on the state of television news and its tendency to trivialise public discourse, I was struck by the response: virtually all the Reuters Fellows present found echoes of what I was describing in the television landscape of their own country. Of course there were differences of emphasis and degree in the extent and nature of the change, but not about the underlying theme which connected television news across countries: the deleterious effect of marketization on broadcast journalism.

Renowned journalist C.P. Scott, the long-time editor of the British newspaper the *Guardian*, remarked on the arrival of television in 1936: 'The word is half Greek and half Latin. No good will come of it'. Seven decades later, television has become the world's most powerful medium for communication and one which continues to evoke strong positive and negative reactions among its producers and consumers, its champions and critics. Despite unprecedented growth in the worldwide expansion of the Internet – in 2007 only 17 per cent of the population was online – it is television that remains the most global and powerful of media. The number of television sets in the world has more than tripled since 1980, with Asia recording the highest growth. Industry estimates show that more than 2.5 billion people around the globe watch on average just over three hours of television a day, on more than 4,000 mostly private channels. Since visual images tend to cross linguistic and national boundaries relatively easily, television carries much more influence than other media, especially in developing countries, where millions cannot read or write (Herman and McChesney, 1997; McChesney, 1999; Thussu, 2006a).

According to an international public opinion poll conducted in ten major countries in 2006 by GlobeScan in conjunction with the BBC, Reuters and the Media Centre (a non-profit think tank), national television news was the most trusted (by 82 per cent), while international satellite TV news was trusted by 56 per cent of those surveyed, who also deemed TV the most 'important' news source. In Europe, television remains the primary provider of information for most people, according to a report on European television produced by the Open Society Institute (Open Society Institute, 2005). According to research conducted by Britain's media regulator Office of Communication (Ofcom), television was by far the most important source for news (68 per cent) among British citizens. For international news, Ofcom noted, television has consistently been the primary point of information, with 72 per cent of the people saying it was their main source for world news (Ofcom, 2005).

If television is so important as a provider of public information, what is happening to television news, globally, becomes one of the key areas of concern, not only for those who study, consume or produce television news but for society as a whole. News is not merely a media product but a vehicle for engagement in the democratic process, feeding off and into domestic politics and international relations. The growing commercialism of airwaves as a result of the privatization of global communication hard- and software, the deregulation of broadcasting and the technological convergence between television, telecommunication and computing industries, have fundamentally changed the ecology of broadcasting. The satellite revolution has, as Lisa Parks argues, redefined the meaning and relations between television and 'the global', creating convergences between televisual and satellite technologies and necessitating an expanded definition of 'television' – one encompassing military monitoring, public education as well as commercial entertainment and public broadcasting (Parks, 2005). The general shift from public to a ratings-conscious television, dependent on corporate advertising and broadcasting to a heterogeneous audience, has implications for news agendas and editorial priorities.

With the globalization of television, the commercial model of broadcasting – with its roots in the United States and largely dependent on advertising – has become the dominant model across the world. In most of the former communist countries, as well as developing nations, the privatization of the airwaves has opened up new territories for transnational media corporations, as the generally discredited state broadcasters have lost their monopolies, generating a debate about the ideological imperatives of a commercially driven media system, dominated by a few extremely powerful multimedia conglomerates (Betting and Hall, 2003; McChesney, 2004; Bagdikian, 2004; Thussu, 2006a; Baker, 2007). One result of the proliferation of news outlets is a growing competition for audiences and, crucially, advertising revenue, at a time when interest in news is generally waning. In the US, audiences for network television peak-time news bulletins have declined substantially, from 85 per cent of the television audience in 1969 to 29 per cent in 2005, partly as a result of many, especially younger, viewers opting for on-line news sources (Project for Excellence in Journalism, 2006; Mindich, 2005). In Britain, the audience for current affairs programming had fallen by nearly 32 per cent between 1994–2001 (Hargreaves and Thomas, 2002).

As television news has been commercialized, the need to make it entertaining has become a crucial priority for broadcasters, as they are forced to borrow and adapt characteristics from entertainment genres and modes of conversation that privilege an informal communicative style, with its emphasis on personalities, style, storytelling skills and spectacles. Its tendency to follow a tabloid approach, its capacity to circulate trivia, blend fact with fiction and even distort the truth is troubling (Downie and Kaiser, 2002; Gitlin, 2002; Anderson, 2004). News-gathering, particularly foreign news, is an expensive operation requiring high levels of investment and, consequently, media executives are under constant pressure to deliver demographically desirable audiences for news and current affairs programming to contribute to profits or at least avoid losses. In the US, one major recent development has been the acquiring of major news networks by conglomerates whose primary interest is in the entertainment business: Viacom-Paramount owns CBS News; ABC News is part of the Disney empire; CNN is a key component of AOL-Time Warner (the world's biggest media and entertainment conglomerate), and Fox News is owned by News Corporation. This shift in ownership is reflected in the type of stories – about celebrities from the world of entertainment, for example – that often get prominence on news, thus strengthening corporate synergies (Bennett, 2003a). These are supplemented by the new genre of reality TV and its relatives – docudramas, celebrity talk shows, court and crime enactments, rescue missions. The growing global popularity of such infotainment-driven programming indicates the success of this hybrid formula. This media concentration has contributed to a tendency in journalism towards a socially dysfunctional focus on the 'bottom line' (Baker, 2007: 28–9).

Real-time news as 24/7 infotainment

The perceived dilution of news and information globally, as a result of market-driven television journalism and its impact on the public sphere, has become a major concern for critical media theorists. In the early 1980s, years before media globalization and rampant commercialisation of the airwaves, Neil Postman formulated the thesis that public discourse in the United States was assuming the form of entertainment. In his influential book *Amusing Ourselves to Death* (1985), Postman argued that television had become:

> the background radiation of the social and intellectual universe, the all-but-imperceptible residue of the electronic big bang of a century past, so familiar and so thoroughly integrated with American culture that we no longer hear its faint hissing in the background or see the flickering grey light. This, in turn, means that its epistemology goes largely unnoticed. And the peek-a-boo world it has constructed around us no longer seems even strange. (p. 80)

Postman also argued that the 'epistemology of television' militated against deeper knowledge and understanding as television's conversations promote 'incoherence and triviality' as television speaks in only one persistent voice – the voice of entertainment.' The very medium of television, argued Postman, is epistemologically compromised: 'Television does not extend or amplify literate culture. It attacks it' (Postman, 1985: 84).

In his book, *Bread and Circuses: Theories of Mass Culture as Social Decay* Patrick Brantlinger charted a trend to what he called 'negative classicism', which found analogies between television as a popular medium and Roman circuses: 'they both substitute immediate visual experience for anything deeper or less immediate; they both impinge from above or outside on mass audiences of non-participatory spectators; they both seem to substitute false experiences of community for something more general and the sex and violence of commercial television appeals like the Roman games to sadomasochistic instincts' (1985: 279).

By the early 1990s, the explosion in the number and reach of television channels, especially news, only reinforced this view of the negative impact of the medium on the polis. Investigative journalist Carl Bernstein, of Watergate fame, in an essay in *The New Republic*, lamented that the speed and quantity of news was undermining its quality, accuracy and context and normalising a 'sleazoid infotainment culture'. 'In this culture of journalistic titillation,' Bernstein wrote, 'we teach our readers and our viewers that the trivial is significant, that the lurid and the loopy are more important than real news. We do not serve our readers and viewers, we pander to them. And we condescend to them, giving them what we think they want and what we calculate will sell and boost ratings and readership' (Bernstein, 1992: 24–5). A forum of journalists and academics organized by the *Columbia Journalism Review* concluded that the US news media had reached a new low with the Clinton/Monica Lewinsky scandal and that this reflected 'the rise of the tabloid and the trivial on our pages and screens, and the increasing pressure to conform to the values of our corporate owners' (*Columbia Journalism Review*, 1998: 44).

In Britain, Bob Franklin noted that 'news media have increasingly become part of the entertainment industry instead of providing a forum for informed debate of key issue of public concern.' He observed: 'journalism's priorities have changed. Entertainment has superseded the provision of information; human interest has supplanted the public interest; measured judgment has succumbed to sensationalism; the trivial has triumphed over the weighty; the intimate relationships of celebrities, from soap operas, the world of sport or the royal family, are judged more 'newsworthy' than the reporting of significant issues and events of international consequence. Traditional news values have been undermined by new values; 'infotainment' is rampant' (Franklin, 1997: 4).

It seemed to many that television news was taking on the worst aspects of the tabloid newspapers, which had always understood their entertainment remit. For Colin Sparks, the tabloidization of news showed in it giving 'relatively little attention to politics, economics, and society and relatively much to diversions like sports, scandals and popular entertainment,' and 'relatively much attention to the personal and private lives of people, both celebrities and ordinary people, and relatively little to political processes, economic developments, and social changes' (Sparks, 2000: 10). The proliferation of all-news channels and the fragmentation of their audiences was being accompanied, according to Tracey, by a 'linguistic poverty and therefore a mental and moral poverty, daytime soaps, tabloid television, the trivialization of public discourse, an evangelism of the ephemeral, the celebration of the insignificant, and the marginalization of the important' (Tracey, 1998: 264).

In Western Europe, too, though the home of public-service broadcasting, there was a tendency to move away from a public-service news agenda – privileging information and education over the entertainment value of news – to a more market-led, 'tabloid', version of news, with its emphasis on consumer journalism, sports and entertainment. The growing intrusion of media into the political domain in many countries has led critics to worry about the approach of the 'media-driven republic', in which media will usurp the functions of political institutions. German scholar Thomas Meyer detected trends towards depoliticization, noting that even 'in overtly political television broadcasts there is a preponderance of programming with extremely scanty informational content and little room for debate, with much of it offering an image of the political that would more likely distract viewers from actual events than help them understand what is happening.' The result of this, Meyer wrote, is that 'the most crucial informational inputs emanating from an important segment of the mass-media system, in short, simply do not meet the standards of appropriate information for a democratic polity' (Meyer and Hinchman, 2002: 129). Commentators in Germany started talking of 'politainment' (Dorner, 2001).

A 2005 comparative survey of European television by the Open Society Institute noted that despite availability of thousands of channels, there was remarkable similarity of content across Europe. 'The distinction between public-service broadcasters and their commercial competition, in terms of programme content and quality,' the Survey, the largest of its kind, covering 20 countries, concluded, 'has become increasingly blurred. Investigative journalism and minority programming are scarce commodities in both public and commercial television. Newscasts have often become markedly tabloid, particularly on commercial television channels' (Open Society Institute, 2005: 22). In India, where television news has grown phenomenonally in the last decade, infotainment was rife, as one well-known television critic observed: 'Currently TV news is a study in the poverty that comes with plenty. More channels means more frenzied competition, and the less sense the viewer gets of the reality behind the political spokesman's bluster, or the anchor's chummy wrapping up of some non-discussion' (Ninan, 2006a).

Dumbing down?

Some have blamed television for creating a 'lowest-common-denominator society', arguing that 'the news media have contributed to a decrease in attention span and the death of curiosity, optimism, civility, compassion for others, and abstract and conceptual reasoning' (Arden, 2003: 48). Richard Hoggart, the founder of the now-defunct Centre for Contemporary Cultural Studies in Birmingham, has lamented this 'dumbing down' in Britain and the tendency among the intelligentsia to practice 'a little cultural slumming' to claim to enjoy such programmes as *Big Brother* (Hoggart, 2004: 124).

John Simpson, the veteran BBC correspondent alleged that 'thanks to the diminishing effects of appealing to the lowest common denominator,' the United States 'is turning into an Alzheimer nation, unaware of its own or anyone else's past, ignorant of its own or anyone else's present' (Simpson, 2002: 288). Other senior journalists, including John Humphrys of the BBC, have expressed serious concerns about 'dumbing down' and called for the strengthening of the public-service ethos of news (Humphrys, 1999; Lloyd, 2004). Similarly Andrew Marr has commented: 'The idea of news has altered. It stopped being essentially information and became something designed to produce – at all costs, always – an emotional reaction, the more extreme the better' (2004: 381).

What seems to be at stake is the public-service ethos of journalism, critical for fostering democratic practices among citizens (Curran, 2002). This ethos was very much that of the founder of the BBC, John Reith, who argued that the role of the new broadcaster would not only be to 'inform, educate and entertain', but within that to provide information free from the influence of both government and commerce, unlike the print media: 'Broadcasting is now bringing direct information to the homes of the people, information which formerly was not obtainable, or only in a form which had suffered considerable adjustment [by the press]' (Reith, 1924: 112). According to a UNESCO definition: 'Public Service Broadcasting (PSB) is broadcasting made, financed and controlled by the public, for the public. It is neither commercial nor state-owned, free from political interference and pressure from commercial forces. Through PSB, citizens are informed, educated and also entertained. When guaranteed with pluralism, programming diversity, editorial independence, appropriate funding, accountability and transparency, public service broadcasting can serve as a cornerstone of democracy' (UNESCO, 2006a). In Britain, for example, the BBC has been partly financed through the licence fee paid by British citizens so that, at least in theory, programme makers do not have to chase ratings and can make quality programmes which 'inform, educate and entertain' in that order.

Supporters of popular communication paradigms have tended to valorise the rise of infotainment, suggesting that it expands and democratizes the public sphere. It has been argued that sex, scandal, disaster and celebrity have been intrinsic to modern journalism since its inception, and discourses on 'dumbing down' and 'tabloidization' are associated with a rather pessimistic, not to say, elitist and idealised view of television news (Hartley, 1999). This reflects a tendency among Western democracies towards a post-modernist 'restyling' of politics centred around consumerism, celebrity and cynicism (Corner and Pels, 2003: 7). As this trend is replicated world over, the present work will attempt to make sense of what appears to be a dominant characteristic of television news and one that requires critical scrutiny, given the crucial significance of television in public life.

Defining global infotainment

Infotainment – a neologism which emerged in the late 1980s to become a buzzword, a handy catchall for all that was wrong with contemporary television – refers to an explicit genre-mix of 'information' and 'entertainment' in news and current affairs programming. By 1992, the word 'infotainment' had made it into *Roget's Thesaurus*. According to the *Oxford*

English Dictionary, infotainment is 'broadcast material which is intended both to entertain and to inform', while *Key Concepts in Political Communication* defines it as 'the combination of the words information and entertainment, suggesting a practice of blending together of their presentation within the broadcasting of news and current affairs' (Lilleker, 2006). The phenomenon of infotainment denotes a type of television news where style triumphs over substance, the mode of presentation becoming more important than the content.

This new news cannibalizes visual forms and styles borrowed from contemporary TV commercials and a MTV-style visual aesthetics, including fast-paced visual action, in a post-modern studio, computer-animated logos, eye-catching visuals and rhetorical headlines from an, often glamorous, anchor person. Such news, particularly on the rolling 24/7 channels, appears to be the answer to attracting the 'me' generation of media users, prone to channel hopping and zapping as well as more inclined towards on-line and mobile news. This style of presentation, with its origins in the ratings-driven commercial television news culture of the US, is becoming increasingly global, as news channels attempt to reach more viewers and keep their target audiences from switching over.

For the purposes of this study I define 'global infotainment' as 'the globalization of a US-style ratings-driven television journalism which privileges privatized soft news – about celebrities, crime, corruption and violence – and presents it as a form of spectacle, at the expense of news about political, civic and public affairs.' The global circulation of such television news, made possible by the creation of an international infrastructure of policies, trade and hardware, has undermined the public-service ethos of television but, at the same time, a 'global infotainment sphere' is emerging as a potential site for competing versions of journalisms, including an increasingly vocal and visible blogosphere.

Infotainment as diversion

In his book, *The Power of News*, Michael Schudson has shown how news media act as a central institution in the evolution of a modern society and a key repository of 'public knowledge' and cultural authority (Schudson, 1996). The mediatized politics and the symbiotic relationships between journalists, spin doctors, and politicians within contemporary tele-visualized politics makes television an extremely powerful medium for political persuasion (Louw, 2005). Building on Guy Debord's concept of the 'society of the spectacle', Douglas Kellner has observed that we are increasingly becoming part of 'networked infotainment societies,' where 'media spectacle is invading every field of experience, from the economy to culture and everyday life to politics and war (2003: 10).

While this mode of communication may seem more inclusive and potentially liberatory, the implications for the transmission of the public information necessary for democratic discourse may be less reassuring. There is a concern that too much news is creating an information overload, contributing to a structural erosion of the public sphere in a Habermasian sense, where the viewer, bombarded with visuals, is unable to differentiate between public information and corporate propaganda. Some 40 years ago, the renowned British historian Eric Hobsbawm defined advertisers as 'the most effective mass ideologists since the decline of the churches' (Hobsbawm, 1968: 321). However, news 'should be a stimulus to new thinking' as Jean Seaton reminds us, 'not an anaesthetizing escape from it' (2005: 296).

Entertaining news entails much more than a carnivalseque communication experience. As Garcia Canclini has observed, 'argumentative and critical forms of participation cede their place to the pleasure taken in electronic media spectacles where narration or the simple accumulation of anecdotes prevails over reasoned solutions to problems' (2001: 24). There is also an important ideological dimension associated with such modes of interactions. Herbert Schiller argued that Western media corporations are integral to capitalist systems and thus play a core role as ideological agents: 'They provide in their imagery and messagery, the beliefs and perspectives that create and reinforce their audiences' attachments to the way things are in the system overall' (Schiller, 1976: 30). In this age of ever-shortening sound- and sight-bites, does television news allow a critical assessment and reflection of the content presented, or does the sensory overload reduce the very concept of information to a mere surface impulse? What are the social and political implications of such a news discourse?

This book argues that there is a pressing need to go beyond the debate about 'dumbing down', which seems to have dominated critical commentary on marketization of television news, some of which is referred to above. Infotainment, especially in its global context, entails much more than dumbing down: it works as a powerful discourse of diversion, in both senses, taking the attention away from, and displacing from the airwaves, such grim realities of neo-liberal imperialism as witnessed in the US invasion and occupation of Iraq; the intellectual and cultural subjugation by the tyranny of technology; of free-market capitalism and globalization of a profligate and unsustainable consumerist lifestyle. In this 24/7 global cultural economy, the 'mechanisms of television', which Adorno warned 'often operate under the guise of false realism' (1991: 158), are creating a false global 'feel good' factor, predicated on the supremacy of the market as defined by the West, led by the United States.

In this multimodal communication era, new digital delivery mechanisms offer unprecedented levels of media as content flows from around the globe from anywhere to anywhere at any time, creating what has been termed a 'mobile network society' (Castells et al., 2006). In this broadcasting ecology, there will be little need for schedules and specific channels. Rupert Murdoch sees digitalization as 'the prelude to a new golden age of media', noting that 'technology is liberating us from old constraints, lowering key costs, easing access to new customers and markets and multiplying the choices we can offer' (News Corporation, 2007: 9). As market-driven broadcast journalism becomes the norm, this process is not just confined to homes: TV monitors in public places – railway stations, airports, shopping malls – are legion, making television a pervasive and ambient phenomenon, transforming 'waiting room populations' into advertising audiences, influencing brand visibility and consumer behaviour (McCarthy, 2001). This global infotainment culture will be increasingly supported by infomercials – combining information with a product or service placement, further blurring the distinctions between news and advertising, creating what is sometimes termed as 'advertainment'.

Such liberating technology has been harnessed by infotainment conglomerates who bestride the globe and the public imagination with a cornucopia of media products, the paradigm of which is Murdoch's News Corporation, a key player in creating global infotainment, undermining and in some countries replacing the public-service ethos of television. In this respect, it is not dissimilar to the 'bread and circuses' of the Roman Empire, when the spectacle of the arena gradually won out over the theatre: 'Tragedy and comedy had to compete with gladiatorial combats and chariot races for spectators ... Theatres themselves came to be used for combats and displays of wild beasts. Cruder types of dramatic entertainment, pantomime and farce, evolved partly to meet the competition of the games, and these relied heavily on stage effects, obscenity, and other forms of sensationalism. Gradually the viciousness of the stage approximated the viciousness of the arena' (cited in Brantlinger, 1983: 75).

The structure of the book

The key arguments of the book follow these propositions:

- Despite the unprecedented growth in on-line media, television continues to be the world's most powerful medium, and television news helps shape the world views of millions of people across the globe.
- In the battle between public-service and private, commercially driven television, the commercial model of broadcast journalism has won.
- As the epicentre of such a television journalism, the United States has a major role in the globalization of the commercial model of television news.

- In a market-driven, 24/7 broadcasting ecology, television news is veering towards infotainment – soft news, lifestyle and consumer journalism are preeminent, a conduit for the corporate colonization of consciousness, while public journalism and the public sphere have been undermined.
- The globalization of infotainment is detectable across the world, exemplified by new synergies between Hollywood-based and Bollywood-based television news cultures.
- Even conflict and wars are portrayed on television news in an entertaining manner, drawing on conventions of Hollywood and thus legitimizing a neo-imperial ideology predicated on the superiority of free-market democracy.
- New technologies and alternative modes of global communication have created possibilities of a 'global infotainment sphere'.

The book is divided into seven chapters. In the first chapter, the infotainment phenomenon is discussed in its historical context. It is argued that infotainment has a long history and any standard text book of the history of journalism will show that 'tickling' the public has been central to the growth of journalism as a business and as a profession. The different frameworks within which television news has evolved are analysed: the public service model dominant in Western Europe; state-controlled television news in communist and many developing countries, and the commercial US model. The focus then moves on to the changing nature of television news in the United States, where commercial imperatives seem to have come to dominate broadcast journalism, and the impact of importing such a model on public-service television in Europe is discussed.

The second chapter sets out the political, economic and technological context of this change, examining the impact of neo-liberal policies in the post-Cold War era – liberalization, deregulation and privatization of television – and the shift from public-service to private television journalism. This is framed within the macro structural changes in broadcasting as a result of the privatization of audiovisual and communications sectors as part of transnational liberalization undertaken under the auspices of the World Trade Organization. The chapter also maps the developments in communications technologies, such as satellites and the availability of digital broadcasting, that made the global expansion of news and current affairs channels possible. The creation of infotainment conglomerates through deregulating media ownership and the merger of entertainment and information corporations, and changes in the media marketplace are analysed, in relation to their contribution to the growing commercialism of television news, primarily in the US as the centre of free-market media. The dependence of news channels on corporate advertising is also investigated to establish to what extent such factors influence news content. The impact of all these factors on infotainment in news is exemplified by Murdoch's Fox News.

The focus of the third chapter is on the globalization of this phenomenon of infotainment, as the US model of market-led broadcast journalism is imposed or is adopted across the world, influencing news and current affairs. As the home of key players in global television news – both as providers of raw footage as well as round the clock news through such channels as Cable News Network (CNN), part of AOL-Time Warner, the world's biggest media corporation, the US has a major role in this process. The implications of rolling 24/7 news operations for news agendas and priorities is analysed, drawing illustrative examples from Europe, Russia, Japan and many other countries. The chapter demonstrates how globalization and homogenization of a news culture is taking effect, with localized global infotainment gaining ground. The parallel rise of reality television, from documentaries to docusoaps, is also discussed through a case study that demonstrates the symbiotic relationship between these new factual entertainment genres and entertaining news.

Chapter 4 examines the impact of infotainment on television news in India, which, with 40 dedicated 24/7 television news networks, is the world's largest television news market. The chapter provides an analysis of how the Indian newsscape has been transformed, looking at the main players in the field and their growing global ambitions. A special focus of the chapter is on what I term the 'Bollywoodization of television news', examining the impact of a celebrity entertainment and ratings-driven environment on the broadcasting of news and current affairs. As India integrates in the world of global infotainment, the synergies between the US model and the Indian broadcasting experience are also discussed.

Given the characteristics of television news - arresting visuals, dramatic pictures – wars and civil conflicts are particularly susceptible to infotainment. Chapter 5 considers the representation of war on television news, where increasingly the trend is to show it as a form of macabre infotainment. The chapter examines the obsession of TV news with high-tech war reporting, analysing how it has evolved since the 1991 US invasion of Iraq, the first internationally televised war. The sanitisation of state-sponsored violence and its resistance by extremist Islamic groups, it is argued, is creating a greater degree of acceptance of violence in the popular imagination, helped in no small way by the growing popularity of digital war games. The chapter also notes the role of Siliwood (Hollywood and Silicon Valley) and the development of 'militainment' – the mutually beneficial collaboration between Hollywood and the Pentagon and how these have contributed to the rise of militaristic infotainment in the news and in factual entertainment.

In Chapter 6, the discussion takes a more theoretical turn, with its focus on the politics of global infotainment, and analysing the phenomenon as an ideology for a neo-imperialism of neo-liberalism. It explores the relationship between television news and political, economic, military and cultural processes, and examines the role that TV plays in shaping our worldview. Global massification and the role of television as an apparatus of power and ideology is revisited, drawing on key theoretical approaches that inform the study of infotainment, from Marxist to postmodernist, analysing infotainment as a 'feel good' vector in the corporate colonialism, masquerading as globalization. The chapter delineates the major implications of global infotainment for the formation of public opinion and its manipulation in an age of neo-imperialism, characterized by the display of US military might. The average consumer of the 24/7 infotainment bombardment may not be able to differentiate between public information and propaganda from a powerful military-industrial-entertainment complex. Global infotainment, the chapter argues, is the soft emissary of a hard-nosed new imperialism. It is also a form of diversion, distracting attention away from this project to dominate and control, as well as displacing alternative views and information that is essential for public debate. Given the growing power of global infotainment conglomerates and their local clones, there is a danger that the potential for an informed citizenry, essential for genuine democratic discourse, is undermined, while corporate propaganda masquerading as infotainment reaches billions of people in their living rooms.

Chapter 7 offers a more positive assessment, noting that infotainment has the capacity to provide greater diversity than traditional hard news, thus a liberatory potential and a more democratic character. It observes that popular factual television could be used to raise global awareness of contemporary issues and argues that a 'global infotainment sphere', created through the globalization of television and growing importance of the Internet, could be harnessed for the public good. Despite their commercialization, such phenomena as web-casting and blogging and on-line infotainment sharing sites like YouTube and MySpace may have a role in influencing global news agendas. The chapter also examines the area of knowledge television – so-called 'edutainment' – a sector into which major international broadcasters such as the BBC are expanding. The book suggests a new approach for the study of international television news for the twenty-first century by developing the idea of 'global public media' as a 'global public good' to counter the increasing power of commercial 'global infotainment', which characterizes the 'breads and circuses' of the twenty-first century avatar of the Roman Empire – the US-managed neo-liberal imperialism.

As a former journalist with an academic background in International Relations, what is happening to global news has been the central concern of my research and writing over nearly two decades. At a time when infotainment is hailed as empowering individuals and societies around the world, to argue that it may be a diversion, masking a covert agenda to embed neo-liberal imperialism, is unfashionable. Nevertheless, it is an argument that needs to be made and made unambiguously and without apology.

This book has had a long gestation period and in writing it I have accumulated a range of debts: first and foremost, to the writings of fellow academics, journalists and activists passionate about the need to defend public media. Colleagues at the University of Westminster – many of whom, especially Colin Sparks, still wedded to the idea of a critical communication project – provided a robust academic environment within which such scholarship can be sustained, and this book is a modest contribution to what James Curran has called 'the Westminster School' of research (Curran, 2004).

For her generosity and patience I want to thank Julia Hall, who commissioned this book but left Sage before it saw the light of day. Others at Sage, especially Gurdeep Mattu, Mila Steele and Ian Antcliff were extremely helpful and cooperative. Close to home, my family, including my mother, who would complain that I was always 'cuddling the computer', coped very well with my extensive and intensive work schedule. During the final weeks of writing, my daughter Shivani, preparing for her GCSE exams, was a constant source of inspiration, reminding me the worth of hard work, while my son Rohan, meticulous as he is, helped with checking the references, as well as alerting me to the militaristic nature of many computer games. My deepest gratitude as ever goes to my wife Elizabeth for her intelligent and professional support and to whom this book is dedicated.

1

THE EVOLUTION OF INFOTAINMENT

The following verse appeared in a book published to mark the centenary of the *Daily Mail*, Britain's oldest surviving popular newspaper, established in 1896:

> Tickle the public, make 'em grin,
> The more you tickle the more you'll win;
> Teach the public, you'll never get rich,
> You'll live like a beggar and die in a ditch.
>
> (Anon, cited in Engel, 1996)

These four lines of verse sum up rather well the importance of 'tickling the public'. That crime, celebrity and human interest stories are more marketable than coverage of political or policy issues is well attested in most histories of journalism. News as entertainment has a long and venerable tradition, from the broadside ballad to the yellow and tabloid press, from cinema newsreels to television. The complaint about such 'infotainment' dumbing down the public, or at least not using the opportunity to raise them up has just as long a history. Since the advent of mass media, there has been a tension between informing and educating the public and entertaining the crowd in the market place. This tension has been framed in terms that John Stuart Mill identified in relation to the purpose of politics, whether the 'will of the people' or the 'good of the people' should prevail. In nineteenth-century Britain, the rise of mass society and fear of the illiterate masses claiming rights to democratic power was inextricably linked with the urgent demand to educate and inform them as the only bastion against barbarism (Carey, 1992).

From the earliest days of printing and publishing, the dialectic between the market and the moral has been reflected in media production and consumption. In Britain, the emergence of the newspaper press in the eighteenth century was aimed at gentlemen and the merchant classes. The broadsheet 'quality' newspapers were read by 'the quality' and made little concession to entertainment, providing the public with a sphere for debate (even if only for the ruling elite), while the masses were entertained by street literature: 'Newspapers were dull, over-clever or pompous and, with a tax rising from 1d to 3½d at the end of the eighteenth century, a broadside ballad was the only sheet most poor people could afford' (Shepard, 1973: 64). These offered cheap and cheerful verses about sensational news and entertaining topics on crudely printed sheets to the general public, whose literacy was on the rise at the turn of the nineteenth century. Street literature was also made more entertaining and attractive by appealing to the visual through its typography and crude woodcut illustrations.

The battle to use this new literacy for religious education and moral uplift, led by Hannah More and the Sunday School movement, prompted a huge revival of street literature through the great success of their religious 'tracts' or pamphlets that had borrowed its entertaining features. Jumping on this bandwagon, one of the most successful printers of street literature in London in the early decades of the nineteenth century, James Catnach published hundreds of 'crudely written ballads that became the poor man's newspapers, dealing with politics, sport, fashions, murders, dying speeches and confessions. Catnach became famous for his '"cocks and catchpennies", fictitious narratives printed up when news was scarce' (Shepard, 1973: 72).

When in 1846, the world's first illustrated weekly newspaper, *The Illustrated London News* was launched, the poet William Wordsworth was appalled by what he considered a return to barbarism. This weekly publication printed graphic woodcuts of sensational crimes, royal events and battles, attracting new readers by appealing to the drama of the visual. His sonnet 'Illustrated Books and Newspapers' included the lines:

> ... Avaunt this vile abuse of pictured page!
> Must eyes be all in all, the tongue and ear
> Nothing? Heaven keep us from a lower stage.
>
> (cited in Brantlinger, 1983: 278)

The development of the popular press owed much to street literature, with clear influences in their typographic and journalistic styles, their attractive format of illustrations alternating with text and forceful headings, as well as their vivid and dramatic news topics, sensationalist and often macabre (Shepherd, 1973: 115).

Given its founding principles and the composition of its inhabitants through migration, it is not surprising that popular media witnessed its greatest success in the New World, where the masses and the market were celebrated from an early age. The US, the home of the idea of a mass society and mass communication, could also be said to be the inventor of the infotainment industry, starting with the penny press in the 1830s. Established in New York in 1833, copies of Benjamin Day's *Sun* sold for one penny when all other newspapers were sold for six cents, with a high quota of human interest stories, particularly relating to crime and punishment, using the police courts as a source of material (Mott, 1962). During the American Civil War in 1861–65, some journalists, Mott notes, became little more than 'news scavengers' (ibid: 236). The renowned journalist, Joseph Pulitzer (after whom the prestigious Pulitzer Prize in US journalism is named) was also one of the first media magnates and his newspapers offered readers investigative journalism, undercover reports, contests, opinion surveys, and even stunts to boost circulation. The penny press provided diversions for working people, as Neal Gabler noted:

> For a constituency being conditioned by trashy crime pamphlets, gory novels and overwrought melodramas, news was simply the most exciting, most entertaining content a paper could offer, especially when it was skewed, as it invariably was in the penny press, to the most sensational stories. In fact, one might even say that the masters of the penny press *invented* the concept of news because it was the best way to sell their papers in an entertainment environment. (cited in Gitlin, 2002: 51)

What became known as 'yellow journalism' was characterized by intense competition between Pulitzer and his rival magnate William Randolph Hearst, reflected in sensationalist and scandalous reporting, often tinged with staged events or half-truths. As Michael Schudson has argued in his history of journalism in the US, from the nineteenth century onwards a 'journalism of entertainment' (with its distinct formats and style – accessible language and more pictures – the *Illustrated Daily News* being a good case in point) has paralleled with that of 'analysis' (Schudson, 1978: 89). This 'journalism of entertainment' was exported back to Europe and then to the rest of the world, as part of the globalizing American mass culture that began in the mid-nineteenth century, with circuses, amusement parks, vaudeville, mail-order catalogues and dime novels, which increasingly became agents of American popular culture. The tour of

Buffalo Bill's *Wild West* show to Europe in the late nineteenth century was a major success in promoting a US version of the 'good life', and its popularity was such that it was staged twice at Queen Victoria's Jubilee Day festivities and was reported widely in the press (Rydell and Kroes, 2005).

Versions of the American penny press were adopted in many European countries. In Italy, for example, new illustrated weekly magazines such as *Illustrazione Italiana*, founded in 1875, combined human interest with infotainment stories on the wonders of science and industry, and served as a backdrop for the popularization of new consumer goods, like patent medicines, bicycles and kitchen equipment, in the process creating a new constituency of buyers for branded consumer products (Arvidsson, 2003: 16). In Japan too, the success of the penny press was noted and replicated, with popular newspapers such as *Yomiuri* adopting US-style populist journalism, creating a 'black third page', with regular reports centred on 'scandals about politicians and businessmen' (Chapman, 2005: 109).

In Britain, as the taxes and duties on the press were progressively reduced during the late nineteenth century, newspapers became an increasingly important commercial enterprise, thriving on sensationalist stories. The economic and entertainment power enhanced their political position and their capacity to control the masses (Berridge, 1978). This 'new' journalism demonstrated 'a shift away from parliamentary and political news to sport, gossip, crime and sex' (Wiener, 1988: 54). The extensive and lurid coverage of the 'Jack the Ripper' murders in 1888 by the London newspapers – both quality and popular – reflected the beginnings of a mass newspaper culture, one predicated on sensationalist journalism (Curtis, 2001). The cult of celebrity also began in earnest during the Victorian period, particularly in relation to Queen Victoria and the royal family. Benjamin Disraeli, the Prime Minister (1868 and 1874–80), could be said to have been one of the first 'spin doctors', recognizing the potential of the mass media to promote the Queen as Empress and Britain as an imperial power. There was a huge appetite for royal news and editors made sure that Queen Victoria's pictures were adjusted to hide her double chin and make her look younger than her age (Plunkett, 2003).

The development of the popular press was also underpinned by the rise of the advertising industry in the US. By the end of the nineteenth century, advertising had become a powerful element in the making of the world's most consumerist society, and in 1899, US-based advertising company, J. Walter Thompson, had established a 'sales bureau' in London and by the end of the First World War, the United States already boasted an advanced network of culture industries that served to promote American values.

New visual media for infotainment

Building on the success of and demand for illustrated news, the advent of film and cinema at the turn of the twentieth century provided an appealing new visual medium for news and journalism. Invented by the Frenchman Charles Pathé in 1907, the first British newsreel appeared in 1910 as an offshoot of the French Pathé-Journal, founded by him in 1908. Pathé's *Animated Gazette* was already putting out a daily edition of the newsreel in London before the First World War. It was possible for cameramen to accompany George V to France in 1914 and the film to be shown in the West End by 8p.m. the same day. On its showing, the film trade paper *The Bioscope* predicted that the illustrated newspaper would be superseded by the news film, 'which depicts the actual scenes of contemporary history in living and moving reality' (*The Bioscope*, 9 June 1910, cited in McKernan, 2002: 12). 'Motor racing at Brooklands, manoeuvres on Salisbury Plain, Caruso on the street, Modes in Paris' were typical of the fare on offer.

The global potential of the new medium was quickly recognised. In 1912, a book on the new *Moving Pictures* by F.A. Talbot reported that the newsreels were gaining a very favourable reception all over the British Empire, as it 'serves to bring the world's happenings far more vividly before the public than can be done in a brief newspaper cablegram…' (cited in McKernan, 2002: 19). This was quickly borne out during the First World War. Between May 1917 and February 1919, the British War Office took over one of the commercial newsreels, *Topical Budget*, which produced one of the most successful and memorable news films, of General Allenby's entry into Jerusalem in 1917, showing him as he entered the walls of the holy city on foot to receive its surrender after 400 years of Ottoman rule. This provided a powerful symbolic image that was shown around the world (McKernan, 2002).

The vital role of film in managing public opinion at home and abroad, as well as propaganda overseas was demonstrated during the war, as noted by Lasswell: 'During the war period it came to be recognized that the mobilization of men and means was not sufficient; there must be mobilization of opinion. Power over opinion, as over life and property, passed into official hands' (1927: 14). Entertainment and popular culture were appropriated by the authorities for ideological purposes. The Committee on Public Information in the United States liaised with Hollywood to produce patriotic films, and senior government figures were not averse to be seen with film stars, recognizing the power of moving pictures and infotainment.

The films were so successful that the German Chief of Staff General Ludendorff wrote in a letter to the German Ministry of War in 1917: 'The war has demonstrated the superiority of the photograph and the film as means of information and persuasion' (quoted in Jowett and O'Donnell, 1999: 115). The Soviet Union and other communist countries also recognized the ideological and strategic importance of cinema, deploying it to propagate Communist ideologies. Films with deft use of emotion-inducing montage, visible in such classic propaganda films as Sergei Eisenstein's *Battleship Potemkin* (1925) and newsreels, supplemented radio as an ideological instrument.

Increasingly a part of cinema-going life in the interwar years, newsreels in Britain had a diet largely of 'racing and royalty.' Despite the fact that Pathé and Movietone had foreign bureaux all over the world and Gaumont an affiliation with Hearst's Corporations Metrotone News in America, the newsreels in Britain ignored the signs of war in Europe in the 1930s and were preoccupied with 'a cavalcade of mind-stupefying trivia such as the man who tried to take flight with rockets attached to his trousers' (cited in McKernan, 2002: 10). Interestingly, the strongest anti-Nazi news reels were in America, so much so that in some areas of the country they were banned from cinemas.

This period saw the rise of mass media in the US and Europe with the press, cinema and the radio, and emerging synergies between media, consumption and politics. Walter Lippmann described this as the 'manufacture of consent' in a democratic mass society, driven and dependent on advertising, promoting consumerism and an idea of free choice and enterprise in an increasingly depoliticised public opinion. A mirror image of this could be seen in the use of mass media entertainment for direct state propaganda in the totalitarian regimes of Soviet Union and Nazi Germany. In Nazi Germany, this reached new heights of sophistication under Propaganda Minister Joseph Goebbels, who encouraged both the indoctrination of the masses with racist ideologies as well as escapist entertainment through newsreels, documentaries and 'cultural' films. One senior member of the Propaganda Ministry wrote in 1942: 'In comparison with the other arts, film, from a mass psychological and propagandistic viewpoint, has a particularly deep and lasting impact because of its property to affect the visual and emotional, i.e. the non-intellectual' (cited in Hoffmann, 1996:194).

John Reith, the first Director General of the British Broadcasting Corporation (BBC), identified the potential of the new media of radio and television, in his famous words, 'to inform, educate and entertain' the public. The ranking of these aims reflects his strong Scottish Presbyterian view of social and moral improvement. While these values were for him the driving spirit behind the public-service broadcasting ethos, he also recognized that entertaining the public was key to its success. Under Reith, who in 1940 became Minister of Information and resented being referred to as 'Dr Goebbels' opposite number' (Hickman, 1995: 29), the government-funded BBC Empire Service, established in 1932, broadcast anti-German propaganda such as *The Shadow of the Swastika*, a series of dramas about the Nazi Party to reach the scattered parts of the British Empire.

During the Second World War, cinema played a key role both domestically and globally: Hollywood was integral to the war effort, as films were able to 'entertain and propagandize at the same time' (Jowett and O'Donnell, 1999: 120), while Britain's Ministry of Information realised that 'for the film to be good propaganda, it must also be good entertainment' (Taylor, 2003: 219). Their counterparts in the Soviet Union produced over 500 newsreels from 1941–45 with 250 cameramen filming on the different fronts. *Stalingrad*, produced only a few weeks after the German surrender in 1943 had 'stunning combat footage, realistic portrayal of street fighting, maps and diagrams' and showed the surrender of the German commander (ibid: 237). After the Second World War, as the reach of television grew, the cinema newsreels lost their monopoly on news on film and their audience. Henceforth the cinema was only for entertainment, though entertainment could be harnessed to provide information and ideology. Interestingly, the very first television news broadcast was produced on the old newsreel film (Petersen, 1993).

Broadcasting: for public service or private profit?

From the very beginning of the broadcasting era, different models and approaches emerged on either side of the Atlantic, characterized by how they viewed and defined the public interest. Broadcasting in the United States – both radio and television – had a commercial remit from its very inception: the US Radio Act of 1927 defined radio broadcasting as a commercial enterprise, funded by advertising. It was argued that public interest would be best served by largely unfettered private broadcasting and therefore the Act made no provision for supporting or developing non-commercial broadcasting (McChesney, 1993). Television, too, followed the market model, driven by advertising and dependent on ratings. Although the Public Broadcasting Act of 1967 created the Corporation of Public Broadcasting (CPB), the Public Broadcasting Service (PBS) and National

Public Radio (NPR), to produce and distribute non-commercial radio and television programming across the US, their presence was largely appreciated by a minority of educationalists and activists. For the mass audience, the trio of television networks – CBS (Columbia Broadcasting System), NBC (National Broadcasting Corporation) and ABC (American Broadcasting Corporation) – provided both entertainment and information.

As the networks' revenue was based on audience ratings, 'tickling the public' was an important ingredient of their programming (McChesney, 1993; Barkin, 2002). Lazarsfeld and Merton, back in 1948, lamented that 'our commercially sponsored mass media promote a largely unthinking allegiance to our social structure' (1948: 108). Such infotainment programming as *Candid Camera*, using entertaining footage involving unsuspecting people reacting to pranks, was launched in 1948 and is still in operation in some shape or form around the world. By the 1950s, game and talent shows had become the staple diet of American television. Glamour and celebrity programming, too, has a long history: The *Miss America* pageant was broadcast for the first time in 1954, while the celebrity talk programme *The Tonight Show* has been successfully running on NBC since 1954.

In such a television culture, the notion of the citizen as consumer was deeply entrenched. The idea that the 'public interest' should be defined only by market logic was clear during the first Reagan Presidency, when in 1982 the Federal Communications Commission (FCC) chairman, Mark Fowler, wrote in an article with his aide Daniel Brenner: 'Communication policy should be directed toward maximizing the services the public desires. Instead of defining demand and specifying categories of programming to serve this demand, the Commission should rely on the broadcasters' ability to determine the wants of their audience through the normal mechanisms of the marketplace. The public's interest, then, defines the public interest' (cited in Calabrese, 2005a: 272). As the FCC overturned its 'public trust' requirement, and commercialism became more acute – Fowler reportedly claimed that television was basically 'a toaster with pictures' – the broadcasters 'began to conflate ratings and relevancy' (Mindich, 2005: 52).

By the late 1980s, scholars were already expressing concerns about declining political interest among citizens, creating a 'vicious circle', leading to an apathetic or the cynical public undermining quality journalism. In his judiciously titled book *Democracy without Citizens*, Robert Entman (1989) noted this 'decay' in American politics:

> Because most members of the public know and care relatively little about government, they neither seek nor understand high-quality political reporting and analysis. With limited

> demand for first-rate journalism, most news organizations cannot afford to supply it, and because they do not supply it, most Americans have no practical source of the information necessary to become politically sophisticated. Yet it would take an informed and interested citizenry to create enough demand to support top-flight journalism. (1989: 17).

In Western Europe, and especially in the case of Britain and the BBC, a fundamentally different kind of model – a not-for-profit, public-broadcasting monopoly – was the norm. This model was replicated among virtually all Western European nations and in several other countries, including Canada, Australia, New Zealand and Japan, as well as Commonwealth countries such as India. In communist nations, a state-controlled media system developed that was more akin to a rigid and regulated information bureaucracy than professional journalism and was sustained by a strong regime of censorship and thought control. In the ideological battles for hearts and minds during the Cold War years, many communist countries and their allies in the developing world followed this model, in which all information was controlled and media explicitly used for propaganda purposes. In a fourth model of state broadcasting, the ruling party, or in many cases, unelected leadership (whether of left or right political affiliation) used the media for self-aggrandizement in the name of development and 'nation building'. With the possible exception of a few broadcasters in Western Europe and the Japanese NHK (Nippon Hoso Kyokai), most other broadcasting organizations had to contend with one of two hugely powerful and competing forces: the state machinery, in the case of most communist and developing countries or the vagaries of the market, for those operating in a commercial environment. For the former the governments set the news agenda; for the latter advertisers and ratings.

In Britain, broadcasting evolved within a public-service framework, with the BBC at its core. From being granted its first Royal Charter in 1927 and starting regular television broadcasts in 1936, the corporation was exempted from commercial pressures, as it was funded by a licence fee. Although the BBC lost its monopoly in 1955 with the launch of independent television (ITV) that carried advertising (unlike the BBC), it continued to dominate both radio and television in a uniquely British broadcasting 'duopoly'. Even the commercially run ITV had to meet certain public-service obligations. The establishment of Channel 4 in 1982, although advertisement based, retained and even widened the public-service ethos, particularly in relation to the provision of news and current affairs. Even in a multi-channel multimedia age, its flagship Channel 4 News remains the most highly regarded newscast on British television. While it could be argued that the idealized version of public-service broadcasting reflected the class values of a social and political elite, the professional autonomy that the system could guarantee journalists provided British broadcasting with a cultural capital which contributed to the quality of the public debate. As James Curran observed: 'Public-service broadcasting diminished the knowledge gap between the political elite and the general public because it made informing the public an institutional priority. It consciously sought to offset the 'two nation' division of the country (supported by a polarized, elite and popular press) by scheduling flagship news and current affairs programmes in prime time, and developing a distinctive style of journalism that was both popular and informative. This strategy succeeded in the sense that television became the principal source of news for the majority of the population' (Curran, 2002: 6–7).

The principles at the heart of public-service broadcasting have been enumerated as: universality of availability; universality of appeal; provision for minorities; a commitment to the education of the public; distance from vested interests; structured to encourage competition in programming standards not for audiences; freedom for the programme maker; and fostering a public sphere (Tracey,1998: 26–32). According to Britain's Ofcom, the characteristics of public service broadcasting are programming which is of high quality, original, challenging, engaging and widely available, and among its purposes is 'to inform ourselves and others and to increase our understanding of the world through news, information and analysis of current events and ideas' (Ofcom, 2007). Such public communication, according to the BBC, creates public value in five main ways: 'democratic value', supporting civic life and national debate by providing 'trusted and impartial news and information' that helps citizens make sense of the world and encourages them to engage with it; 'cultural and creative value', by enriching cultural life and broadening 'the national conversation'; 'educational value', by offering audiences formal and informal educational opportunity; 'social and community value', by enabling social cohesion and understanding in a multicultural Britain, and lastly 'global value', being 'the world's most trusted provider of international news and information' (BBC, 2004a: 8).

The end of the Cold War and the triumph of commercial television

Culture wars were an integral part of Cold War ideological battles, with the superpowers striving in the 'century of the masses' to keep the masses entertained. During the early years of the Cold War, as Nancy Bernhard has shown, the US government used television networks to 'sell' the ideological war against communism to the American public, persuading networks to broadcast news and current affairs programmes approved by the government, sometimes even produced or scripted by government agencies, and thus making them act as unofficial state propagandists (Bernhard, 1999). By the fading years of the East-West rivalry, television had become a powerful harbinger for neo-liberalism. The shift in broadcasting that came about after the end of the Cold War in 1989 was heralded by one of the most spectacular media events – the fall of the Berlin Wall. Television news itself had played an important role in the 1989 revolutions in Eastern Europe, broadcasting images of mass demonstrations which had a domino effect. The transition to capitalism was largely peaceful, except in Romania, where at least some of the violence was simulated, including the 1989 Timisoara massacre ostensibly staged for the Western TV cameras, in what Baudrillard called, 'a hijacking of fantasies, affects and the credulity of hundreds of millions of people by means of television' (1994: 69).

Similarly, the 1991 coup in Moscow, which led to the break-up of the Soviet Union, was hailed as the 'first true media event in the history of the Soviet Union', which was 'profoundly and decisively shaped by the electronic eye that transformed instantly and continuously, elements of a political confrontation into meaningful scripts with their corresponding images, styles, and symbols' (Bonnell and Freidin, 1995: 44). These scripts had a Western or more specifically American writing on them: freedom, democracy and choice – with television roles for populist leaders such as Boris Yeltsin, who skilfully used the visual media, with not inconsiderable help from his Western backers and Russian oligarchs, to provide new meanings to such Russian words as *glasnost* (openness) and *perestroika* (restructuring).

The triumph of market capitalism inevitably undermined the state-driven model of public broadcasting. In Eastern Europe and part of the former Soviet Union, state broadcasters were exposed as little more than propaganda networks, losing all credibility. As the airwaves were privatized, public-service as well as state-run broadcasting was threatened. In Britain, commercial broadcasters had accepted their obligations to deliver public-service programming in return for privileged access to the limited analogue spectrum and the right to broadcast, under the so-called public-service broadcasting 'compact'. This was gradually undermined by a set of developments, including the advent of digital broadcasting, the end of spectrum scarcity and the proliferation of channels, resulting in keen competition and, crucially new sources of funding from pay-TV, sponsorship and interactive revenues. Figures from Ofcom demonstrate clearly the differences in

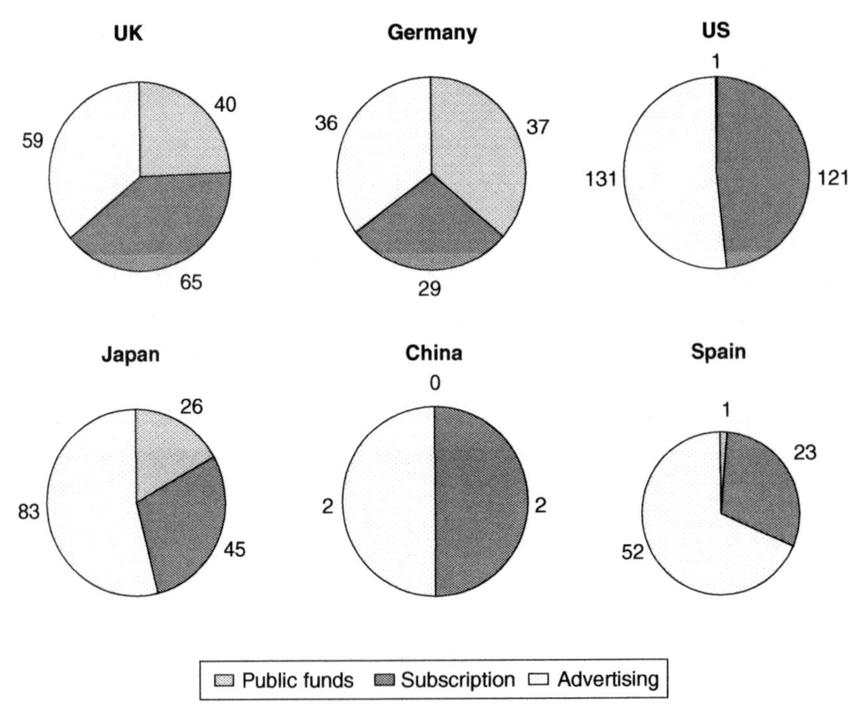

Figure 1.1 How television is funded: selected countries (funding per head from different sources of revenue in £)
(Source: Ofcom, 2007)

revenue sources between private and public broadcasters. According to Ofcom, in terms of television industry revenue per head of population, in 2005, Britain (£164) was second only to the US (£253), with advertising constituting 36 per cent of total TV industry revenue, while subscription revenue accounted for 40 per cent and public funds for the remaining 20 per cent. As Figure 1.1 shows, this was broadly similar in countries like Germany and France with strong traditions of public-service broadcasting but in striking contrast to the US and Japan, where television is predominantly funded by advertising (Ofcom, 2007).

Advertisement-driven broadcasting is inevitably more susceptible to commercial imperatives. Michael Tracey puts it succinctly: 'In a public system, television producers acquire money to make programmes. In a commercial system they make programmes to acquire money' (1998: 18). The proliferation of television channels and news in particular came at the same time as a historic decline in the audience for news programming. Thus in an increasingly competitive market, broadcasters were chasing to increase market share – but only a bigger slice of a diminishing cake.

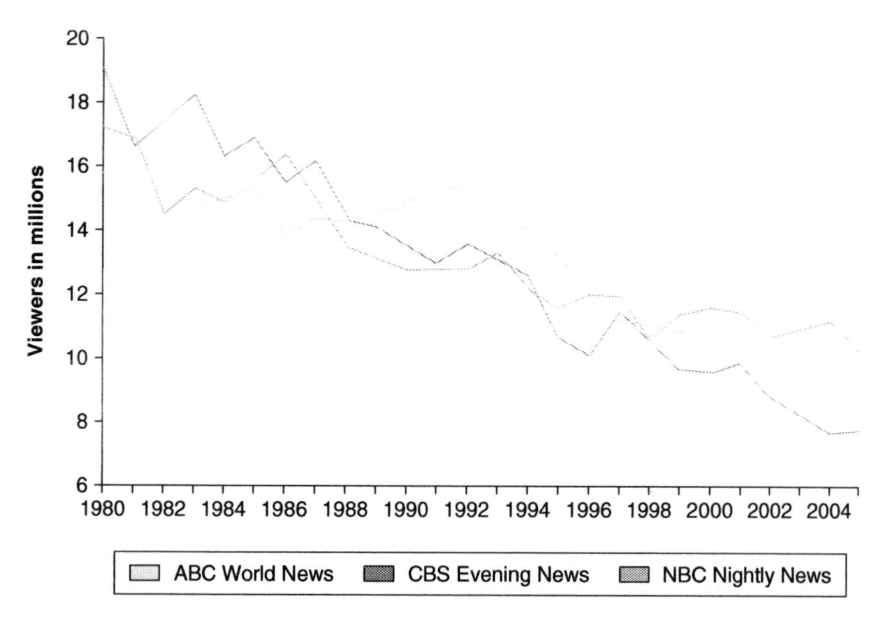

Figure 1.2 Evening news viewership in the US, by network 1980–2005
(Source: http://stateofthemedia.org/2006/printingthereport.asp)

The rise of infotainment in US television news

The Project for Excellence in Journalism in their 2006 Annual Report on American Journalism, *The State of the News Media* traced the decline in viewership for the nightly network newscasts by using two landmarks: 1969, the historic peak of nightly news viewership, and 1980, the launch of the cable news network CNN. As Figure 1.2 demonstrates, based on data from 2005, viewership share has fallen 56 per cent since 1969 and 51 per cent since 1980.

The steady loss of audience and advertising forced US networks to adapt to the new multi-channel broadcasting environment. Academic studies in the early 1990s tried to measure the trend to infotainment on television news, demonstrating that the framing of news stories was deliberately dramatic so that the policy-relevant aspects of news were often overshadowed by entertainment features (Graber, 1994). This trend towards entertaining news could be seen in 1996 when the President, Bill Clinton, answered questions from an MTV audience. Evidence of such trends was also found in a major study conducted in 1997 by the Project for Excellence in Journalism, which examined the US mass media over the previous two decades. The study noted: 'There has been a shift toward lifestyle, celebrity, entertainment and celebrity crime/scandal in the news and away from government and foreign affairs'. Looking specifically at television networks, it reported: 'The greatest new shift in emphasis of network news was a marked rise in the number of stories about scandals, up from just one-half of one per cent in 1977 to 15 per cent in 1997. The next biggest shift in emphasis in network news is a rise in human interest and quality of life stories. On network TV, human interest and quality of life stories doubled from 8 per cent of the stories that appeared in 1977 to 16 per cent in 1997' (Project for Excellence in Journalism, 1998).

As the commercialization of the US news media proceeded apace during the 1990s, commentators on broadcast journalism grew ever more critical of standards. As a recent history of television wryly notes, the 1990s 'marked a period of unprecedented decay in broadcast journalism', when the networks 'greased the slippery slope with pointed suggestions for news stories that were little more than promotions for upcoming entertainment shows' (Marc and Thompson, 2005: 121). Marketing consultants were employed by broadcast networks to spruce up news with suggestions about news programmes and talents including 'more soft-feature stories, more emotive delivery, more use of graphics, and the close attention to the youthful and attractive appearance of (female) on-air talent' (Calabrese, 2005a: 278).

An historic moment in the encroachment of entertainment into news was the infamous 1995 O. J. Simpson story, with its 'multitude of story lines involving murder, sex, celebrity, and race', and 'a dream story' for a new media era (Thaler, 1997: 132). Defining the Simpson saga as a 'mega spectacle', a key event in the decline of journalism, in a nation and perhaps a globe that is 'hooked on infotainment and tabloid culture' and marking the 'shift from journalism to infotainment', Douglas Kellner noted: 'For TV news, 1995 was the year of the Simpson spectacle, thus making clear that the priorities of corporate journalism are infotainment and profits, merging news into entertainment and journalism into business'. Between 1 January and 29 September 1995, the nightly news programmes on ABC, CBS, and NBC devoted 1,392 minutes to covering the Simpson trial, exceeding by a vast margin the reporting of the war in Bosnia (Kellner, 2003: 100–1). TV news exploited the violent aspects of the case, with re-enactments of the murders, featuring actors playing the victims and the assailant. A regional television report recreated the murders 'using a computer-animated figure, depicted as an African-American, slashing the throat of another computer-animated figure, white and blonde' (Thaler, 1997: 133).

That such commercialism was impacting on television news was identified by many scholars (Jamieson, 1992; Cappella and Jamieson,1997; Delli Carpini and Williams, 2001; Sabato et al., 2001). Cappella and Jamieson noted cynical tendencies in journalism about politics, politicians and public issues, arguing that such journalism fostered cynicism among the population. Blumler and Kavanagh described the changing nature of the relationship between media and politics. In their view, the first age of political communication – post Second World War – was characterized by stable political institutions and democratic values, followed by the second age when the relationship was 'professionalized', with political communication being adapted to the requirements of television. In 'the third age of political communication', the significant increase in competitive pressures, coupled with post-modern anti-elitist populism, were transforming the way citizens received news and engaged with political issues. Noting the 'rush to embrace infotainment' and 'the sway of politics-smearing journalism', they observed that:

> much of the increased competition stems from entertainment, 'infotainment' approaches to politics are here to stay and may proliferate. This is reflected not only in the explosion of subgenres designed as hybrids – breakfast shows, news magazines, talk shows, crime watches, tabloid television, and so forth – but also in the further mixing of information with drama, excitement, colour, and human interest in the topics, formats, and styles of most programmes. (Blumler and Kavanagh, 1999: 218)

Others, such as Bill Kovach and Tom Rosenstiel, argued that profit-oriented journalism and a 'corrosive' combination of infotainment and political spin had affected news agendas. They suggested four main reasons for this: the 24/7 news cycle with its appetite for 'live' news; the proliferation of news networks; increasingly sophisticated methods of news management and the growing importance of 'spin'; and a ratings-driven news industry that promotes a 'blockbuster mentality', privileging dramatic and entertaining reports over more staid forms of political news (Kovach and Rosenstiel, 1999). Harvard political scientist, Thomas Patterson's study of US media content, published in 2000, showed that there was a tendency among American journalists to opt for 'soft' rather than hard news stories. His analysis of a national sample of more than 5,000 news stories – from television network news as well as newspapers – from 1980 to 1999, revealed that half of all stories had no public policy content in 1999, up from 35 per cent in 1980, while sensationalism surged from 25 per cent to 40 per cent, and human interest stories more than doubled in the period of study (Patterson, 2000).

Entertainment had truly entered politics in the US by the presidential elections in 2000. Both Democratic and Republican presidential candidates appeared on a special prime-time edition of *Saturday Night Live* the night before the election. In April 2000 ABC asked actor Leonardo DiCaprio to interview Bill Clinton on the environment as part of an Earth Day special, straining the credibility of the network's professional journalism (Bishop, 2004). By 2003, the Democratic Party presidential candidates debated on MTV and each of the candidates used 'fast-cut MTV-style video' with driving music to put their case to a young audience (Mindich, 2005: 126). In the same year, Hollywood actor Arnold Schwarzenegger announced his candidacy for Governor of California on *The Tonight Show* with Jay Leno, and Senator John Edwards declared his candidacy for President on *The Daily Show* with Jon Stewart. By early 2004, most of the Democratic presidential candidates were guests on either *Real Time with Bill Maher* or *The Daily Show* (or both), being interviewed by comedian-hosts who rarely operated within traditional journalistic boundaries or mindsets (Jones, 2004: 5).

One of America's leading media commentators, Ken Auletta summarized the problems of contemporary journalism in the United States, based on the discussions of a select task force, comprising journalists and teachers of journalism, as follows:

> business pressures to achieve ratings or circulation gains and how this often trivializes news and produces infotainment; the journalistic game of Gotcha! And how this spurs reporters to chase headlines without understanding what they're after; the bimbo factor of dumb reporters (or dumb questions) without a clue what to ask or who to pursue mindless stories without context; reporters who are full of attitude, not information, who think it is okay to be cynical, as opposed to sceptical, and who adopt a fake adversarial pose without having done the legwork; the conformity of pack journalism; the lack of time that leads to hurried stories. (Auletta, 2003: xviii)

To cope with competition, all types of tactics were being employed to retain ratings: CNN, for example, appointed a senior executive with a background in entertainment television rather than in news 'to rework its staid format', which included encouraging 'personality-driven shows' and employing former *NYPD Blue* star Andrea Thompson as an anchor for *Headline News* (Bernstein, 2001). In 2002, ABC announced that it was dropping Ted Koppel, a respected anchor for the 22-year old programme *Nightline*, an analytical look at the day's news and replacing it with an entertainment programme. American journalist Bonnie Anderson, who has also worked as a network executive, argues that the networks had been co-opted by 'bottom-line thinking' that places more value on a telegenic face than on substantive reporting. Network executives are increasingly employing tactics and strategies from the entertainment industry. They 'cast' reporters based on their ability to 'project credibility', value youth over training and experience, and often support coverage only if they can be assured that it will appeal to advertiser-friendly demographics (Anderson, 2004). This type of blurring of boundaries between entertainment and news has evolved into forms of 'representational theatre' in the era of what one commentator called 'casual spectatorship' (Woodward, 2006).

The former chief foreign correspondent for ABC News and NBC News, Garrick Utley, reported that in the 1990s the US networks substantially cut back on their international coverage as their news executives felt that foreign news was 'expendable, unless it is of compelling interest to a mass audience' (Utley, 1997: 5). This observation was supported by the former CBS News foreign correspondent Tom Fenton, who chronicled the effect on quality reporting from abroad of a news media steeped in an 'entertainment-industry mindset' and executives for whom often distant yet important stories are 'obscure' (Fenton, 2005).

How can one make sense of these changes in the television news industry of the world's most powerful nation? Economist James Hamilton provides a useful model to analyse the situation, deploying market logic to explain the production and consumption of news, which he defines as 'the subset of information offered as news in the marketplace' (2003: 8). The decision-making process among what Hamilton calls 'news directors' about what information to offer as news depends 'on audience interests, costs of assembling stories, readers'/viewers' expectations about their treatment of the news, and the likely actions of their competitors.' He lists five key questions: 'Who cares about a particular piece of information? What are they willing to pay to find it, or what are others willing to pay to reach them? Where can media outlets or advertisers reach these people? When is it profitable to provide the information? Why is this profitable?' (Hamilton, 2003: 14).

Hamilton comments that entertaining 'soft news' – which he defines as programmes with 'low levels of public affairs information', in contrast to political 'hard news' with 'high levels of public affairs information' – is likely to fare better in a market-led system where 'broadcasters sell audiences to advertisers'. He argues that:

- Soft news programmes will be more prevalent if advertisers value those viewers more highly...
- If programmers pay less for soft news, then they will be more likely to programme this type of information...
- As the number of channels increases, the number of soft news programmes will increase...
- The number of soft news shows grows as the number of viewers attracted to this genre increases.
(Hamilton, 2003: 15–16)

He describes a cycle that is self-perpetuating: 'As the number of viewers attracted to programmes with low public affairs content increases, profits from offering this type of programming will attract more channels into this market. As the number of viewers of soft news programming increases, holding other factors constant, programmers will find it more profitable to offer shows with low public affairs content to attract these viewers' (ibid: 15–16).

Infotainment is a sign and a signifier of what McChesney (2004) has called the 'age of hyper-commercialism' where almost every aspect of mediated communication is commodified. As he notes: 'After watering down and dumbing down TV news until it is a joke while making a killing with inexpensive and inane fare, stations eventually found that their shrinking audience made news programmes untenable. Accordingly, some local commercial television stations have discontinued their news programming' (ibid: 96). The proliferation of infotainment has not left untouched the non-commercial and generally marginal US Public Broadcasting Service (PBS), which has been integrating into a commercial broadcasting culture, by increasingly adopting market-oriented business practices, including building brand identity by licensing its logo, selling new forms of advertising and developing PBS brand name product lines (Hoynes, 2003).

Not immune to infotainment: public-service broadcasters in Britain

Despite the well-established tradition of public-service broadcasting in Britain – exemplified by the BBC but including commercial broadcasters such as Independent Television (ITV) and Channel 4 – and its record of providing serious, informative programmes on national and international public affairs, British television programming has also been affected by the trend to infotainment, following the US experience. The role of entertainment – the last of the Reithian triad of 'informing, educating and entertaining' the public – gained ever greater prominence during the 1990s.

Though advertisement-driven but operating within a public service remit, ITV had been particularly innovative in the genre of hard-hitting current affairs programming. Granada Television's *World in Action* (1963–65 and 1967–98), a major prime time series with its mixture of 'profiles, inquiries and exposes', reflecting a robust tradition of investigative journalism in public interest, had a key role in maintaining an informed citizenry in the best tradition of public-service broadcasting (Goddard et al., 2001). The 'buzz' of 'inquiry and dissent' was also important for another ITV current affairs series *This Week* (1955–92), which, in its long history, as Patricia

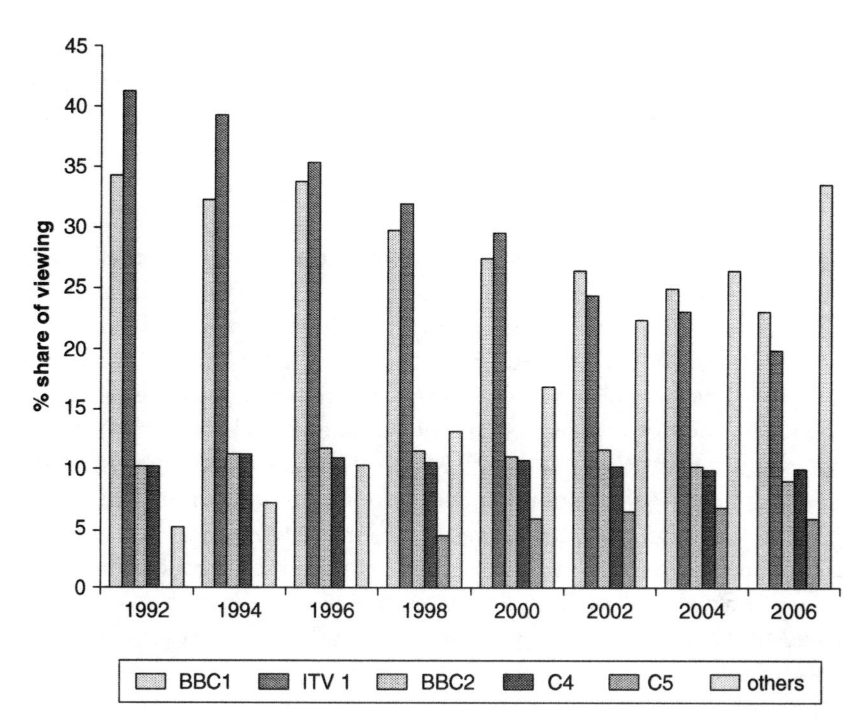

Figure 1.3 Share of TV viewing in Britain
(Source: Adapted from BARB data)

Holland has shown, brought to the British public serious documentaries about such sensitive issues as sectarian conflict in Northern Ireland and famine in Africa, thus strengthening the democratic project (Holland, 2006).

The biggest challenge to such public television came from commercially driven satellite and cable television. The undermining of the public-service ethos started with the advent of satellite television (Murdoch's Sky network) in 1989, the audience for which grew steadily during the 1990s, accounting for more than a third of British television households by 2006 (see Figure 1.3). In the early days of cable and satellite television in Britain, in a bid to grab attention and ratings, the station became notorious for its 'dumbing down', including *Live TV*'s 'news bunny', a journalist dressed up in a rabbit suit which approved or disapproved news stories, as well as topless darts and Tiffany, who undressed as she read the financial news (Horrie and Nathan, 1999).

As an increasing number of programme makers began chasing ratings, which translated into advertising revenue in the cases of ITN and Channel 4, and threatened the licence fee for the BBC, a serious news agenda started to give way to a more populist one, with its emphasis on celebrity, crime and consumer journalism. The 1990 Broadcasting Act, passed at a time when ITV was becoming more commercially driven, with a top management drawing their inspiration from corporate boards rather than newsrooms, was partly responsible for this change as it relaxed ITV's public-service responsibilities, prompting critics to claim that ITV had 'dumbed down'. The network's Independent Television News (ITN), whose flagship *News at Ten* was moved after 30 years in 1999 from its customary 10p.m. slot, was another striking example of this change of attitude. From its launch by ITN in 1967 – the first television news channel to give 30 minutes to news – *News at Ten* had played a successful role in making news accessible to viewers. More informal in style than the 'stuffy' BBC, it appealed to both popular and more serious audiences. ITV lobbied the broadcast regulators for permission to move the news programmes to later in the schedule, in order to screen entertainment programmes, especially Hollywood films, to retain its audience in the face of competition from Murdoch's satellite television channels offering the latest Hollywood blockbusters and live sporting events.

The BBC's flagship current affairs series *Panorama*, broadcast since 1953 had set the standards for current affairs reporting for half a century, with a dedicated audience of up to 10 million in its heyday in the late 1950s. It, too, was shifted to a late weekend slot and its content diluted to retain steadily declining viewership (Lindley, 2002). This shift affected not just news and current affairs but also art and ideas programmes, with series such as BBC's *The Late Show, Arena* and *Omnibus* giving way to intellectually less challenging television fare. As multi-channel broadcasting grew in the early 2000s, serious documentary and other programming was moved to specialised, some would say, ghettoized, niche channels such as BBC Four – the arts and culture channel available only on digital networks launched in 2002. While this seemed to be re-emphasizing the BBC's commitment to serious television, the audience for this worthy channel, with its high-minded motto 'we all need a place to think' has been miniscule: in its initial year it was just 0.2 per cent of the British audience. Interestingly *Panorama* was re-launched on BBC1 in January 2007, but reduced to 30 minutes and though it was broadcast on a weekday at 8.30p.m., a prime time slot, it was strangely scheduled against its two key rivals *Tonight with Trevor McDonald* on ITV and *Dispatches* on Channel 4, thus fragmenting the already declining audience for current affairs.

In Britain, as in the US, news channels tried to retain their declining audiences by transforming their presentation styles. When in 1997 the

BBC launched *News 24*, its domestic digital rolling news channel, a promotional video stated that it was 'not going to be stuffy... it might even be fun', an attitude necessitated by the changing consumption pattern of news, as an internal programme review document released to the press noted candidly: 'World economics, wars and famine make little impact unless there is some frothy presentation. The groups at the bottom are looking for entertainment, not information' (quoted in Culf, 1997). Channel 5, launched the same year, brought more glitz and glamour to television news. In 2000, Channel 5 News hired glamorous Kirsty Young to read the evening news, standing up in a brightly lit and graphically designed studio set, a trend followed by other broadcasters, including the generally sober Channel 4 News. Infotainment was deemed a necessary mechanism to connect with the rapidly fragmenting news audiences. Broadcasters started dealing with growing competition by 'increasing the dosage of trivia and spectacle in their shows' (Meyer and Hinchman, 2002: 82).

In order to succeed in the changing media environment, politicians, too, started to adapt their presentational styles, thus, it was argued, impoverishing 'political debate by oversimplifying and trivialising political communications'. 'Packaging politics' one commentator noted, 'places a premium on personalities and presidentialism. Persistent television portrayals of a select clique of "telegenic" politicians, mouthing pre-rehearsed slogans and automaton sound-bites, has supplanted the rational and sustained advocacy of policy' (Franklin, 2004: 12). The blurring of boundaries between entertainment and politics could also be detected in British Prime Minister Tony Blair's appearance in an episode of *The Simpsons*, aired in Britain in 2004. The decline of serious journalism may also be connected with the growth of the public relations industry, which is increasingly setting the news agenda. Even in Britain, where a tradition of public-service broadcasting has been very strong, this trend has been noticed by seasoned commentators. 'The fear among journalists is that they no longer have the resources to counter the increasingly sophisticated munitions of their traditional enemy: that journalism is being hung out to dry by the not-so-hidden persuaders' (Hargreaves, 2003: 180).

This trend to infotainment is not just a question of 'dumbing down', there is also an opportunity cost in terms of what is left off the news agenda. A report by the British government's Department for International Development noted: 'Few programmes about the developing world are now made and wanted by British broadcasters, outside news and current affairs. Broadcasters have marginalized this output, driven single-mindedly by the ratings imperative, and are eliminating audiences for international output.

Britain is getting increasingly insular and the television industry is not in tune with the international marketplace which wants more global, universal output (DFID, 2000: 173).

Infotainment blockbusters

A close look at the top programmes in the non-fiction category (apart from sport) over the past 25 years since systematic audience monitoring began by BARB (Broadcasting Audience Research Board), shows that infotainment-type programming dominates (see Table 1.1). The key themes to emerge are connected with what might be called very British concerns – royalty, pageantry, spectacles, celebrity game shows and talent shows.

The BBC's increasing commercialism can also be seen in its very successful development and marketing of blockbuster factual entertainment programme series in collaboration with such global operators as the Discovery Network: an indication of the scale of this can be gauged from the fact that 135 of the 225 factual productions presented at the BBC Showcase between 2002 and 2005 were co-produced with Discovery. Through its commercial arm BBC Worldwide, it has become one of Europe's biggest television programme exporters (Steemers, 2004). The production of spectacular documentary series, influenced in no small measure by the Hollywood 'blockbuster mentality' has employed formulas and sequels that guarantee 'a few global hits that can be marketed across different media outlets as opposed to many small projects with lower profit margins' (Fürsich, 2003: 135). The debut of this form of infotainment documentary was the very successful *Walking with Dinosaurs* (1999), for which an important 'cultural reference point' was the Hollywood film *Jurassic Park* in 1993 and its 1997 sequel *The Lost World* (Scott and White, 2003: 320). *Walking with Dinosaurs* was among the top ten programmes of 1999 in the UK and was rapidly replicated as a brand by other infotainment documentary series: *Walking with Beasts* (2001); *Walking with Cavemen* (2003); *Walking with Spacemen* (2004) and *Walking with Monsters* (2005). A global branding and packaging exercise, together with the series' spectacular visuals and eye-catching computer-generated graphics contributed to their global sales success (Steemers, 2004). Other examples of this public/private media marriage successfully mixed the genres of drama and documentary in such productions as *Pompeii: The Last Day* (mixing history and reconstruction), produced in 2003; and *Supervolcano* (when computer aided graphics mixed with real science), broadcast in 2005.

Table 1.1 Infotainment British-style: non-fiction programmes in the top ten, 1981–2006

Date	*Programme*	*Type*	*Channel*	*Audience (million)*
29/07/1981	*Royal Wedding*	Ceremonial	BBC1/ITV	39.00
25/04/1982	*ITN News*	Falkland War	ITV	17.25
17/11/1983	*Miss World 1983*	Pageantry	ITV	14.95
15/11/1984	*Miss World 1984*	Pageantry	ITV	17.10
20/10/1985	*Prince & Princess of Wales*	Royalty	ITV	18.60
22/09/1986	*Prince & Princess of Wales in Private and in Public*	Royalty	ITV	18.45
27/11/1987	*Challenge Anneka*	Charity gala	BBC1	17.20
05/02/1988	*Comic Relief*	Charity gala	BBC1	16.40
06/02/1992	*Elizabeth R*	Royalty	BBC1	17.85
20/11/1995	*Panorama: Princess Diana*	Royalty	BBC1	22.78
06/09/1997	*Funeral of Diana*	Royalty	BBC1	19.29
02/12/1998	*Celebrity Stars in Their Eyes*	Game show	ITV	16.34
07/03/1999	*Who Wants To Be A Millionaire*	Game show	ITV	19.21
04/10/1999	*Walking With Dinosaurs*	Documentary	BBC1	15.00
19/01/2000	*Who Wants To Be A Millionaire*	Game show	ITV	15.88
01/01/2001	*Who Wants To Be A Millionaire*	Game show	ITV1	12.65
03/02/2001	*Popstars*	Talent show	ITV1	12.37
09/02/2002	*Pop Idol Live Final*	Talent show	ITV1	13.34
03/06/2002	*Jubilee 2002: Party At The Palace*	Music show	BBC1	12.54
09/02/2002	*Pop Idol Result*	Talent show	ITV1	12.52
03/02/2003	*Tonight Special: Michael Jackson*	Interview	ITV1	15.32
21/04/2003	*Tonight Special: Millionaire*	Game show	ITV1	16.10
12/05/2003	*I'm A Celebrity – Get Me Out Of Here!*	Reality TV	ITV1	12.73
09/02/2004	*I'm A Celebrity – Get Me Out Of Here!*	Reality TV	ITV1	14.99
11/03/2005	*Comic Relief: Red Nose Night Live 05*	Charity gala	BBC1	10.94
05/12/2005	*I'm A Celebrity – Get Me Out Of Here!*	Reality TV	ITV1	12.35
17/12/2005	*Strictly Come Dancing*	Talent show	BBC1	10.76
23/12/2006	*Strictly Come Dancing*	Talent show	BBC1	12.11

(Source: Based on data from BARB, 2007)

Impact of infotainment on European public service broadcasting

The international success of the US-originated commercial model of television has had a profound effect on broadcasting, not only in Britain, but in the rest of Western Europe, the world's second richest media market and home to a strong public-service broadcasting ethos (Tracey, 1998; Price and Raboy, 2001; Lowe and Per, 2005). The deregulation and privatization of the European airwaves, which started in the late 1980s, undermined public-service monopolies with an explosion of new private channels, and, by the beginning of the twenty-first century, the television landscape in Europe had been dramatically altered. The most powerful force for the homogenization of media systems, wrote Hallin and Mancini, was 'the commercialization that has transformed both print and electronic media in Europe' (2004: 273). Such commercialism has challenged the television monopolies or duopolies in Western Europe, as elsewhere, and resulted in 'rush to commercialized communication and news' (Mazzoleni and Schulz, 1999: 257). All Western European countries had a monopoly of public television channels, except for Britain and Italy (with dual systems) and Luxembourg (all commercial) (Norris, 2000). The number of television channels in Western Europe grew exponentially from 36 state-run terrestrial channels and only 3 private channels in 1980 to 1,700 in 2005, most of which were privately owned and entertainment-oriented, though news and documentary channels also witnessed unprecedented growth (see Table 1.2).

Public-service broadcasters have been forced to follow the American model of broadcasting, as the European Union (EU) opened up its internal broadcasting borders as a result of policies to liberalize and deregulate. In such a decentralized market, entry to one of the national markets allowed free mobility to the totality of the EU market and regional space. This was particularly useful to the US television industry

Table 1.2 Expansion of TV channels in Europe

Channel type	*1990*	*1995*	*2000*	*2005*
Entertainment	14	31	90	170
News/Business	6	24	65	119
Documentary	2	9	65	108
Total channels*	93	242	768	1703

Note:
*Including all other channel types

(Source: Based on data from *Screen Digest*, August 2005)

'that now need[ed] only to deal with the same set of rules across Europe, making significant savings in resources and time' (Chakravartty and Sarikakis, 2006: 103).

One argument governments made for the regulation of television during the analogue period was that, due to scarcity of electromagnetic spectrum, state regulators could ensure that it was used for the public good by restricting the number of television operators. However, with digitalization and consequent capacity to squeeze 'more channels within existing pipes' the government tutelage of television was gradually being undermined,' although governments could also benefit from the process of charging for access to this capacity (Galperin, 2004). In fact a comparative study of digitalization and funding among four public broadcasters, which included two from Europe: the BBC, Radiotelevisione Italiana, the Australian Broadcasting Corporation, and the Canadian Broadcasting Corporation, showed that these four major public broadcasters enjoyed relative stability precisely because they embraced competition and commercialism, though in the process they were losing their distinctiveness and purpose (Padovani and Tracey, 2003).

There was an unmistakably neo-liberal character to media policy-making in Europe during this period of expansion, which will be discussed in more detail in the next chapter. Reflecting on the US experience, Robert McChesney argues that there has been a progressive deterioration of transparency and public participation, and a 'decisive increase in the business domination of media policy making' (2004: 48). In Britain, the Communication Act of 2003 demonstrated a clear shift in language from protecting the public interest towards the concept of the individual 'citizen-consumer', a phrase that began to be used in government policy papers, for example, in Ofcom reports (Feintuck and Varney, 2006). The Act also simplified media ownership rules, paving the way for greater consolidation in the field of television. For example, the rules which prevented the joint ownership of ITV were repealed, making it possible for it to be consolidated, with Carlton TV and Granada TV merging in 2004 to form one main company – ITV plc. Similarly, media ownership rules for Britain's fifth terrestrial channel, Channel 5, were relaxed and ownership of television licences by non-EU persons was permitted – since 2005 Channel 5 has been owned by the German television company RTL, while Murdoch acquired a nearly 18 per cent share of ITV in 2006 (Ofcom, 2006).

Colin Leys notes how public policy in every area of British public life, including what he calls 'public service television', has been adapted to suit 'the interests of corporations' (Leys, 2001: 56). The inspiration for such media policy-making, according to this perspective, may have come from the US. After studying the dynamics of media policy-making in Britain and the US, one commentator concluded:

> Key decision-makers operate in close ideological conformity with the *broad* interests of one key constituency – that of business – in a way that structures the parameters of the debate, dictates what forms of participation are most effective and conditions the balance of power in the policy process. While a range of voices may be heard, there is little opportunity to question the assumptions about the desirability of 'competition' and 'consumer sovereignty' that increasingly dominate media policy-making. The process is therefore skewed by a fundamental imbalance in both resources and influence between public and private interests. (Freedman, 2006: 921)

Television policy-making has been increasingly affected by transnational or regional actors, and, with pressure from market forces, public-service broadcasters have been forced to justify their special position within the broadcasting marketplace, with questions being raised about the appropriateness of support from their respective governments as well as special provisions, such as the licence fee in case of the BBC and other subsidies which have traditionally bolstered public broadcasting. The European Commission's Competition Directorate, for example, monitors public-service television channels to ensure that the strict 'state aid' rules are not breached. In 2006, the EU decided that its member states could authorize product placement in television drama and entertainment programmes, though such blatant commercialism was prohibited in news, current affairs and children's programmes. Advertising rules vary between what the EU calls the 'linear' television broadcasts (broadcasting via traditional TV, the Internet or mobile phones), which 'pushes' content to viewers, and 'non-linear' on-demand services (video-on-demand), which the viewers 'pull' from a network: rules for the latter being less stringent than the former. As a report of the advisory panel for the Council of Europe Steering Committee on the Mass Media (on media concentrations, pluralism and diversity questions) noted: 'The main concerns raised by transnational media concentrations are the negative effects on freedom of expression and information in Europe, especially by the diminishing diversity of content production and the reduced contribution of commercial European media outlets to the public sphere' (Council of Europe, 2004: 33).

The deregulation of television in Germany and the consequent 'dualization' of its broadcasting system, which kick-started intensive competition between the public and commercial stations, has had an impact on news coverage. A study of television news comparing the presentation of politics in 1986, immediately after the deregulation of television, and in 1993, when the dual broadcasting system was well established, showed that 'serious'

Table 1.3 Daily audience market share (%) of public television in Europe, selected countries

	1995	*2003*
Hungary	79.0	17.5
Slovakia	73.7	21.8
Slovenia	61.5	34.7
Poland	80.0	51.2
UK	54.3	46.2
Italy	48.2	48.6
France	43.9	46.4
Germany	40.1	44.4

(Source: Open Society Institute, 2005)

politics on television was limited to the traditional news broadcasts, while at the same time new formats had appeared mixing political information with entertainment (Pfetsch, 1996).

In eastern Europe the discourse of 'liberty' and 'free media' has been 'used quite extensively in policy, to provide the normative justification of the liberalization of airwaves, licences and other means of communications transmissions, especially by neo-liberal, right-wing governments who played a significant role in this process' (Chakravartty and Sarikakis, 2006: 88). It is scarcely surprising then that the audience share for public broadcasters in Eastern European countries has drastically declined, as Table 1.3 demonstrates, while in countries with longer tradition of public service broadcasting such as Germany and France, the audience share has in fact increased, bucking the trend witnessed among most countries. In Europe's so-called 'transition' countries, sometime also referred to as 'the new Europe', journalists have taken to the market road with a convert's zeal. However, as a report from Open Society Institute's EU Monitoring and Advocacy Program cautions: 'Journalists working within commercial television in the transition countries are underpaid – although in some cases they earn more than those working for public-service broadcasters – and have limited or no labour protection. These factors all compromise the independence of the newsrooms in commercial television stations' (Open Society Institute, 2005: 66).

What seems to be happening is that a clear distinction between private and public television is becoming increasingly difficult to sustain. The Open Society Institute's report on European television mentioned above covering 20 European countries, the largest comparative survey of its kind, notes: 'the distinction between public-service broadcasters and their commercial competition, in terms of programme content and quality, has become increasingly blurred. Investigative journalism and minority programming are scarce commodities in both public and commercial television. Newscasts have often become markedly tabloid, particularly on commercial television channels' (Open Society Institute, 2005: 22). Television in Europe as elsewhere has been profoundly affected by larger, transnational changes in the broadcasting industry, triggered by multilateral institutional and technological transformations which have altered television news, as well as other sectors of media, to which we turn in Chapter 2.

2
THE INFRASTRUCTURE FOR GLOBAL INFOTAINMENT

How did this Americanized or American-inspired infotainment reach a global audience? It is crucially important to understand the creation of the infrastructure for global infotainment, which took place during the 1990s, when fundamental ideological changes in the post-Cold War global political arena and claims of the 'end of history' and the triumph of free-market neo-liberalism were routinely bandied about in media and policy discourses. The creation of the 'informational state' (Braman, 2006) and pro-market international trade regimes, that included the media sector, transformed the global television landscape. The processes of deregulation and privatization in the communications and media industries, combined with new digital information and communication technologies, resulted in a quantum leap in television news channels. The convergence of the telecommunications, computer and media industries enabled the instantaneous delivery of infotainment across a digitally linked globe. As the new technologies put in place a global communication infrastructure based on regional and global satellite networks, used for telecommunications, broadcasting and electronic commerce, a policy shift from state to private control and from a state-centric view of television to one governed by the rules of the free market also gained growing acceptance around the world (Oslund and Pelton, 2004).

In this free market environment, multilateral organizations such as the World Trade Organization (WTO), International Telecommunication Union (ITU) and the World Bank argued for a strong communications infrastructure as a foundation for international commerce and economic development. Dismantling barriers to the free flow of information was seen as essential for growth and significant trade in goods and services would not be possible without a free trade in information (World Bank, 1998; UNDP, 1999; ITU; 1999). The globalizing ideology of these multilateral organizations drove the establishment of a pro-market television and telecommunication infrastructure. This reversed the traditional national frameworks for television and telecommunication, which, for most of the twentieth century, were owned or regulated by the state, which was also involved in providing their networks and equipment and regulating international traffic. By 2007 most of the world's telecoms organizations were privatized, revolutionizing the delivery of sound, pictures, videos and data. Such changes have undermined national telecommunication monopolies and created a competitive environment which has hugely improved services and drastically reduced costs.

This decisive shift from the public-service role of television and telecommunications to private competition and deregulation had a major impact on international communications policy, shaped by the US and by European Union countries, which are also home to companies with global ambitions (Braman, 2004, 2006). By including telecommunications (telephone, telegraph, data transmission, radio, TV and news services) in its remit, the 1995 General Agreement on Trade in Services (GATS), the first multilateral, legally enforceable agreement covering trade and investment in the services sector, played a key role in creating a global market for information and entertainment, along with many other products and services (Geradin and Luff, 2004). The most significant component of this agreement for communication was the GATS Annex on Telecommunications, which effectively extended the 'free flow of information doctrine' to cover both the content of communication and the infrastructure through which such messages flow. Its one guiding principle stated that foreign and national suppliers of telecom facilities should be treated equally, obliging countries to ensure that foreign services suppliers had access to public networks and services on an equal basis, both within the national market and across borders, thus exposing domestic telecommunications industries to international competition. The Annex also encouraged the establishment of international standards for global compatibility and interoperability (WTO, 1998). In parallel, the ITU advised countries to dismantle structural regulations preventing cross-ownership among broadcasters, cable operators and telecom companies.

The policy of liberalizing the global telecommunication system was also greatly influenced by the 1996 US Telecommunications Act, which not only transformed the industry within the US but enabled private US telecommunications corporations to operate globally. These US-based corporations have in turn played a leading role in pushing the WTO and the ITU to further liberalize global communication. Always a champion of free trade, US Government policy was to further reduce the role of its state regulatory mechanisms: the FCC, for example, saw its role changing from 'an industry regulator to a market facilitator', promoting competition in the global communications market. As a result of the opening up of the global market, telecommunications has become one of the largest and fastest-growing service sectors, doubly significant, as it is not only a service itself but also the delivery mechanism for many other services – by 2004 the overall network-generated revenue had reached $1.3 trillion (UNCTAD, 2005).

Infotainment beaming from the sky

With the increasing privatization of global satellite networks, the satellite industry benefited the most from the liberalization of communication. At the dawn of the twenty-first century, satellites were seen as the new 'trade routes in the sky' (Price, 1999). Just as the cabling of the world in the nineteenth century helped the establishment and maintenance of the British Empire, so satellite links were providing the global infotainment and information networks for an American commercial empire and were crucial in disseminating infotainment in a global television marketplace (Parks, 2005). Ever since the mid-1960s, when geostationary communications satellites first began to beam pictures across nations and oceans, unrestricted by geographical terrain, satellites have played a key role in the globalization of television (Oslund and Pelton, 2004). The 1989 decision of the FCC to authorize a private company, Pan American Satellite Inc. (PanAmSat) to provide international carrier services between the US and Latin America, triggered the privatization of satellite-based international communication. The WTO's Fourth Protocol, also referred to as the Basic Agreement on Telecommunications Services, endorsed the US position that the distinction between 'domestic' and 'international' satellite systems was no longer valid in a digitally connected world and that satellite transmissions could cross national borders, thereby revolutionizing satellite television. ITU's World Radio-communication Conferences (WRC) in Istanbul in 2000 and Geneva in 2003, further liberalized the global communication infrastructure and worked towards spectrum harmonization allowing satellite systems to deliver 3G mobile voice and high-speed broadband services.

With communication satellites being launched by many countries (such as India, and, especially, China, which has launched 30 satellites since 1990) and by regional consortia (Eutelsat, Arabsat, AsiaSat and Hispasat), there are many more providers of infotainment hardware in a crowded geostationary spectrum. Since satellites are a lucrative and highly competitive industry, in which a few big players operate, given that there are a limited number of orbital slots in the geostationary orbit and multiple satellites covering the same footprint, even intergovernmental organizations have adopted the market-based solutions: Inmarsat (International Marine

Satellite) an international co-operative of 86 countries and the sole provider of a broad range of global mobile satellite communications, became in 1999 the world's first international treaty organization to transform itself into a commercial company.

The pan-European intergovernmental organization Eutelsat, the first satellite operator in Europe to broadcast Direct-To-Home (DTH), was also privatized in 2001 after a long 'restructuring process' of privatization: by 2005, Eutelsat was operating 23 satellites, broadcasting more than 1,700 television channels to 120 million households in Europe, the Middle East, North Africa and parts of Asia and North America. In an international context, a more significant change has been the gradual commercialization and privatization of the International Telecommunications Satellite Organization (Intelsat), created in 1964 as an intergovernmental treaty organization (in the spirit of the UN), offering affordable satellite capacity on a non-discriminatory basis (Thussu, 2002). In 2005, a consortium led by four major US-based private investment groups bought Intelsat, the world's largest satellite service provider – with a fleet of 53 satellites. In the same year, Intelsat announced the takeover of PanAmSat, exploiting synergies between communication and broadcasting interests as PanAmSat has a strong presence in DTH services, while Intelsat has its core strength in telephony and data services (Thussu, 2006a).

The satellite industry demands substantial investment and only transnational corporations and other large businesses and governments are able to exploit this communication hardware. With digital technology, modern satellites have experienced a nearly 500-fold capacity increase over 1960s spacecraft, and the WTO-sponsored deregulation and rapid privatization of national telecommunications organizations have accelerated the flow of infotainment and information across national borders. This has resulted in a flourishing global telecommunications industry led by commercial international satellite and cable communications operators offering a wider range of services. US companies and a French-led European consortium dominate the world market for the manufacture of geostationary satellites. In 2005, the US-based Satellite Industry Association, which represents the leading US commercial satellite corporations, reported that the commercial satellite industry generated $97.2 billion in revenue in 2004, a figure which has more than doubled since 1996, driven primarily by the DTH services, which accounted for $49.5 billion, or about 51 per cent of the entire industry's revenues.

The three largest US contractors – Hughes Space and Communications, Lockheed Martin, and Loral – have between them built more than 70 per cent of the geostationary communications satellites in orbit, while a European satellite consortium, led by the French Aerospatiale, has built more than 20 per cent. Among Hughes' main customers is the Luxembourg-based Société Européenne des Satellites (SES), the owner and operator of Astra, Europe's leading DTH satellite system. In less than a decade, the market share of satellite reception in Europe has risen from virtually zero to more than 26 per cent of TV households, and, by 2007, Astra was carrying broadcast (1,400 TV channels) and broadband services to more than 102 million homes across the continent. SES Global, set up in 2005, owned five satellites and shared 'complementarity' with Americom (which it acquired in 2001) in North America and Star One in Latin America. It also holds a 34 per cent share of AsiaSat, Asia's premier satellite operator.

In Latin America, PanAmSat, the first private satellite service for the continent, established in 1988, launched three satellites for the Latin American region in 1997 to support the DTH services operated by Sky Latin America and Galaxy Latin America. By 2005, when it was taken over by Intelsat, PanAmSat was operating a global network of 23 geosynchronous satellites. The launch in 1990 of AsiaSat 1, signalled China's entry into the world of commercial satellites, and AsiaSat 2, launched in 1995, covers 53 countries and two-thirds of the world's population, beaming such pan-Asian television networks as STAR (Satellite Television Asian Region). In the Arab world, DTH services have been available since the launch of Arabsat 1C in 1992, by the regional satellite operator, the Arab Satellite Communications Organization (Arabsat).

Though the geostationary systems continue to grow, they have been brought under the control of large corporations, through mergers, takeovers and regional alliances. From a commercial perspective, this makes market sense, since large systems create economies of scale and boost the argument for further deregulation of satellite communication, especially in the DTH sector, to which several countries have been resistant. Unable to compete with global carriers, many state-run operators have privatized their own satellite systems, as have the intergovernmental satellite operators. The result of these changes is that the market for satellite services has become increasingly commercial, a trend which is likely to grow, with the convergence of digital media delivery systems and the increasing worldwide use of satellites for Internet and mobile communication and commerce. Satellite communication has another, highly critical role, providing images for military intelligence and security (Thussu, 2002). In 2007 Intelsat was serving more than 60 US government and military users, as well as NATO entities. According to the 2002 annual report of the US Department of Defense: 'A key objective of the Department's space surveillance and control mission is to ensure freedom of action in space for the United States and its allies and, when directed, deny such freedom of action to adversaries' (US Government, 2002a). The role this plays in providing images for the news coverage of war will be discussed in Chapter 5.

The expansion of global satellite networks is having a significant impact on the international infotainment industry. The growing availability of DTH television has ensured that infotainment can be beamed literally direct to homes across the world, circumventing national regulatory and censorship mechanisms and thus provide a feast of commodified images and ideologies. With a global communication infrastructure in place, media and communication corporations have harnessed liberalization, deregulation and privatization of broadcasting to good effect, leading to unprecedented rates of merger activity and corporate consolidation, resulting in the domination of a few hugely powerful infotainment conglomerates.

Creation of infotainment conglomerates

The neo-liberal global policy regime established in the 1990s, in conjunction with the new communication technologies of satellite, cable, digital and mobile delivery mechanisms, have created a global marketplace for infotainment (Betting and Hall, 2003; Geradin and Luff, 2004; Hoskins et al., 2004; Caves, 2005; Croteau and Hynes, 2005; Thomas, 2005; Thussu, 2006a). Media products constitute one of the largest uses of commercial satellites, making it imperative for media conglomerates to plan their strategies in a global context, with the ultimate aim of profitable growth through exploiting economies of scope and scale. The convergence of both media and technologies, and the process of vertical integration in the media industries to achieve this aim, have resulted in the concentration of media power in the hands of a few large transnational multi-media corporations (Betting and Hall, 2003; Bagdikian, 2004; McChesney, 2004; Croteau and Hynes, 2005; McPhail, 2006; Thussu, 2006a; Baker, 2007).

The privatization of broadcasting across the globe, coupled with the relaxation of cross-media ownership restrictions, especially in the US and Britain, have enabled television companies to broaden and deepen their existing interests, cashing in on a wave of mergers and acquisitions, which have characterized the media industry in the last two decades. In 1985, Rupert Murdoch bought Twentieth Century Fox in order to acquire a base in the US and in 1989 Sony purchased Columbia TriStar. In the same year Time Inc. merged with Warner Communication, forming Time Warner to which Turner Broadcasting Systems was added in 1995. Disney bought Capital Cities/ABC in 1995, thereby adding a broadcast network to a traditionally entertainment company. The $80 billion merger in 1999, of two major US corporations, Viacom and CBS, created at that time the world's largest entertainment and media corporation, to be overtaken a year later by the merger of America on Line (AOL) and Time Warner. In 2003, the FCC, arguing that ownership concentration was not a threat to democracy, further reduced restrictions on media mergers, despite strong public opposition (McChesney, 2004; Baker, 2007). Such mergers have reduced the number of corporations controlling both production and delivery of media content internationally. By 2006, fewer than ten corporations, most based in the US, owned a large section of the world's media industries, with AOL-Time Warner being at the forefront, followed by Walt Disney, Viacom-CBS, Bertelsmann, News Corporation, Telecommunication Inc. (TCI), Sony and NBC, which entered into partnership with the Paris-based Vivendi Universal in 2003 to create NBC-Universal. All the major television corporations – Disney, Time Warner, News Corporation and Viacom – own multiple broadcast and cable networks and production facilities.

As the media and telecommunications sectors intersected globally, the vertical integration of the media industries from content origination through to delivery mechanisms enabled multi-media conglomerates to dominate global media: newspapers, magazines, books, radio, broadcast television, cable systems and programming, movies, music recordings, DVDs, mobile and on-line services. With the revolution in digital distribution, a whole range of new revenue-earning opportunities emerged. The expanding bandwidth, combined with the rapid globalization of fixed and mobile networks, as well as the digitization of content and growing use of personal computers worldwide, have considerably helped global media conglomerates to capitalize on new markets and experiment with innovative media products. One of the most important drivers in the US economy, contributing nearly 60 per cent of the growth of US exportable products and services, the 'core' copyright industries (also referred to as 'convergence industries' that include software publishers, film, video, sound recording, advertising, printing, and video and disk rental) added $33 billion to export revenues in 2003 (Siwek, 2005).

Infotainment conglomerates have benefited hugely from the exponential growth in the reach of the media and the diversification of its forms and modes of delivery, exploiting corporate synergies by promoting their products across virtually all media sectors, including broadcast and cable television, radio and on-line media, mobile telephony and personal digital devices – for example, TNT films can be advertised on the CNN networks, while clips from Fox News can be broadcast on Murdoch's British television news operation – Sky News (Vogel, 2004). The logic of synergies operates, as Meehan notes, when entertainment intrudes into news provision. Time Warner, for example, circulates brief items about movie stars, television actors, singers, and other personalities associated with the entertainment industries on CNN's *The Hollywood Minute* or *Showbiz Today*, 'served up as if they were part of the news cycle – as just more information that regularly passes by our window on the world. In one sense, these items are filler, but in another sense they are mini ads masquerading as news. The items plug both the celebrities and the media products associated with them' (Meehan, 2005: 2).

Corporations such as Disney have their own central synergy departments charged with maximizing company product sales, through cross-selling and cross-promotion strategies involving hundreds of media markets round the world. The model has been compared with a wheel: 'At the hub lies content creation. The spokes that spread out from it are the many different ways of exploiting the resulting brands: the movie studio, the television networks, the music, the publishing, the merchandising, the theme parks, the Internet sites. Looked at this way, the distinction between manufacturing and distribution begins to blur, because the various ways of selling the brand also serve to enhance its value' (*The Economist*, 1998: 8). Despite intense competition among infotainment conglomerates, they also exploit synergies by sharing international markets. Consortia such as Latin America Pay TV (News Corporation, Universal, Viacom, MGM), HBO Ole and HBO Brasil (Time Warner, Sony, Disney), and HBO Asia (Time Warner, Sony, Universal and Viacom) are some of the examples of these overlapping operations. Disney shares programming with TCI in E! Entertainment while STAR works with Disney-owned Entertainment and Sports Network (ESPN) in televising sports in Asia (Thussu, 2006a).

Outside the US ambit, the other infotainment conglomerates include Germany's Bertelsmann, Japan's Sony, Paris-based Vivendi Group, which owns the Canal+ Group (one of Europe's biggest pay-TV networks) as well as Vivendi Universal Games (a major European producer and distributor of on-line and computer games); Britain's Pearson and ITV; Italy's Mediaset; Brazil's Globo group; Zee Network (India's largest multimedia company), and Shanghai Media Group in China. While these 'old' media companies continued to set the global media agenda, by 2007 'new' media corporations such as Internet giant Google, Microsoft and Yahoo! were also emerging as powerful global infotainment providers.

Fears about excessive power concentration among a few mainly American conglomerates have been expressed by commentators, labelling these as communication cartels, controlling production and distribution of global information and entertainment (Herman and McChesney, 1997; Bagdikian, 2004; McChesney, 1999, 2004; Kunz, 2006). Monitoring this concentration of media power, in his 1983 book *Media Monopoly*, Ben Bagdikian argued that the US media were dominated by 50 private corporations. By 2004, when the book was republished in its seventh edition, now called *The New Media Monopoly*, the number of corporations controlling most of US media had dropped to just five – Time Warner, Disney, News Corporation, Bertelsmann and Viacom, with NBC as a close sixth. As Bagdikian writes:

> In 1983, the men and women who headed the 50 mass media corporations that dominated American audiences could have fit comfortably in a modest hotel ballroom. The people heading the 20 dominant newspaper chains probably would form one conversational cluster to complain about newsprint prices; 20 magazine moguls in a different circle denounce postal rates; the broadcast network people in another corner, not being in the newspaper or magazine business, exchange indignation about government radio and television regulations; the book people compete in outrage over greed of writers' agents; and movie people gossip about sexual achievements of their stars. By 2003, five men controlled all these old media once run by the 50 corporations of 20 years earlier. These five, owners of additional digital corporations, could fit in a generous phone booth. Granted, it would be a tight fit and it would be filled with some tensions. (2004: 27)

Global trade in infotainment

International trade in infotainment should be considered within the larger dimensions of the economic system in which it operates as it is affected by many of the same economic forces that apply to other types of commercial enterprises (Gershon, 1997, 2005). As noted by Picard, media in the US 'are for the most part capitalist ventures operated by private parties for the purpose of generating profit, and are thus subject to the operational principles of the market system. Even not-for profit media – such as public broadcasting or organizational operated media – are influenced by the principles of the market system and are thus affected by its operations' (Picard, 1989: 14). Infotainment products form part of the rapidly expanding and highly lucrative global market in cultural and creative industries, valued at $1.3 trillion. According to UNESCO, between 1994 and 2002, international trade in cultural goods increased from $38 billion to $60 billion, with the US being the leading exporter of cultural products, and the entertainment industry one of its largest export earners (UNESCO, 2005). As Table 2.1 shows, of the world's top five entertainment corporations in 2005, four were based in the US, while the remaining one had substantial US business and corporate connections.

Despite impressive growth in on-line delivery mechanisms and increasing use of broadband, most of the world's entertainment output is transmitted

Table 2.1 The world's top five entertainers

Company	*Revenues ($ bn)*	*Profits ($ bn)*
Time Warner (US)	43.6	2.9
Walt Disney (US)	31.9	2.5
News Corporation (US)	23.8	2.1
Bertelsmann (Germany)	21.2	1.0
CBS (US)	14.5	–0.7

(Source: *Fortune*, July 24, 2006, figures for 2005)

through digital terrestrial as well as satellite and cable television, increasingly transnational in its operations, technologies and audiences (Barker, 1997; Smith, 1998; Spigel and Olsson, 2004; Chalaby, 2005). Unlike print-based traditional transnational media, such as *Time* magazine or *Wall Street Journal*, which has always had an elitist readership, television has the potential to create transnational popular audiences. The volume of US trade in visual entertainment and the capacity of its infotainment conglomerates to produce and distribute to an international audience ensures that US-based networks are the most prevalent in the global television system – see Table 2.2.

Hollywood-imported or inspired programming, whether in music (MTV), factual entertainment (Discovery), sports (ESPN), news (CNN) or children's entertainment (Cartoon Network), produced by them or their localized clones, forms a significant part of the television schedules around the world (Thussu, 2007a). In addition to the presence of US entertainment programmes (in original, dubbed or localized versions), syndication companies that are largely US-based but also European sell 'format rights' for programmes that are more nationally specific, such as game and reality shows, constituting what has been termed as 'copycat TV' (Moran, 1998). Some

Table 2.2 Top five global TV networks in 2005

Network	*Type*	*Ownership*	*No. of households (millions)*
MTV Networks	Music	Viacom	418
CNN International	News	AOL-Time Warner	260
BBC World	News	BBC	258
Discovery	Documentaries	Discovery Comm.	180
Star	Entertainment	News Corp.	103

(Source: Company websites and trade press, figures for 2005)

genres of television, notably animation, music, wildlife documentaries and live sporting events, are relatively easy to sell into different cultural contexts, which may go some way to explaining the global success of a factual entertainer such as Discovery Network (Fürsich, 2003). Through its 90 networks, including themed digital channels, ranging from travel, to lifestyle; from children's programming to wildlife, to history and adventure, available in 35 languages, this 'real-world media and entertainment company' had a pre-eminent position, reaching 180 million households in more than 160 countries in 2007.

Other global factual networks with portable content and a generally high infotainment quotient include National Geographic Television, which was broadcasting to 151 countries, reaching 230 million households in 27 languages; the History Channel and The Sci-Fi channel. American style infotainment has also entered the world of religious broadcasting, which is being increasingly commercialized and globalized. By 2007, the Family Channel, a platform for US evangelist preacher Pat Robertson, was reaching 200 countries, broadcasting programmes in more than 70 languages, while the Trinity Broadcasting Network, the 'largest worldwide religious network' promoting evangelism through 47 satellites and the Eternal Word Television Network, the world's largest Catholic television network, was accessible in 110 countries. Reflecting the 'Christianization' of secular media, these networks work closely with the evangelical movement, targeting converts and consumers to spread a 'Christian lifestyle' message (Hendershot, 2004).

One result of the privatization and proliferation of television outlets and the growing glocalization of US media products is that American film and television exports witnessed extraordinary growth. According to the US government's Bureau of Economic Analysis, receipts for film and television tape rentals, covering 'the right to display, reproduce and distribute US motion pictures and television programming abroad', have shown a nearly five-fold increase – from $2.5 billion in 1992 to $10.4 billion in 2004 (US Government, 2005a) (see Figure 2.1).

Advertising for global infotainment

The global expansion of television and other media could not have been possible without the support of advertising revenue. In a market-led broadcasting system, the role of advertising is crucial – a role that has become increasingly powerful. Given the historical importance of advertising in American domestic commercial radio and television, the US is the world's biggest advertising market, three times bigger than its nearest rival Japan in

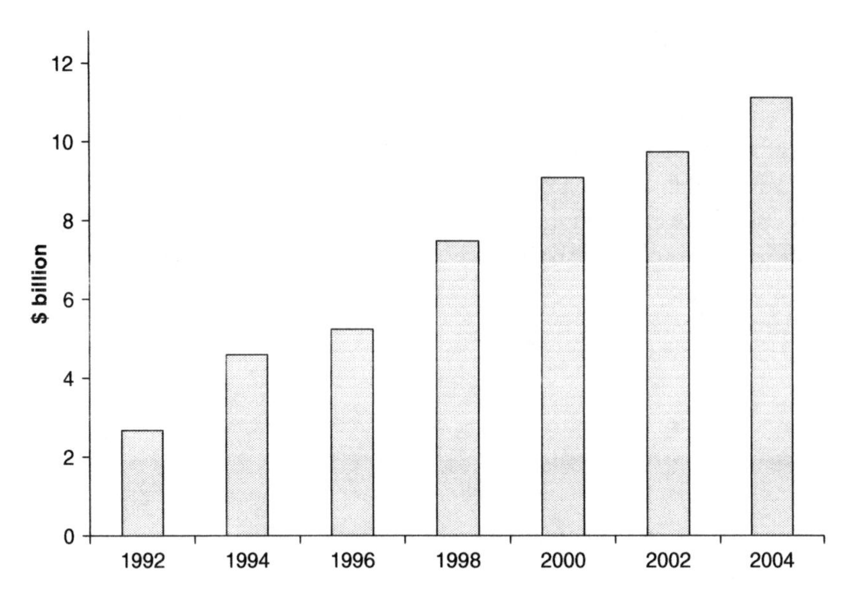

Figure 2.1 US film and TV programming exports ($ billions)
(Source: US Government, 2005a)

terms of spending on advertising. In common with many other countries, especially in Latin America, product placement is an integral part of US television culture: in the last three decades product placement spending on US television has increased by more than 26 times, as Table 2.3 shows. By 2003, television product placement had reached such levels that a formal independent rating service iTVX was introduced, to evaluate product placements on the basis of how long the product is on screen, how prominently it was displayed and whether it was incorporated into the story line (McChesney, 2004: 150). The proliferation of digital channels and shifting of advertising to on-line media has forced television networks to set up departments to promote what is variously described as 'advertainment', 'branded content' and 'advertiser-funded programming' (AFP), ranging from short infomercials to series sponsorship and branded entertainment programming shown around the world: according to industry estimates, global investment in such content in 2005 was $4.2 billion (*Television Business International*, 2006).

Global advertising expenditure, according to McCann Worldgroup, one of the world's largest advertising companies, has doubled in the past decade and a half – from nearly $276 billion to an estimated $604 billion in 2006 (see Figure 2.2).

Television is one of the fastest growing advertising media, especially internationally, with the proliferation of television channels across the world and

Table 2.3 Product placement spending on US television

Year	*Spending ($ million)*
1974	71
1979	104
1984	188
1989	330
1994	464
1999	709
2004	1,878

(Source: PQ media, www.pqmedia.com)

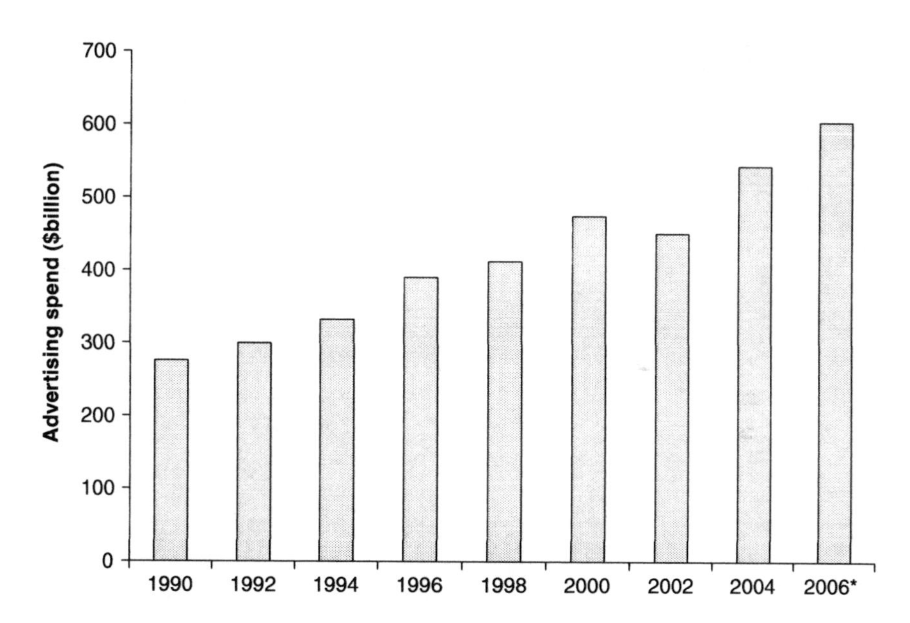

Figure 2.2 Growth in worldwide advertising 1990–2006
*Estimates
(Source: McCann Worldgroup)

growing acceptance of new digital and mobile delivery mechanisms. As a result, advertisements promoting transnational corporations – such as Procter & Gamble (US); Toyota (Japan); L'Oreal (France) – are ubiquitous on television screens around the world, adapted to suit local languages and cultural parameters. It is no coincidence that five of the top ten advertisers in 2005 were US-based corporations (see Table 2.4). A glimpse through

Table 2.4 Top ten global marketers by advertising spend ($ million), 2005

Advertiser	*Worldwide*	*US*	*Europe*	*Asia*	*Latin America*
Procter & Gamble (US)	8,190	3,410	2,553	1,743	216
Unilever (UK)	4,272	761	2,107	1,048	227
General Motors (US)	4,173	3,004	800	138	92
Toyota Motor (Japan)	2,800	1,076	511	1,096	19
L'Oreal (France)	2,773	794	1,633	236	35
Ford Motor (US)	2,645	1,583	801	108	69
Time Warner (US)	2,479	2,061	272	91	20
DaimlerChrysler (Ger.)	2,104	1,590	375	46	32
Nestle (Switzerland)	2,033	561	1,048	274	105
Johnson & Johnson (US)	1,968	1,386	324	190	17

(Source: Based on data from *Advertising Age*, http://adage.com/datacenter, accessed February 2007)

Advertising Age magazine's annual advertising spend will show that corporations based within the trading triad – US, Western Europe and Japan – dominate the top hundred list: the magazine defines a 'global' operation when media spending covers at least three continents.

As Table 2.5 shows, a Western, and more specifically, Anglo–American stamp is visible on global advertising conglomerates. With their extensive affiliates and subsidiaries around the world, these major advertisers help to propagate the neo-liberal agenda by localizing advertisements, using national languages and cultural codes. The opening up of new markets has ensured that advertising conglomerates can expand their operations without restrictions, installing new networks and facing fewer problems in the repatriation of royalties or profits. Having grown substantially during the 1980s as a result of the deregulation of television, primarily in the US (Mattelart, 1991), the advertising industry has been transformed into a transnational marketing service for conglomerates. In this role, the advertising industry has gone beyond its traditional business, offering a global package which includes advertising, marketing, promotion, media services, public relations and management consultancy (Dicken, 1998; Mooij, 1998; Jones, 1999).

It is often the case that the same transnational corporations are the main users of advertising in different regions. The major conglomerates are the advertisers and the advertising agencies are themselves part of major conglomerates, both of which are global in their strategies and approach (Jones, 1999). Some advertisers can also play an important part in television programme production: US corporations had a historic role as the originator

Table 2.5 The world's top marketing organizations, ranked by worldwide revenue ($ million), 2005

Agency	*Worldwide*	*US revenue*	*Outside US*
Omnicom Group (US)	10,481	5,744	4,737
WPP Group (UK)	10,032	3,912	6,112
Interpublic Group (US)	6,274	3,461	2,813
Publicis Groupe (France)	5,107	2,182	2,926
Dentsu (Japan)	2,888	48	2,839
Havas (France)	1,808	713	1,095
Aegis Group (UK)	1,578	446	1,132
Hakuhodo DY (Japan)	1,364	0.0	1,364

(Source: Based on data from *Advertising Age*, April 2006)

of the 'soap opera,' and sponsorship of television programmes, including of news programmes in many countries, by corporations is not uncommon. There is, therefore, a community of interest between the advertisers and the advertising medium. In the twenty-first century, the increasingly international nature of advertising, marketing and public relations has led to 'Globally Integrated Marketing Communications', that ensures a co-ordinated global management of products across country offices and disciplines.

The trend is towards global branding, a brand which 'shares the same strategic principles, positioning and marketing in every market throughout the world, although the marketing mix can vary. It carries the same brand name or logo. Its values are identical in all countries, it has a substantial market share in all countries and comparable brand loyalty. The distribution channels are similar' (Mooij, 1998: 16). Like the corporations and non-governmental organizations, even governments are now forced to employ professional branding companies to 'sell' themselves in the global market place. The existence of Anholt Nation Brands Index, the first ranking of the world's nation brands, which surveys consumers to determine how countries are perceived in terms of cultural appeal, political stability and investment potential, is one such example.

Television news from entertainment conglomerates

The major media conglomerates are at the heart of the globalization of the infotainment industry. Their internal structures and organization embody the convergence of the key media products of news and entertainment.

Hollywood-generated entertainment is often launched on news networks, as they belong to the same conglomerates which produce them: Paramount Pictures (part of Viacom) can use CBS News to highlight a new release; Universal Studios (part of NBC-Universal) can push a soft feature story on NBC News about a show; Warner Brothers (part of AOL-Time Warner) can publicize a new star on CNN; Disney can use ABC News for its latest offering; while Fox News can give airtime to the latest fare from Twentieth Century Fox. News thus becomes a part of the organizational and corporate strategy and an advertising medium for infotainment conglomerates, and, since it is supposed to be a serious, factual-based medium, part of 'the knowledge system', it carries a greater degree of trustworthiness and therefore can be more effective in influencing audiences.

An examination of the main infotainment conglomerates shows that selling visual spectacles is their primary business. AOL-Time Warner, the world's largest entertainment and information company, has an international television presence in news through CNN, the 'world's most extensively syndicated television news service', though the company's primary revenue is drawn from entertainment – Turner Network Television (TNT) and Turner Classic Movies and Cartoon Network, the international children's channel, 'the most widely distributed 24-hour animation network in the world'. Apart from owning such media brands as *Time* magazine, the group's other major interest is in filmed entertainment through Warner Brothers, whose businesses range from film and television production and product licensing to a broadcast television network such as Home Box Office (HBO), drawing on its vast library: more than 5,700 feature films, 32,000 television programmes, 13,500 animated titles, including 1,500 classic cartoons, also distributed on-line through its ownership of AOL.

Another major news network, CBS, is part of the entertainment giant Viacom (though since 2005 both operate as separate companies), 'a cradle-to-grave advertising depot', catering to toddlers, with children's channels such as Nickelodeon, to youth by way of Music Television (MTV), and to the older generation through CBS. The group also owns Paramount Pictures, a leading film producer, with more than 2,500 titles in its library and co-produces films with Nickelodeon Movies and MTV Films, utilizing their expertise with children and youth respectively. Paramount Television is one of the largest suppliers of television programming for broadcasters worldwide, drawing on a library of 16,000 television episodes. MTV is the most widely distributed network in the world, while Nickelodeon, one of the world's largest producers of children's programming, was accessible in 178 million households in over 100 countries. Other entertainment channels which were part of the conglomerate included: VH1, Showtime and The Movie Channel.

The third main news network, ABC News, is part of the Walt Disney company, the world's second largest media corporation after AOL-Time Warner, with primary interests in global entertainment. The Disney Channel and Toon Disney are two major cable channels in the US. In addition, Disney owns ESPN and partly owns, with Hearst and GE, Arts and Entertainment Television (A&E), as well as shares in The History Channel and E! Entertainment channel (the world's largest producer and distributor of entertainment news and lifestyle-related programming, in 2006, reaching 300 million homes in 120 countries worldwide). By 2006, Disney was operating country or area-specific Disney channels in Britain, Taiwan, India, Australia, Malaysia, France, Italy, Spain and the Middle East. In addition Disney Channel Worldwide, with 120 million subscribers in more than 70 countries, was operating 24 Disney Channels, eight Playhouse Disney Channels, nine Toon Disney Channels and 18 international Jetix channels, as well as branded blocks of programming distributed to viewers worldwide. In the area of television production and distribution, the company has a global presence with Buena Vista Television, Touchstone Television, Walt Disney Television and Walt Disney Television Animation, with production facilities in Japan, Australia and Canada.

The same is the case in movie production and distribution through Walt Disney Pictures, Touchstone Pictures, Hollywood Pictures, Caravan Pictures, Miramax Films, Buena Vista Home Video, Buena Vista Home Entertainment and Buena Vista International (in 2005, Buena Vista International distributed more than 30,000 hours of programming to 1,300 broadcasters across 240 territories). The company established a joint digital cable venture video-on-demand movie service in Britain, FilmFlex, where it already had stakes in GMTV. In addition, Disney had investments in Super RTL and RTL 2 in Germany and HBO services in Central Europe and Latin America. Media networks were the main revenue generators for the company – in 2005, for example, they accounted for just over $13 billion out of the total revenues of nearly $32 billion (Disney website).

Another infotainment conglomerate NBC (owned by General Electric), which by 2006, was broadcasting approximately 5,000 hours of TV programming each year, transmitting to more than 200 affiliated stations across the US (including 15 Telemundo stations, the fastest-growing Spanish-language network in the US, which NBC acquired in 2002). Its business news channel CNBC, launched in 1989, has become a major international presence, as were its film interests in Universal Studios.

The most important infotainment conglomerate to emerge in the past two decades is Rupert Murdoch's News Corporation – 'the only vertically integrated media company on a global scale' – whose primary financial interests are in the arena of entertainment – including Fox entertainment as well as Hollywood blockbusters produced by Twentieth Century Fox. The 'Fourth Network' – with such 'signature' series as *The Simpsons*, *The X-Files*, and *America's Most Wanted* – has redefined contemporary US television (Kimmel, 2004). Murdoch made skillful use of the liberalization of cross-media ownership regulations in Britain and the US during the 1990s and the entry of private satellite operators into the arena of broadcasting, risking an enormous amount of money by leasing time on new satellite ventures such as Astra and AsiaSat, to create a truly international media corporation, at the heart of which is satellite television. Murdoch's global influence is likely to be consolidated with the acquisition of DirecTV in 2004, the largest DTH platform in the US and investment in DTH operations elsewhere (including Tata-Sky in India and Sky Italia), and growing engagement with on-line media by buying internet-based operations like MySpace.com and entering a deal with Google in 2006 for maximizing visibility of Murdoch's media on the web, as well as the introduction in Britain in the same year of Sky-by-broadband and Sky-by-mobile. The title of the 2006 Annual Report of News Corporation *Imagining the future...today* is indicative of this. A triumphant Murdoch notes:

> For the first time in media history, complete access to a truly global audience is within our grasp. No company is better positioned to seize this opportunity than ours. Some boast higher traffic but little content. Others have plenty of content but little traffic. Only News Corporation combines high traffic with vast amount of compelling content. Our situation is unique – and powerful. And we are taking advantage of it. (News Corporation, 2007: 5)

Murdoch's control of both communication hardware and software makes him, in the words of Robert McChesney, 'the visionary of a global corporate media empire' (1999: 96). Apart from having extensive interests in newspapers and publishing, News Corporation is particularly strong in the television industry. In Britain, it holds majority shares in British Sky Broadcasting (BSkyB), which since its 1998 launch of a multiple-channel subscription service, Sky Digital, has also come to dominate interactive digital television. Though the US remains its primary market and since 2004 also News Corporation's headquarters, accounting for more than 55 per cent of its 2006 revenue of $25.32 billion, Murdoch has wide-ranging media interests in the world's two biggest consumer markets – India and China. It also owns the Hong Kong-based STAR TV, the first pan-Asian network which in 2007 was operating over 50 television services in seven languages to reach more than 300 million viewers across 53 countries, including STAR Plus, India's most popular Hindi-language entertainment channel, and with stakes in Phoenix, a Mandarin-language channel. In Latin America, Sky network has agreements with Televisa, the Mexican television giant and other regional broadcasters for a DTH operation, while among News Corporation's pan-regional Latin American programming channels are Canal Fox, 'the Hollywood channel' one of the most widely distributed channels in the region, as well as minority share in Cine Canal and Telecine. With television operations on four continents, News Corporation's reach into the world's living rooms is unequalled. Television, delivered by broadcast, cable and satellite, remains the fastest growing part of the company: in 2006, it accounted for half of News Corporations' income of $3.86 billion (News Corporation, 2007). Unlike its close competitors, News Corporation was uniquely created and globalized by the vision of one individual, Rupert Murdoch, the 76-year old chairman and Chief Executive Officer of News Corporation, who has had a profound impact on global broadcasting, especially television journalism (Page, 2003).

The 'Murdochization' of media and the rise of Fox News

Among the major trends in US journalism enumerated by the Project for Excellence in Journalism in their 2006 *The State of the News Media: An Annual Report on American Journalism* the growing marketization and managerial control of news is most striking. 'At many old-media companies, though not all, the decades-long battle at the top between idealists and accountants is now over. The idealists have lost,' it ruefully declares, adding that 'journalism in the public interest has lost leverage' (Project for Excellence in Journalism, 2006). Murdoch's media has a major contribution in this transformation. The biggest change in television news in the US has been in cable news where Fox News has become the most popular cable television news, witnessing a steady increase in its audience share: according to a 2006 report from the Pew Research Center, 23 per cent of Americans said that they regularly watch Fox News, the majority of these viewers being right-wing Republicans (Pew Research Center, 2006a) (see Figure 2.3).

The 'Murdochization' of television news – with its emphasis on entertainment and infotainment at the expense of the public-service role of the media – has changed the media landscape in the US and in Britain and, increasingly, in other countries where Murdoch has been a major player since the 1990s. In Chapter 4, I discuss how Murdoch's media has contributed to changing the character of television news in India as well as influenced the broader broadcasting ecology. In the US, the impact of the growing importance of Fox News, which has emerged as the highest rated

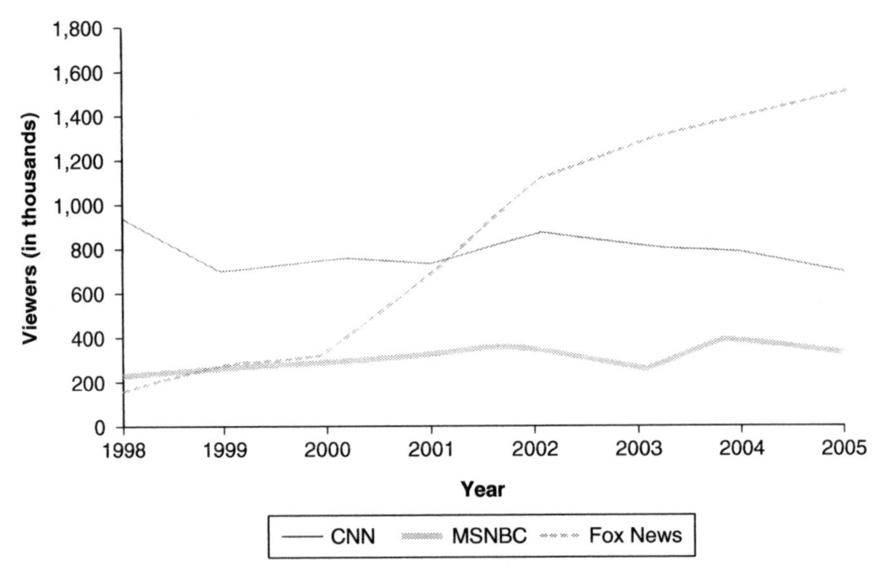

Figure 2.3 Cable news prime time median audience by channel 1998–2005
Source: http://stateofthemedia.org/2006/printingthereport.asp

cable network, reaching 88 million homes in 2006 (News Corporation, 2007), can be seen in attempts by its rivals to 'out-fox Fox News' by developing their own versions of such popular news programmes as the *O'Reilly Factor*, but these have not been very successful (Collins, 2004).

One study of Fox News observed that the channel 'does the best job of attracting Americans with the increasingly common traits of lower political knowledge, higher cynicism, and less political involvement' (Morris, 2005: 73). US comedian Al Franken played on the slogan of Fox News 'Fair and Balanced', in his 2003 controversial book *Lies (and the Lying Liars Who Tell Them): A Fair and Balanced Look at the Right*, prompting Fox News to take him to court for infringement of copyright, as well as attempting to squash him under the weight of such adjectives as 'shrill and unstable', 'unfunny' even 'intoxicated or deranged', broadcast leading up to the trial but Fox News lost the case and made Franken's book a commercial success.

Fox News appears to privilege opinions of a certain political affiliation as against facts, appointing right-wing commentators and journalists, as outlined in Robert Greenwald's 2004 documentary *Outfoxed: Rupert Murdoch's War on Journalism*. Eileen Meehan has noted: 'News Corporation's decision to run opinion programmes instead of news coverage means that it has allocated money to hire personalities, money that could have been used to hire journalists and fact checkers. O'Reilly's show is an outcome of that decision. Like the other hosts on Fox News, O'Reilly espouses the same neo-conservative views as News Corporation's owner, Rupert Murdoch. Fox News' preference for neo-conservative opinions over news should be recognized as a matter of corporate policy' (Meehan, 2005: 2).

This corporate policy is based on an unabashedly right-wing political agenda, at the heart of which is global expansion and consolidation of neo-liberalism through Murdoch's 'electronic empires'. In Chapter 5, I discuss how Murdoch's television news networks acted as cheerleaders for US invasion of Iraq. Murdoch's networks are operating in a commodified television system where fact and fiction, half-truths and quarter truths mingle. The growing encroachment of corporate agendas into television news both 'pervasive and secretive' has in some cases reached crisis proportions. 'Fake news' produced by public relations companies and distributed to broadcasters for free, is seamlessly integrated into newscasts through pre-packaged video news releases (VNRs). A Center for Media and Democracy report noted:

> television newscasts – the most popular news source in the United States – frequently air VNRs without disclosure to viewers, without conducting their own reporting, and even without fact checking the claims made in the VNRs. VNRs are overwhelmingly produced for corporations, as part of larger public relations campaigns to sell products, burnish their image, or promote policies or actions beneficial to the corporation. (Center for Media and Democracy, 2006: 8)

Neoliberal news imperialism?

Just as the big transnational media conglomerates dominate the global flow of entertainment, the US-led Western media – and within it an US–UK core – dominate production and distribution of international news (Boyd-Barrett, 1998; Thussu, 2006a). From global news agencies to transnational newspapers and radio stations, from providers of television news footage, to 24-hour news and documentary channels, the US/UK-based media organizations demonstrate what has been called 'the US/UK news duopoly' (Tunstall and Machin, 1999: 88). Of the three biggest international news agencies (Associated Press, Reuters and Agence France Presse), the American AP, is the largest, with an average daily news output of 20 million words, more than double that of its closest rival Reuters, and over three times the output of the French agency. These news agencies contribute significantly to the globalization of news (Boyd-Barrett and Rantanen, 1998) and though traditionally these sold news reports and still photographs, today they have diversified their operations by offering video news feeds for broadcasters and on-line information and financial databases. AP claims to be 'the essential global news network', and that 'more than a billion people every day read, hear or see AP news' (APTN website). Reuters is 'the largest financial information provider in the world', dealing in 'the business of information', and makes its main profit by transmitting real-time financial data and collective investment data to global financial markets. The companies which run the world's two biggest wire services also own the world's two top international television news agencies – Associated Press Television News (APTN) and Reuters Television – dominating the global trade in news footage. No self-respecting broadcaster can manage without access to one of these two news giants, especially for coverage of international news. APTN, launched in 1998 following the acquisition from ABC of TV news agency Worldwide Television News (WTN) by AP, integrating it with the operations of APTV, the London-based video news agency launched by AP in 1994.

Through dedicated 24-hour uplinks in Beijing, Hong Kong, Moscow, Jerusalem, New York and Washington, APTN offers individual regional services for Europe, North America, Latin America, Asia Pacific and the Middle East through its Global Video Wire, a 24/7 operation to cover breaking news, fed to more than 500 broadcasters, major portals and websites with video from APTN's 83 bureaux. Since 2003, the agency has also been operating APTN Direct, live news coverage to cater to 24/7 networks (APTN website). By 2007, Reuters Television (formerly Visnews), was providing, in addition to its flagship 'World News Service', coverage of financial news, sports, showbiz ('from Hollywood to Bollywood') and ready-to-air packages, as well as 'World News Express', a digital service primarily geared to the needs of web-casting as well as rolling news broadcasters, to its subscribers worldwide (Reuters TV website). Acknowledging the importance of visual media, AFP also launched an English-language television service, AFP TV, based in London.

With access to global satellite networks, APTN and Reuters Television offer satellite news-gathering deployments around the world. Their feeds are sent, both with ready scripts to allow immediate broadcasting, or with natural sound which can be re-edited with local voice-overs. Broadcasting material – news, photos, graphics, audio and video – is supplied to news organizations worldwide in English and other major international languages, while subscribers translate news agency stories into many more languages. As media outlets shrink their foreign coverage, news agencies have started selling packaged news to non-media organizations, such as governments and corporations. These two companies largely define global flow of audio-visual news material, thus potentially influencing television journalism around the world.

In global financial journalism too, major providers and shapers of real-time news, data and analyses of financial markets and business have a distinctive American-English accent, with Reuters being the leading international presence, closely followed by Bloomberg; AP-DJ economic news service, formed as a result of AP's teaming with Dow Jones; and AFX News, produced by AFP and *The Financial Times*. In the globalized free-market world where speedy and regular transmission of accurate financial intelligence is crucial, the blurring of boundaries between financial news and financial data, broadcast 24/7 side-by-side or even on a single screen on news channels, can carry a sea of information formed and framed by transnational corporate interests, a point I explore further in Chapter 6. In this crucial sub-field of journalism, too, US-based business news channels, themselves parts of infotainment conglomerates, have global presence and influence: notably CNBC, formed after the merger of NBC and European Business News (EBN) (which is owned by Dow Jones) and its sister channel Asia Business News (ABN); and Bloomberg Television – broadcast via ten networks operating in seven languages and reaching 200 million homes.

Globalization of Anglo-American television news

The globalization of American television news journalism is probably best symbolized and exemplified by the rise of CNN, undoubtedly the world leader (Volkmer, 1999). CNN, 'the world's only global, 24-hour news network', influenced news agendas across the world and indeed contributed to shaping international relations, through the so-called CNN effect (Robinson, 2002). One reason for the rapid expansion of CNN was its use of satellite technology. Satellites gave CNN first a national audience in the US, and it was one of the first international broadcasters to take advantage of this technology to 'blanket the globe', using a mixture of Intelsat, Intersputnik, PanAmSat and regional satellite signals (Flournoy and Stewart, 1997). CNN contributed also to the development of media systems in the former socialist countries: it was involved, for example, in the 1993 launch of TV 6, the first private television network in Russia; it entered into an agreement with China's CCTV to receive and selectively distribute its programmes; and CNN was one of the first Western news organizations to open a bureau in Cuba. CNN's on-the-spot reporting of global events gave it unparalleled power to mould international public opinion and even contributed to influencing the actions of people involved in the events it was covering (Flournoy and Stewart, 1997; Volkner, 1999; Robinson, 2002).

Europe has been one of its key markets, making CNN one of Europe's most watched news channels, broadcasting 24 hours a day to 37 countries, with programming from its London centre. Recognizing that there is a greater need for news in local languages it started to localize its feeds. In 1997, it launched CNN Deutschland, a half-hour daily German language slot for the German market and CNN en Español, a Spanish language channel for the Latin American market, followed two years later by CNN Plus in Spain, its first branded local-language version and CNN Turk. In Asia, CNNJ, a Japan-specific network, has been in operation since 2003 and in 2005 it entered a joint venture with a leading Indian television company TV18, to launch a new network CNN/IBN.

By 2007, CNN was available in more than 260 million television households in 200 countries and territories worldwide. CNN News Group was one of the largest and most profitable news and information companies in the world, available to two billion people worldwide. It was the only network capable of covering international news instantly, given its wide network of correspondents – in 2007 it had 36 international bureaux with 150 correspondents and its communications resources – and was beaming its programmes through a network of 38 satellites to cover the entire globe. The group's assets included: 14 cable and satellite television networks (including CNN Headline News, CNN International, CNN Money, CNN/SI and CNN en Español); two radio networks (CNN Radio and a Spanish version CNN Radio Noticias); 6 websites on CNN Interactive (including in Arabic and Japanese); CNN Airport Network; and CNN Newsource, the world's most extensively syndicated news service, with 900 international affiliates. CNN Mobile, launched in 1999, was one of the world's first mobile news and information services (CNN website).

Though financially not as resourceful as CNN, BBC World, the BBC's, 24-hour global news and information channel, has greater international credibility and remains a major global presence: in 2007 it was available in more than 270 million homes across 200 countries and territories. Unlike CNN, BBC World provides news only in English – except in Japan where it broadcasts limited dubbed programming and in Latin America where it provides Spanish subtitles. Murdoch's Sky News, the first 24-hour news channel to broadcast to Britain and Europe when it was launched in 1989, is the third key player of the US–UK news trio. By 2007, it was available to 80 million people across 40 countries (including Israel, South Africa and Australia), though most of its audience was in Europe, and predominantly in Britain. Its international coverage has increased through alliances with other broadcasters including CBS, ABC and Bloomberg Television. Sky also has an alliance with Reuters, which provides its news gathering: as part of News Corporation, it can also draw on the resources of the Hong Kong-based Star News Asia, and Fox News in the US.

The US–UK news duopoly is based on professional output – a reputation for speed and accuracy in the coverage of international events. However, does their interpretation of global political and financial events reflect US corporate priorities? CNN, for example, is part of the world's biggest media and entertainment conglomerate, and its version of world events – more often than not an American one, which might be delivered by one of its multinational staff (usually US-educated or domiciled), sometimes even in local languages – is likely to define the worldview of millions of viewers around the globe. CNN as well as BBC World are advertisement-based channels, dependent on the vagaries of the news market. Their viewership is relatively small, though significant, what CNN calls 'influentials' – government ministers, top bureaucrats, company chief executives, military chiefs, religious and academic elites (Flournoy and Stewart, 1997). Such 24/7 networks are also constantly monitored by informational bureacucrats, journalists and news organizations worldwide for any breaking news stories.

As competition grows – TV news is a $3 billion business – and more and more national, regional and international all-news channels appear with the expansion of digital broadcasting, the pressure to be first with the news is likely to grow. Already, there is a discernible tendency among news channels to sacrifice depth in favour of the widest and quickest reach of live infotainment spectacle to an increasingly heterogeneous, not to say cynical and media savvy, global audience. Larry King, host of one of CNN's most watched chat shows *Larry King Live*, has no hesitation in calling himself an infotainer. CNN has spawned imitators across the world and the existence of global round-the-clock news networks has created a new genre of rolling news, which has facilitated the globalization of infotainment, to which we turn in the next chapter.

3

GLOBAL CIRCULATION OF 24/7 INFOTAINMENT

One key outcome of the globalization of television is that the US model of market-driven television news has been adopted or at least adapted, to suit local characteristics, across the globe. As Shoemaker and Cohen's comparative study of news shows, the nature of news and notions of newsworthiness in different countries are not that dissimilar around newsrooms and news audiences (Shoemaker and Cohen, 2005). This may be congruent with the broader shifts in media systems, from state to market, in evidence around the world, a result of changes in the political economy of the media, as outlined in the previous chapter. Examining media systems in different cultural and political contexts, Hallin and Mancini noted the 'triumph of the liberal model' (2004: 251) and argued that the 'liberal model' is likely to be adopted across the world 'because its global influence has been so great and because neo-liberalism and globalization continue to diffuse liberal media structures and ideas' (ibid: 305). Despite the specificities of world television cultures, it is difficult to disagree with Hallin and Mancini's assumption that 'differences among national media systems are clearly diminishing. A global media culture is emerging, one that closely resembles the Liberal Model', which is represented by central features of the American media system (ibid: 294). This 'convergence of media systems and ... homogenization of contents', sometimes referred to either as 'modernization' or 'Americanization', have also been found in recent comparative studies of political communication, which address among other issues, concerns about 'mediatization of politics', where 'media logic' tends to overwhelm the 'political logic' (Esser and Pfetsch, 2004). Making news and politics interesting is an integral part of this media logic, as demonstrated by the growing infotainment quotient in news programmes and the ascendancy of political public relation mandarins, creating fun-filled, image-driven politics.

Fierce competition between proliferating news networks for ratings and advertising has prompted them to provide news in an entertaining manner and broadcasters have adapted their news operations to retain their viewers or to acquire them anew. In the process, symbiotic relationships between the news and new forms of current affairs and factual entertainment genres, such as reality TV have developed, blurring the boundaries between news, documentary and entertainment. Such hybrid programming feeds into and benefits from the 24/7 news cycle: providing a feast of visually arresting, emotionally charged infotainment which sustains ratings and keeps production costs low. Television news is an expensive business – especially of the 24/7 variety: even well established brands such as ITN had to close down ITV News in 2005, a round-the-clock digital news channel which was not receiving sufficient audience ratings.

International news is an expensive operation and demands huge resources for programming, compared with other types of television production. Thus only large media conglomerates or well-funded state organizations can hope to run successful news channels. They are often flagship programmes, loss leaders providing a key global electronic presence and have to be cross subsidized. The BBC has had to supplement its UK-based licence fee income by operating commercially in its international activities. It is not surprising then that the rise of cheap and cheerful reality television has paralleled the proliferation of news channels. Not only does it bring broadcasters a high return on investment, it breeds from the human interest stories and feeds the news channels with an endless diet of manufactured celebrity and media events.

The spread of 24-hour news factories around the world

ITV News was one of the many 24/7 news clones to have come into life as a result of the success of CNN, a phenomenon sometimes labelled as the 'CNNization' of television news. As one study of the global broadcaster noted: 'CNN redefined news from something that *has* happened to something that *is* happening' (Kung-Shankleman, 2000: 79, emphasis in the original). By 2007, as Table 3.1 (p. 70) shows, several 24/7 news networks were operating internationally, in a 'dynamic, rapidly expanding and increasingly differentiated' broadcasting ecology (Rai and Cottle, 2007: 72). Rolling news relies on live coverage of unfolding events and, as hiring time slots on satellites can be expensive (every second of being live costs money), news networks have been forced to depend on a staple of relatively cheap, studio-bound coverage to fill the airtime, especially when it involves international news. Celebrities, crime and sport are always popular, irrespective of cultural differences. Such coverage also helps promote corporate synergies between

Table 3.1 Global 24/7 TV news networks

Network	*Where based*	*Launch year*
CNN International	US	1985
Sky News	UK	1989
BBC World Television	UK	1992
EuroNews	France	1993
Al-Jazeera	Qatar	1996
Globo News	Brazil	1996
Fox News	US	1998
Star News	India	1998
Channel NewsAsia	Singapore	1999
CCTV-9	China	2000
Star News Asia	Hong Kong	2000
Phoenix Infonews	Hong Kong	2001
NDTV 24x7	India	2003
DD News	India	2003
Telesur	Venezuela	2005
Russia TV	Russia	2005
France 24	France	2006
Al-Jazeera English	Qatar	2006

(Source: Compiled from company websites)

news networks and their entertainment-based parent conglomerates, as described in Chapter 2.

Economic globalization, with its attendant flexible and mobile work-force, has contributed to a large and growing diasporic televisual market, which private networks have been quick to exploit, benefiting from the extension of satellite footprints and the growth of DTH broadcasting to feed into transnational geo-cultural spaces. Unlike state broadcasters, which – at least in theory – tend to address traditional, territory-bound citizens, private networks are more interested in subscription-paying consumers, irrespective of nationality and citizenship (Chalaby, 2005). Their synergies – both of soft and hardware – with infotainment conglomerates have made this expansion easy: Murdoch-supported round-the-clock channels, Star News (Hindi) and Phoenix InfoNews (Mandarin) are distributed in Britain through Sky's digital network, partly owned by News Corporation. Murdoch's DirecTV in the US, as well as such platforms as the Echostar DISH system, provide other distribution outlets for various news channels, primarily aimed at diasporic groups.

State and regional broadcasting organizations have also jumped on the 24/7 news bandwagon, ensuring a presence and profile (however low-key) on the global media scene and a vehicle for public relations and diplomacy. While it would be far fetched to describe some of these less than slick productions as infotainment with their cheap and cheerful production values, their presence indicates the importance of being visible. Regional networks include EuroNews (the 24/7 multi-lingual news consortium of Europe's public service broadcasters) and the pan-Latin American TV channel Televisora del Sur ('Television of the South' or Telesur), based in Venezuela and launched in 2005. With its slogan 'News from the South', Telesur promised to be an alternative to CNN. 'It's a question of focus, of where we look at our continent from', Jorge Botero, Telesur's news director told the BBC. 'They look at it from the United States. So they give a rose-tinted, flavour-free version of Latin America. We want to look at it from right here' (quoted in Bruce, 2005).

The intention of providing news 'from a Russian perspective' was behind Russia Today, launched in 2005 with a start-up and annual running cost of around $30 million provided by the Kremlin and Russian commercial banks. It was part of a resurgent Russian public diplomacy, which also included plans to start an Arabic language channel for the Middle East (Khalaf and Ostrovsky, 2006). A year later, the French government allocated $131 million to establish a 24-hour English-language TV news channel, the French International News Channel (CFII) called France 24, a joint venture between state-run broadcaster France Télévisions and commercial television company TF1, that aims to be the French-language CNN – 'CNN à la Francaise'. President Jacques Chirac, whose pet project it was, justified the launch by suggesting that 'France must ... be on the front line in the global battle of TV pictures' (AFP, 2005). This battle was to be waged in future also in Arabic and Spanish to promote French foreign policy interests and to counter US/UK domination of global news (Chrisafis, 2006). However, its sometimes dubbed, sometimes accented news coverage is unlikely to interest many Anglophone viewers. Moreover, government's backing 'could weaken its journalistic integrity, making it more like Voice of America than CNN' (Carlin, 2006).

The biggest impact outside the US–UK news ambit has been exercised by the Qatar-based Al-Jazeera, sometimes labelled as the 'Arabic CNN' (though its editorial approach is closer to the BBC), which, since its launch in 1996, has redefined journalism in the Arab world (Sakr, 2001; Lynch, 2006). It is in a unique position of being neither a commercial nor a state-run channel but an independent and professional global news operation, financed by the Sultan of Qatar, who was also behind the launch in 2006 of Aljazeera English, the international channel, broadcasting live from four centres: Doha, Kuala Lumpur, London and Washington. By 2007, this pan-Arabic 24/7 news network was claiming to reach 50 million viewers across the world, challenging the Anglo-American domination of news and current affairs in one of the world's most geo-politically sensitive areas. Its coverage of the 'war on terrorism' made Al-Jazeera into an international broadcaster whose logo can be seen on television screens around the world. In the region, satellite networks have led to what one commentator has called 'the structural transformation of the Arab public sphere' (Lynch, 2006). By 2007, there were 20 news channels operating in the Arab world, including the Saudi-owned Al-Arabiya, part of Middle East Broadcasting Centre, one of the Arab world's largest media conglomerates, Hizbullah's Al-Manar, Iranian government supported Al-Alam and the US government funded Al-Hurra.

While the proliferation of news channels internationally may give the impression of a multiplicity of languages and perspectives, English-language news networks continue to have a privileged position in the production and distribution of global TV news, as shown by a spate of new English-language networks outside the Anglophone world: Russia Today, France 24, NDTV 24x7, Star News Asia, Channel NewsAsia and Aljazeera English, are some key examples of this trend. Germany's international broadcaster, Deutsche Welle TV, regularly broadcasts news bulletins in English, while Iran has launched an English-language channel, Iranian TV, in 2007. The expansion of CCTV-9, the English-language 24-hour news network of China Central Television, reflects the recognition by the Beijing authorities of the importance of the English language as the key to success for global commerce and communication and their strategy to bring Chinese public diplomacy to a global audience. In 2007, India's state broadcaster Doordarshan made DD News (in English and Hindi) available on the Sky network in Britain, to provide an Indian perspective on global affairs.

By 2007, the number of regional or international news channels had reached three figures, with most noticeable growth witnessed in Asia: India had nearly 40, virtually all commercial, all-news networks (Rai and Cottle, 2007) (see Figure 3.1).

The 'structures and ideas' of a US-inspired liberal media system that Hallin and Mancini (2004) discuss in their book, have had a wider impact on political communication, demonstrable in the embedding of infotainment in the wider political process: in the way politicians of different styles and stripes engage with their respective citizens, and how television news covers public and civic affairs. Around the world there are examples of how infotainment is affecting the role of news in political communication and culture.

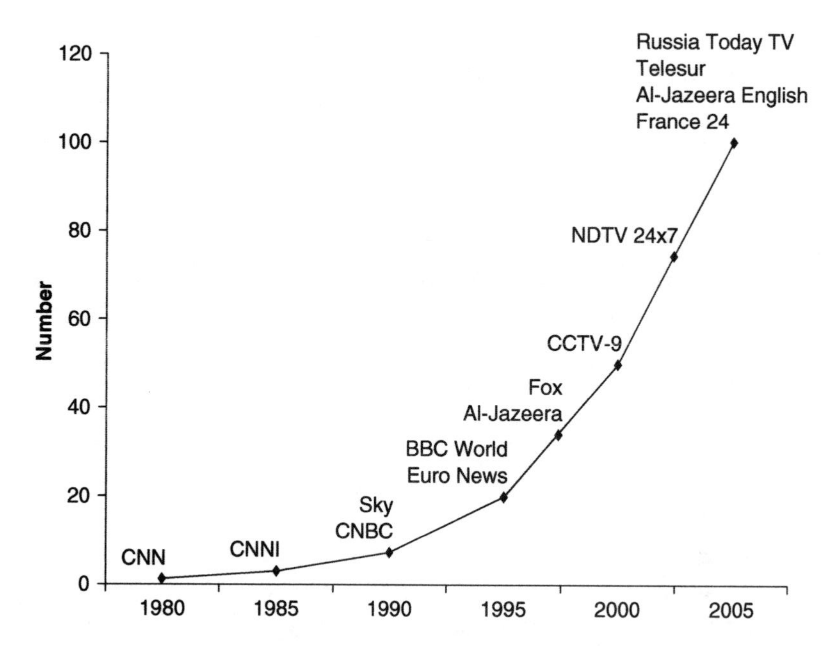

Figure 3.1 The global growth of 24/7 news channels
(Source: Painter, 2007)

Infotainment goes global

Infotainment programming has probably had easiest acceptance in the Anglophone television world, where consumers have naturalized themselves to American entertainment, having been exposed to it – even in prime time – for more than half a century. Given its proximity to the United States, the Americanization of media in Canada has raised questions about media ethics and concerns about the intrusion of entertainment-driven coverage of the private lives of ordinary individuals, making their stories 'public spectacles' for ratings purposes (Cohen-Almagor, 2002). In Australia, during the 1990s, 'the growing desire to mine profits from news and current affairs programmes,' one study noted, resulted 'in a tabloid trend' which emphasised human interest stories, hidden camera stories and set-ups (where the producers contrived a situation to create a story), and in attempts to 'spice up' existing current affairs programmes (Lumby, 2002: 324). Such commercialism was pioneered by Channel Nine's *Burke's Backyard*, a magazine-style show about gardening, Australia's first infotainment hit, which was followed by a raft of programmes on all Australian channels focusing on health, travel, home renovation, money and sex. As a result, the importance of current affairs and television news in a democracy was being undermined by crass commercialism (Turner, 2005). In other countries where US influence is strong – such as Israel – the American style of modern televisual politics, including political advertising, has been enthusiastically embraced, as indicated by a study of election advertising by Israel's Labor Party during the 2003 national elections. This found political advertising indistinguishable in style from American advertisements as the US-based, -trained or -inspired consultants were involved in political communication, predicated on infotainment and one which obfuscated politically complex issues (Perlmutter and Golan, 2005).

Even in Japan, where broadcasting has generally been sober and staid, led by the public broadcaster NHK, infotainment elements have affected news programming. Traditionally, Japanese broadcast stations have allocated large financial and human resources to their flagship current affairs and news programmes and therefore have the ability to 'domesticate' news (relying less on 'homogenizing' international agency footage). However, the news values of programmes such as 'News Station', broadcast on commercial network TV Asahi, a study based on interviews with media experts and news producers reported, may be characterized as 'proximate, interesting and instantly gratifying' (Clausen, 2004: 30).

Television played an unprecedented role in the rise to the premiership in 2001 of Koizumi Junichiro, a media savvy politician, who made a lot of his good looks, so much so that Japanese members of parliament commented that television programmes were being used to promote Koizumi as leader. The upper house elections of July 2001 were preceded by an extraordinary hour-long television programme entitled *One hundred women vs. Koizumi*, in which Koizumi took questions from a studio audience of women. The new marketing of politics by television was illustrated by a Nippon TV weekly drama serial *Let's Go Nagatacho*, which provided a thinly fictionalized account of Japanese politics under Koizumi. In this series, the fictitious prime minister's good looks made women reporters at press briefings hysterical. Meanwhile, the real Koizumi was celebrated in a wide range of marketing spin-offs, including photo books, mobile phone straps and other consumer items. Media coverage of Koizumi focused on such unlikely details as the kind of hair gel he used to maintain his permed mane. Koizumi's team was popularly labelled the 'wide-show cabinet' ('Wide Shows' are infotainment style programmes on day-time TV broadcast on all major commercial stations, generally focusing on scandal or social problems (Mccargo, 2002)). Koizumi reportedly sang Elvis songs with Hollywood star Tom Cruise, when he was visiting Japan in 2003 to promote his film *The Last Sumurai*. The Japanese premier had already released a CD of his karaoke renditions, entitled *Junichiro Koizumi Presents 'My Favourite Elvis Songs'*.

Another example of what Meyer has called the 'theatricalization' of politics (Meyer and Hincham, 2002), was offered by Taiwan, when President Chen Shui-bian allegedly staged his own shooting at a pre-election rally to win sympathy and re-election in 2004 in a tightly contested poll (Watts, 2004). In the Philippines, a former US colony, which, according to a media commentator, was suffering an 'onslaught from unrestrained news media and entertainment industries on its political system', popular actor Josef Estrada was elected as President in 1998, with the biggest ever margin despite having no background in politics and no party structure to depend on. His successor Gloria Arroyo, an economist and daughter of a former president, also came to power partly because of her 'perceived likeness to superstar Nora Aunor', indicating how entertainment was shaping electoral politics (Raslan, 2000).

The commercial model of TV news has been dominant in Brazil since the beginning of television, exemplified by the Globo group, a multimedia infotainment conglomerate that is a major presence in Latin America. The entire in prime-time line-up is devoted to telenovelas and complemented by soccer matches (Globo has the telecast rights for Brazil's top leagues), sitcoms and Hollywood films. More recently, reality TV has become very popular: the 2000 hijacking of a bus in Rio de Janeiro by a homeless person and the attempts by the police to free the hostages and the eventual killing of the hijacker were broadcast live on all Brazilian TV networks, later portrayed in an award-winning documentary, *Onibus 174* (Bus 174), released in 2002. A year later, the siege of one of the country's best-known television presenters, Silvio Santos, held hostage for 7 hours in his mansion in Sao Paulo, was also covered live on national television (Bellos, 2001).

In countries trying to come to terms with years of dictatorial media systems, such as Chile, neo-liberal television has failed to strengthen democratic discourse. According to one commentator, 'commercialization and the triumph of the entertainment model have undermined its potential to invigorate the public sphere during the transition' (Bresnahan, 2003: 55). Infotainment is also common on television networks in Mexico – 'la nota roja' (red news) as it is known in the country, consists of large numbers of both current affairs and news programmes that use sensationalized and dramatic styles of presentation and provide both highly popular and controversial fare. As Hallin observes, 'the tabloid agenda has made powerful inroads into mainstream journalism', noting a dramatic decline in political coverage from nearly 70 per cent in 1994 to 35 per cent in 1999 and nearly doubling of crime reporting in the same period (Hallin, 2000: 272–3).

In the Arab world, where television has traditionally been controlled by governments, globalization of infotainment has brought what Ayish has called a 'liberal commercial television', privately owned, pan-Arabic, even transnational, which draws its inspiration in terms of journalistic practices and approaches from CNN. 'For the first time ever,' Ayish remarks, 'Arab viewers are exposed to American-style news formats and orientations that draw on sensational and technically alluring features' (Ayish, 2002: 151). Such major entertainment conglomerates as the Middle East Broadcasting Centre have invested heavily in news with its 24/7 network Al-Arabiya, emerging as the main rival for Al-Jazeera.

Media in transition: from state propaganda to infotainment

One of the most notable signs of the globalization of infotainment is to be found in the former communist countries, where the shift from Marx to the market has been sudden and on a scale unimaginable during the Cold War (Rantanen, 2002; Zassoursky, 2005). It was only two years after the break-up of the Soviet Union that Moscow allowed commercially-run television networks to share space with state broadcasters. By 2002, three of the four main national networks were commercial, with the most successful, Channel One, being a 'public-private hybrid', while NTV was the largest commercial network. Recognizing the 'dependence on television for news and information for the mass audience' (85 per cent of the prime-time television audience in Russia tuned in to one of the Moscow-based networks), the Russian Government under President Putin has since tightened its control over news networks, directly or indirectly owning them, including private channels once in the hands of such oligarchs as Boris Berezovsky (Mickiewicz, 2005: 374).

Parallel to this state intervention in television, there has also been a huge change in the culture of journalism. The idea of news operating in a marketplace seems to have been normalised in a new world shaped by the market. The following observation sums up the position of journalism in post-Soviet Russia:

> It earns its living in a growing competitive market, and therefore is increasingly directed towards the interests and preferences of consumers and advertisers. The higher the audience ratings the easier it is to sell media products and to earn advertising revenue, and so make a profit. Journalism is adopting a new function: entertaining its audience to promote goods and services in a consumer-driven marketplace. The media sector has turned into a battlefield for audiences and advertisers and is proposing a new role for its workers – as organizers of leisure for the masses. (Pasti, 2005: 99)

Pasti's comparative study of new and old journalism in Russia argues that the 'media aggressively implants hedonistic morals, paying huge attention to the entertainment genre' with young journalists 'willingly accepting' the 'role of entertainer' (Pasti, 2005: 109). The fun element had become so pronounced by 2000 that the weekly late-night newscast *Golaya Pravda* (The Naked Truth), on one of Moscow's most successful commercial television channels, M1, was a ratings hit, with Duma members vying with each other to appear on the programme. Its anchorwoman, Svetlana Pesotskaya, a 25-year-old actress, would read the news in various stages of undress, becoming topless by the end of the 10-minute newscast. 'Our show is popular because it's original,' Pesotskaya told journalists, 'almost every other Russian newscast was just copied from Western television. We were the first to introduce a non-standard approach to the news. In the other shows, the news readers are too serious' (quoted in York, 2000).

Infotainment seems to have taken root also in post-communist Central and Eastern Europe, with companies such as United Pan-Europe Communications distributing a mixed bouquet of largely infotainment programming – predominantly sports and reality television – emanating from the United States. As a former press secretary to the president of the Czech Republic noted, 'most of the formerly serious Czech journalism has moved into infotainment. Many relevant media have traded a comprehensive, analytical coverage for a soft-news, entertainment approach driven by television culture and heavily influenced by the nostalgia for communist times. They have been complicit in perpetuating the stale communist taste, harming the evolution of the civil society in the process' (Klvana, 2004: 40–41).

In China, where the transition from Maoist state controlled and propagandist media to a state-managed marketization has had a different trajectory to that of former communist countries in Europe, new 'capitalist ways' have prompted the media to 'soften the propagandist edges' and replace it with, 'soft', entertaining and apolitical news, which is perceived to be particularly appealing to a mass audience and 'sets the stage for profit' (Chan, 2003). The impact of marketization, as noted by one observer of the Chinese media scene, has been a mixed blessing. 'The media enjoy greater "negative freedom", both chipping away at state commandism and ushering in increasing supremacy of the commercial logic. The non-political range of media discourses has expanded – often to the benefit of urban professional and buying classes at the expense of peasants and workers – but political coverage remains highly controlled' (Lee, P., 2005: 120).

Murdoch's Phoenix channel regularly runs an infotainment news programme called 'Easy Time, Easy News', which the company calls 'soft and diverting news' (Phoenix Experience, 2006). 'Be Chatty, Be Newsy' is another of the channel's slogans. One of the most popular daily magazine shows on Phoenix, hosted by star presenter Lu Yu, concentrates on celebrity infotainment. The media market in Hong Kong – the centre of such pan-Asian news networks as Star News Asia – according to a commentator, 'is highly competitive and the use of sensational material is rampant', with audiences preferring 'entertainment and "soft" information involving lifestyle, shopping tips, food, restaurants, new electronic products and the like instead of "serious news"' (Lee, C.C., 2005: 85). David Bandurski, a researcher at the University of Hong Kong's China Media Project, claims that China's commercialization without liberalization has spun Chinese media into a dangerous vortex (Bandurski, 2006), while others have argued that under a unique marketization regime, the function of post-WTO Chinese media is to act as 'Party-Publicity Inc.' – a quasi-business that seeks profits and to legitimate the ruling Communist Party mandate by promoting its image (Lee, He and Huang, 2006).

The impact of infotainment on public-service broadcasting

The commercialization of broadcasting has also influenced the generally public-oriented networks in Europe. Both Norway's public broadcaster, NRK (Norsk Rikskringkasting) and its Swedish counterpart, SVT (Swedish Sveriges Television), have been made more cost effective, with content and scheduling being 'modernized', by adopting strategies borrowed from commercial broadcasting to increase ratings (Syvertsen, 2003). In Germany the public-service 'networks' ARD (Association of Public-Service Broadcasters in Germany) and ZDF (Zweites Deutsches Fernsehen, 'Second German Television', launched in 1963) have traditionally depended on advertising as well as a licence fee: in the mid-1980s, nearly 37 per cent of the budget of ZDF was from advertising (Humphreys, 1994: 179). Commercial broadcasting in Germany started in 1984 and in 1986 the Federal Constitutional Court provided for the first time a 'legal basis for a deregulated private commercial sector', proposing a dual broadcasting system in which commercial and public broadcasters could operate side by side (ibid: 257). The public-broadcasting corporations 'would remain responsible for providing the basic broadcasting services to the whole of the population and fulfilling their classical public service duties', while commercial broadcasters could operate their stations with lower requirements, with entertainment being a key part of their programming mix (ibid: 255).

This public-private system seemed to work well until the 1990s, when the expansion of commercial digital channels, partly as a consequence of the deregulation of the TV market, with such infotainment conglomerates as the RTL-Group, part of Bertelsmann, Europe's biggest media company, bringing in a great deal of entertainment oriented programming. 'Consequently,' a study of German television consuming patterns reported, 'the viewing habits of the population have changed dramatically' and viewing time increased from a daily average of less than 120 minutes in the early 1980s to 210 minutes in 2002 (Schulz et al., 2005: 65). However, this media plenty has led to infotainment-oriented programming dominating the schedule, especially on such private channels as Sat1 and Pro7.

While the collapse of East Germany as a state ended 'an oppressive monistic media system', the description of East Germany as a 'media colony' was frequently used in the reunited Germany of 1990s as West German media conglomerates took over their eastern state-managed media outlets (Humphreys, 1994: 314), with a concomitant rise in infotainment. Schulz et al. remark: 'As the supply of television programmes has become much more entertainment-oriented, viewers have allotted an increasingly larger share of their daily television consumption to entertainment at the expense of information programmes. Even information viewing has changed in character since the information programmes on television have become more tabloidized with more emphasis on conflict and drama, on soft news and infotainment formats' (Schulz et al., 2005: 65). Such changes in television news may have also affected political communication in Germany: during the 2002 general elections, for example, German chancellor Gerhard Schroder and his challenger Edmund Stoiber featured in Germany's first televised debate on the private networks, RTL and Sat1, following on from the televised American presidential debates, first introduced in 1960 between John F. Kennedy and Richard Nixon.

Such 'Americanization' of political communication was also alluded to in a study of journalists in Austria which found that the American model was becoming increasingly visible. 'The most prominent tendency of Americanization of reporting,' the study observed, was, 'the personalization of politics. Individual actors, their personality, style, and appearance are increasingly the focus of coverage, forming a star system, in which prominence and image force competence into the background and further a shallowing of discussions of political issues in the mass media' (Plasser, 2005: 63). The study also found the ascendancy of a journalism of 'bits and bytes', of 'progressive reduction of messages to sound bites, embedded in ever-faster-changing news cycles', causing 'a more superficial use of sources and citations and accelerating the "breaking news" character of reporting' (ibid: 63). The battle for ratings was found to be promoting a more sensationalist approach to news and current affairs in the Netherlands, where these genres have traditionally been covered in a restrained manner. A comparative study of current affairs programming on television, tracking the output on three Dutch channels in 1992 and 2001, found that competition was contributing to sensationalism in the coverage of current affairs (Vettehen et al., 2006). The case against the suspected killer of Pim Fortuyn, the slain Dutch leader of the far-right, was shown in 2002; the first live broadcast of court proceedings in the Netherlands, while in what was an example of voyeuristic news, SBS6, a private network, broadcast live the digging of his grave and his reburial (Devine, 2002).

In Italy, infotainment-driven private television catapulted Silvio Berlusconi from a businessman to the office of the Prime Minister, elected first in 1994 (for seven months) and then again in 2001 (Ginsborg, 2004; Padovani, 2004). Berlusconi was considered as a formidable force, responsible for changing the face of Italian television, primarily by reorganizing advertising on television through his network Publitalia, which introduced advertising slots in-between programmes and even interrupting ongoing transmissions to insert advertising. After acquiring two rival commercial channels – Italia 1 and Rete Quattro – the 'supply of advertising-financed television time increased radically', and, as one commentator noted, 'private television was now instrumental in spreading a commercial media culture where advertisements mixed with the products of the global, US-dominated entertainment industry, either through direct imports or through imitations' (Arvidsson, 2003: 134).

This popular televised culture was harnessed to shore up support for his political party Forza Italia, which was sold to the masses through such powerful arenas as AC Milan and other football clubs owned by Berlusconi. These served 'as a simulacrum of political participation: they enabled members to feel as if they were part of a new, general political effervescence, almost a revolution, and enabled the party to represent itself as founded on a grass-roots social movement' (ibid: 134). Sometimes referred to as 'Mr Broadcasting', Berlusconi understood the power of the image, of style and of popular imagination through his infotainment conglomerate Mediaset. His channels 'had educated millions of viewers in the values of postmodern society', and Forza Italia represented the revolt of the 'Italy of consumers', of the middle classes socialized into the values and aspirations of a new postmodern consumer culture, against the outdated ideologies of 'politics' (ibid: 144). After he was re-elected in 2001, Berlusconi used his private channels for satire shows such as *Le Iene* (The Hyenas) and *Striscia la Notizia* (Graze the News) broadcast on Italia 1 and Canale 5 respectively, while state broadcaster RAI's best documentary strand, *Report*, was buried late at night on a marginal channel. 'The news landscape is flat,' said a report in the *Guardian*, 'a tundra of deferential, unedited interviews. Chat, chat, chat' (Carroll, 2002: 6).

Commercial pressures have started to impact on media content in France, where government control of television has a long history: the two main national networks – TF1 (established in 1949) and Antenne 2 (established 1964) – were heavily subsidized by the government. Although very restricted advertising was introduced to television in 1970, it has grown substantially in the past quarter of a century, spurred on by the emergence in the 1980s of such cable networks as Canal Plus and the privatization of TF1, acquired by Bouygues, the largest construction company in France. As television has been transformed, it has come to shape the media agenda, dominating 'the journalistic field both economically and symbolically', and as Pierre Bourdieu notes, 'circumventing the rules set by serious journalism' (Bourdieu, 1998: 42). Ratings-obsessed nightly newscasts have raised concerns among media analysts, as indicated by the popularity of programmes such as *Arrêt sur Images* (Freeze Frame), a weekly programme broadcast on the public channel La Cinquième, which examined the infotainment trends seeping into French news reporting. 'The lines between journalism and entertainment have been blurred,' according to Daniel Schneidermann, a former *Le Monde* television critic who hosted *Arrêt sur Images* since its launch in 1995, 'people are being influenced as much by the manner in which information is being presented as by the information itself' (quoted in Crumley, 2000).

In Spain the commercialization of programmes is evident from the dominance of the prime time by docusoaps, reality shows, quiz-shows and soap operas. In 2002, a row erupted over which political party should be allowed to attach its colour to the Spanish equivalent of Pop Idol, *Operacion Triunfo* (Operation Triumph), broadcast on the state-run TVE channel (Tremlett, 2002). Commercial channels, such as Telecinco and Antena 3, thrive on investigative programming about political events and topical murder trials, as well as depend on such US-imported crime dramas as CSI, which became the most successful foreign series in Spanish television history, while the public broadcaster TVE responds by screening Hollywood blockbusters. Often trivial but engaging live news, based on eyewitness accounts, is routinely broadcast on Greek television, presented in a manner to make even mundane everyday events appear newsworthy and credible (Makri-Tsilipakou, 2004). Tabloidization of television news was evident also on Turkish television where the tragedies of the poor and glamorous lifestyles of the rich were the two main topics among commercial broadcasters, as a study of four commercial and one public service channels showed. It found that television news was increasingly presenting political stories in personalized and tabloidized forms, thus 'undermining public knowledge' (Bek, 2004: 383). The commercial imperative set the news agenda in which television news became 'a base for the big media groups,' the study noted, 'to promote their other businesses and compete with their rivals'. To achieve these goals, in the face of 'fierce competition in the ratings war', the Turkish infotainment conglomerates abused television news by even reporting 'fake news' (ibid: 382).

Some underlying themes emerge from this tour of television news: the primacy of market-driven media is well established across the world and the US-model of infotainment, discussed in Chapters 1 and 2, is indeed in the process of globalization: from nominally communist China, to commercialized Brazil, to Russia and even Germany, a bastion of public-service broadcasting. Our survey also shows that the growing importance of ratings has forced journalists to privilege soft stories and present them as sensationalist spectacles. A consistent theme that emerges is that 'tickling the public' can be translated into handsome revenues for infotainment conglomerates. And one indication of this trend is to be detected in the global success of 'reality' television.

Reality TV to the rescue

The blurring of the boundaries between journalism and entertainment have perhaps been most intense in the creation of the globally successful hybrid genre of 'reality television' (Andrejevic, 2003; Kilborn, 2003; Hill, 2005). The extraordinary expansion of 'reality television' in the late 1990s, first in the US and the UK and then globally, is another indication of how market forces have changed broadcast journalism. It is cheap, in more ways than one, and its proliferation makes perfect sense in a ratings-driven privatized television culture (Brenton and Cohen, 2003). A new genre of 'popular factual television' has emerged as a result of mixing tabloid journalism, documentary television and entertainment, demonstrating how 'television cannibalises itself in order to survive, drawing on existing genres to create successful hybrid programmes, which in turn generate a "new" television genre' (Hill, 2005: 24).

The unprecedented success of reality TV has provided television networks with an easy way out of the problems caused by the marketization of news, as two historians of American television note:

> The free-fall of broadcast news standards in prime time was finally offered a plateau – a position from which it could define and defend itself – by the increasing popularity of reality TV. Anything too ridiculous to be called journalism could be classified as a 'reality' show rather than 'news', with production responsibility kicked cleanly to the

lower expectations of the entertainment division. Entertainment producers, for their part, were happy with the arrangement, which freed them, simultaneously, from the two things they liked least: (1) the 'credibility thing', which constrained news magazines from following their entertainment instincts; and (2) the salary of star actors. In fact, reality shows presented opportunities to work without using any professional actors at all, as most performers in a reality vehicle ask nothing more for their services than a chance to appear on national television (Marc and Thompson, 2005: 126).

As with so many ideas of the media age, the concept of reality television emanated from the United States, pioneered by MTV with *The Real World* (the first series was broadcast in 1992 and by 2006 was in its 13th series).This glossy forerunner of *Big Brother* followed a group of good-looking young people sharing a flat, in a different US city each year. Another trendsetter was the US endurance contest, *Survivor*, premiered on prime-time CBS in 2000. By its final episode, some 62 million viewers had seen one or more episodes and the 'Survivor phenomenon' had become the subject of a mass cultural conversation. As Marc and Thompson noted: 'Broadcast network television had found what it needed: an inexpensive programming form that promised to put it, if only occasionally now, squarely at the center of conversation at the office water cooler, above, beyond, and beneath demographic lines' (ibid: 128).

By 2004, the genre had become so big that there were two dedicated 24/7 Reality TV channels – Reality TV and Zone Reality – operating around the world. The variety of reality shows is wide, ranging from lifestyle and makeover shows (for example, *Changing Rooms*, shown on BBC, on and off since 1996), to dating games (*The Bachelor* being a strong prototype); from contests based on skill and talent (*The Apprentice, Pop Idol*), to endurance or the capacity to live in a constricted space with strangers and being monitored 24/7 (*Big Brother, Survivor, I'm a Celebrity, Get Me Out of Here*), as well as sporting contests (*Superstars*, where stars from the sports world are pitted against each other in a series of different sports other than their own). Some of the more successful examples of reality television in the United States included: *The Amazing Race* (9 series), *Big Brother* (7 series) and *Survivor* (12 series by 2006) on CBS; *American Idol* (5 series) and *Temptation Island* (4 series) on Fox; *The Bachelor* (9 series) and *I'm a Celebrity* on ABC; and *The Apprentice* and *Fear Factor* on NBC.

American influence can also be detected in another subgenre of reality television: fly-on-the-wall docusoaps. Its success led to a glut of inexpensive infotainment, making members of the public famous overnight: according to press reports, 12 million viewers tuned in to watch the 1994 British fly-on the wall documentary *Driving School*, one of the first. Later series have ranged from everyday life in an hotel and an airport to even military personnel in war zones (see Chapter 5). In this ostensibly democratizing and empowering experiment in social engineering, ordinary people were turned into minor celebrities – the 'Celetoids', as one commentator called it (Turner, 2006). In 2002, MTV, losing viewers to myriad dedicated music television channels as well as on-line music file-sharing groups, launched the fly-on-the-wall documentary *The Osbournes*, one of the biggest earners for the channel, which has spawned many imitations. The four series based on the everyday life of the British-born former rock star Ozzy, his wife and family spawned a cult following (Gibson, 2005:11).

Despite its public-service remit, the BBC has been one of the most successful public broadcasters to harness reality TV, originating a range of programming in this profitable genre and selling its reality-TV formats to audiences globally. In her study of the BBC, Georgina Born noted the exponential growth in such programming, resulting from the heightened competition and increasing hybridization of 'the trinity of information, education and entertainment', encompassing the notion of 'factual entertainment', which 'delivers the requisite audience share at less risk than sitcoms or drama series; it is relatively cheap and relatively reliable' (Born, 2004: 376). Such factual entertainment falls into what John Corner has labelled as the newest function of documentary – 'diversion' – arising from a privatized television ecology and characterized by the 'lightness' of a topic or its treatment. 'Performing this function,' Corner writes, 'documentary is a vehicle variously for the high-intensity incident (the reconstructed accident, the police raid), for anecdotal knowledge (gossipy first-person accounts), and for snoopy sociability (as an amused bystander to the mixture of mess and routine in other people's working lives)' (Corner, 2002: 260).

Globalizing this form of infotainment was relatively easy: the template was essentially the same – cheap, cheerful and preferably choreographed television, high on drama and emotion but generally low on intellect and ideas. Their potential for localization and indigenization – in terms of language and cultural preferences – made reality television appealing to different networks. Public broadcasters in Europe have taken to such BBC imports as *Strictly Come Dancing*, which has been very successful on Spanish TVE-1, for example. Music talent-show formats such as *Star Academy* have been sold globally: the commercial French channel TF1 has been regularly broadcasting it along with such British game show imports as *The Weakest Link* and *Who Wants to be a Millionaire?*

The globalization of *Big Brother*

European-devised reality television formats have been localized, cloned and copied – both legally and illegally – in various forms around the world, and one of the most widely adapted show has been *Big Brother* (Mathjis et al., 2004; Bazalgette, 2005; Bignell, 2005). Its globalization made its Dutch creator John de Mol a millionaire and the company Endemol a global leader in format sales. In the programme, the contestants are meant to live under 24/7 public scrutiny in the 'Big Brother House', in a time-free zone, while members of the public vote to evict them one by one, the last one to remain winning the prize. The *Big Brother* format was seen to be easily transportable across borders and cultures. After premiering in the Netherlands in 2000, its second airing was in Germany. In 2001, the French commercial network M6 launched *Loft Story*, its own version of *Big Brother*, centred on relationships and sexual tension among eleven young men and women enclosed in a loft-style flat in a Paris suburb.

Peter Bazalgette, the television executive credited to bringing *Big Brother* to Britain, wrote an international bestseller, *Billion Dollar Game*, celebrating this new global voyeurism. He noted how, when the series was broadcast in Denmark for the first time in 2001, MPs and bureaucrats crashed their entire Internet connections as they were all logging on at once to watch the housemates having a shower. In Spain, as *Gran Hermano*, the undisputed king of reality TV in its sixth session, aired by commercial broadcaster, Telecinco, a Basque separatist broke into the *Big Brother* house to stage a one-man protest. A *Big Brother* housemate in Poland joined the television programme with the aim of entering politics, and won a parliamentary seat in the 2001 general elections (Bazalgette, 2005). In Colombia, President Alvaro Uribe became a surprise guest at the local version of *Big Brother* to promote a package of constitutional reforms. A pan-African version was introduced in 2003, while a year later, in Bahrain clerics led a mass demonstration against the Middle Eastern *Big Brother*, claiming it to be un-Islamic and forcing the authorities to stop the programme. *Big Brother* became *Big Boss* on Sony television in India, broadcast in 2006.

As one commentator points out in relation to Europe:

> in all the countries where *Big Brother* has been adopted, domestic national audiovisual systems have lost their state monopoly position. Reality TV programming has often been broadcast on minor or emergent commercial channels, which have successfully displaced the dominance and prestige of the established channels. In this respect, they have distanced themselves from the values of public service, burdened with an image of traditionalism, (self)-censorship and patriarchal stiffness. (Frau-Meigs, 2006: 40–1)

Apart from continuously showing high ratings, such programmes also have significant spin-offs. The news media – and not just the tabloid press – have regularly covered the antics, misbehaviours, successes and failures of participants. It made stars of ordinary people – some even going on to front their own television shows.

The element of interactivity – for those who missed the action on TV – the Internet, with a live, round-the-clock feed from the *Big Brother* house allows the pseudo-voyeuristic pleasure of watching the contestants talk, sleep, get intimate with each other, eat or just sit around. Though its banality may baffle some, programmes such as *Big Brother*, simultaneously distributed across multiple platforms, including on-line and mobile media, are big business for broadcasters as well as telecommunication companies. The growing penetration of broadband has made them more interactive, a marriage of convenience between mobile Internet and television. This interactivity benefits the telecommunication companies and helps keep channel loyalty, in an age of media plenty and ever-shortening attention span, especially among the young viewers. The assumption that the viewers are effecting the outcome of the programme as they vote via telephone, text or Internet for their favourite winners, can be manipulated by clever spin doctors. It is not unusual for programme makers to provoke controversies to retain high ratings. Public rows between contestants, display of raw emotions and intimacy make for compelling viewing.

Celebrity *Big Brother* – the Shilpa Shetty story

A striking example of global circulation of infotainment and the symbiotic relationship between news and reality TV was the international coverage of the controversial *Celebrity Big Brother* broadcast in January 2007 on Britain's Channel 4 television. The racist remarks endured by Bollywood actress Shilpa Shetty – the first Indian contestant in a reality TV show in Britain – provoked over 40,000 complaints to Ofcom, the most to date. Complaints alleged that her three female tormentors hurled racial abuse, purposefully mispronounced her name, and implied that Indians were unhygienic. The story had all the ingredients of infotainment – an exotic celebrity, a foreign female film star, emotionally tormented – facing determined but dim fellow housemates. For the BBC radio's Asian Network it became a big story, with callers recollecting their experiences of racist bullying. Britain's race relations watchdog, the Commission for Racial Equality expressed concern. The issue made it to Parliament, forcing Prime Minister Tony Blair to remark in a parliamentary response, 'we must oppose racism in all its forms'. The story received almost blanket coverage in Britain and India, generated more than 1,200 articles in English-language newspapers alone, including making it to the pages of *New York Times*. Though the coverage was framed as race issue, in fact it may have had as much to do with a clash of class than race. Traditionally, reality TV programmes tend to receive large coverage in the tabloid press and this *Celebrity Big Brother* was

Table 3.2 British quality press coverage of *Celebrity Big Brother* (week ending January 17, 2007)

Newspaper	*Words devoted to the story*
Guardian/Observer	10,674
Independent	7,670
Times/Sunday Times	5,611
Telegraph	4,062

(Source: The *Guardian*, January 22, 2007)

no exception. However, even the quality newspapers devoted extensive space to the story, as shown in Table 3.2.

Fearing that negative publicity might affect its reputation, Carphone Warehouse, the main sponsor of *Celebrity Big Brother*, pulled its £3 million sponsorship of programme. However, for Channel 4, the controversy helped raise the ratings of the show. The Chief Executive of Channel 4, Andy Duncan, who has a marketing background, went on air to apologise for the abuse meted out to Shetty. Given the ingredients of the story, it was to be expected that it would be covered on television in Britain and in India, however, as Table 3.3 shows, the story was headline news around the world, including on 24/7 television networks in US, Russia, Germany and France, indicating how news and reality television feed off each other to attract consumer and advertising attention in a crowded marketplace.

Monitoring the global 24/7 news network on the night when the story broke demonstrated that the content of the reports was remarkably similar, using the same ingredients but in different combinations:

- Footage of the insulting behaviour of the housemates (Endemol/C4)
- Footage of Parliament during Prime Minister's questions with Tony Blair responding to questions from Keith Vaz, Labour MP and of Indian origin
- Footage of protests in India, burning effigies of the producers
- Comments from Chancellor Gordon Brown during his New Delhi visit
- Comments from Shilpa Shetty's parents
- Views of Asian media commentators
- Vox pop comments on the street in New Delhi
- Scenes from Shilpa Shetty's film career

Most of the reports mentioned the fact that, as a result of the row the programme's ratings went up by 20 per cent, and several, especially the Indian channels, focused on how Shetty's career had received a much-needed boost. CNN called it 'a snowballing controversy' and featured a branding expert who called

Table 3.3 International infotainment: world TV coverage of Shilpa's story January 17 2007

Channel	*Where based*	*Duration*
Star News	India	8′ 20″
BBC World	UK	7′
NDTV 24 × 7	India	6′ 5″
Channel 4 News	UK	5′
Al-Jazeera English	Qatar	4′30″
ITN	UK	3′25″
Sky News	UK	3′ 5″
CNN International	US	2′15″
France 24	France	1′40″
DW-TV	Germany	1′20″
Russia Today TV	Russia	1′
EuroNews	Brussels	30″

the programme 'low-brow voyeurism' – talking about the impact on the sponsor's brand; while, Meera Syal, a British-based Indian writer and actress, was quoted by NDTV 24x7 as saying that the episode showed the 'thin line between entertainment and a wild spectacle'. Interviewed on Aljazeera English in their London studio, the British Asian MP Keith Vaz reminded the viewers that they were watching 'edited highlights', i.e. that these were the scenes deliberately chosen by Channel 4 for all to see, stoking up the controversy. Even the BBC's *Newsnight*, the 50-minute long, most serious news analysis programme on British television, gave 16 minutes to the Shetty affair. In India, TV networks competed with each other to give prominence to the story, ignoring the visit of British Chancellor of Exchequer Gordon Brown who was leading an economic delegation, bombarding him instead with question about the Shetty episode. Heated studio-based discussions dominated the airwaves, with NDTV 24x7 broadcasting 'Racism or ratings?', a 30-minute special programme devoted to the Shetty story, under its *Reality Bites* series.

Once considered a serious television channel with an innovative editorial agenda, Channel 4, has become the main source of reality television for the British audience in the past ten years. Such programmes have been ratings successes, bringing much-needed advertisement and telephone revenues to the broadcaster. Even before the Shetty row took off, a Channel 4 executive told the *Times of India*: 'Shilpa is part of a varied and eclectic bunch of celebrities who, in the confines of the house, will undoubtedly entertain and surprise us. The unpredictability of the mix of this year's celebrity housemates makes the line-up our most exciting yet.' Shetty's London agent told the newspaper that Shetty viewed the show as a 'huge opportunity ... a blank template for the UK market ... a challenge to become a name in a country where only British Asians know her despite the fact that she is a huge star in India' (quoted in Lall, 2007).

Is it at all possible that in this age of commodification, that perhaps a Bollywood actress with a fading career but with new ambitions to operate within a lucrative Western market, acted in a certain manner to create a controversy with the blessings of the producers? As *The Hindu*, India's most serious newspaper, noted in an editorial: 'A B-grade Bollywood actor, who shed finely wrought tears over racial slurs, has metamorphosed into an international celebrity.' The newspaper added: 'Because somewhere in the huge controversy over *Celebrity Big Brother* – one in which a Prime Minister weighed in, sundry Ministers held forth, academics vented spleen, celebrities frothed at the mouth, and television anchors crammed the airwaves with all manner of bits and bytes – something seems to have been forgotten. Should the world have worked up such a lather over a possibly orchestrated spat between two women in a tasteless reality show?' (*The Hindu*, 2007).

Shetty graciously accepted the apologies from her housemates, receiving the support of liberal opinion and emerging the winner of the show. Soon after leaving the house, Shetty took advice from Max Clifford, Britain's highest-paid and best known public relations manager who specializes in celebrities, to advise her on how to sell her story to the media. Subsequently, Shetty appeared in various newspaper and magazine interviews (including *Hello!* magazine), and Murdoch's Sky News ran a 30-minute interview with the star, while Sky One, his general entertainment channel in Britain, broadcast an hour-long biopic on March 19, 2007, called *The Real Shilpa Shetty*.

Why did this story receive such global coverage? No one will dispute that racism in all its manifestations is a serious social and political question and one which should be discussed in the media. Some commentators even argued that programmes such as *Big Brother* help bring these latent issues out into the public sphere. While the media circus focused on a foreign celebrity, other less famous foreigners living in or visiting Britain, especially if they sport a beard and have a Muslim name, continue to be arrested on 'terrorism' charges, stopped at airports or deported. It is debatable whether Shetty would have won without the row: when she entered the *Celebrity Big Brother* house the betting odds against her were 16/1. Shetty's winning demonstrates something more than just the fact that infotainment sells. The Indian element is important here, as Britain is home to 1.3 million Indians. The migration pattern – from villagers with a limited education working nightshifts in factories, to a more professional, highly educated group of individuals, representing the increasingly globalized middle class in India – may have contributed to the globalization of this story. That Indian businesses are one of the biggest investors in London, as the city's mayor Ken Livingstone reminded the BBC, may also have been a consideration. Another reason may have been the Bollywood factor – globalization has created much greater awareness of non-Western popular culture and Bollywood – the world's largest film industry, has certainly helped make the Shilpa Shetty story global infotainment fare. The Indian case offers interesting insights into how infotainment has entered and prospered in the world's largest democracy. This is the focus of discussion in the next chapter, which also addresses the nascent synergies between Bollywood and Hollywood-originated infotainment.

4

INDIAN INFOTAINMENT: THE BOLLYWOODIZATION OF TV NEWS

One of India's most respected television news channels, NDTV 24×7, broadcasts a regular popular comedy programme, *The Great Indian Tamasha*. Loosely translated, 'tamasha' means 'show', but the word has other connotations that could make it a metaphor for the state of television news in India. Tamasha has its roots in a popular form of folk theatre in Western Maharashtra (the state in which Mumbai is located): with its suggestive dances and lyrics, it has traditionally been immensely popular among rural communities. Generally bawdy, often funny, its aim is not just to tickle the public but to make them roll in the aisles. The genre has been adapted skilfully by the Mumbai-based Bollywood, the staple diet of which are the song and dance numbers. It is not a coincidence that many of India's television news networks are also based in Mumbai, India's commercial capital and a centre of its cultural industries, particularly film and television.

In this chapter, I want to examine how the case of Indian television news demonstrates a global trend towards infotainment. Given the size and diversity of India's television landscape, it is arguably the world's most complex television market, not comparable to any other country. The closest it gets to in terms of size of audience is China, but, unlike its giant eastern neighbour, India is a multilingual democracy. The constitution of India recognizes 18 languages, most of which have huge geo-linguistic constituencies, both within the country and among the diaspora that can sustain language-based television industries. Perhaps a more useful comparison would be with the European Union, although its television audience is smaller and incomes much larger. Like the EU, India has a well-established democratic polity, which gives its press a level of autonomy unthinkable elsewhere in the developing world. In addition, as part of the British colonial legacy, India embraced the public-service model of broadcasting for both radio and television, though, unlike the BBC, its public broadcaster was more akin to a state-controlled information and entertainment network than an autonomous entity in the best tradition of West European public-service broadcasting.

Following the general trend, India has also seen its public media being undermined by the forces of the market. The scale and scope of the change, given the size of India's population and the potential of its television industry, is truly remarkable and one which has so far not been sufficiently recognised in academic studies of media globalization. More than 70 per cent of India's billion-plus population is below the age of 30 and a sizeable segment of these young Indians is increasingly mobile, harnessing the opportunities offered by the globalization of the trade and service industries and especially using their skills in the English language, the vehicle for global communication and commerce. The mainly US-based media transnational corporations have successfully made use of this demographic, benefiting at the same time from the growing geo-political and economic convergence between the governments of India and the United States. India offers a unique market opportunity for media conglomerates, given its exposure to Western-dominated global culture through a British-inspired educational and institutional framework, and its religious, linguistic and ethnic plurality.

The development of Indian media: private press and public broadcasting

Traditionally presenting itself as a leader of the developing world, ostensibly following a 'non-aligned' foreign policy (which in reality meant pro-socialist), and championing 'Third World' causes in international forums, India saw its role as a spokesman for the global South. It was a vocal advocate, for example, during the 1970s UNESCO-sponsored New World Information and Communication Order debates, for a more balanced and equitable global news flow, and a founding member of the Non-aligned News Agencies Pool (Boyd-Barrett and Thussu, 1992). Such internationalist sentiments were rooted in the Nehruvian version of socialism, which emphasized a liberal worldview anchored in an indigenous cultural space and which dominated intellectual life and the 'Brahaminical press', which was serious, staid and sober.

The press was a crucial element in 'nation-building', transforming India from a feudal to a modern, multi-party democratic nation-state. Newspapers have a long association with modernity in India: *The Times of India* – today the world's largest circulated quality English-language newspaper – was established in 1838 and by the 1870s, more than 140 newspaper titles were in circulation in various Indian languages, many set up by nationalist leaders, who were involved, in later years, in campaigning journalism, most notably Mahatma Gandhi, the 'father of the nation' who edited *Young India* (later renamed *Harijan*). India inherited from the British the combination of a private press and a government-controlled broadcasting system, though an element of anti-colonialism continued to influence journalism. A privately owned broadcasting regime, it was feared, could destabilise the nascent Indian republic and its fragile democratic system, given its traumatic birth, which saw one million people killed and more than 15 million displaced as a result of Partition. Consequently the government was compelled to keep broadcasting under its firm control.

The introduction of television in 1959 reflected the attitude to the medium as a means for disseminating government policies, public information and propaganda, while entertainment, which was almost exclusively the preserve of the privately financed film industry, was hardly a priority for the state broadcaster. Ostensibly the main aim of the national broadcaster Doordarshan was to educate and inform, and to create an Indian identity: in reality, it was a dull, over-bureaucratized public-broadcasting monopoly and was perceived as little more than a mouthpiece for the government of the day. Its news coverage rarely rose above what critics derided as 'protocol news' – reports on government ministers inaugurating a major industrial project or receiving a foreign dignitary (Thussu, 2007b).

Unlike television news, private print journalism, professionally organized and ideologically diverse, helped create a space for democratic discourse on socio-political and economic issues affecting millions of Indians. The diversity of the mainstream press reflected the wide variety of political and linguistic affiliations in a vast, multi-ethnic, multi-religious and geographically and culturally complex country. Its sometimes adversarial role contributed to the evolution of an 'early-warning system' for serious food shortages and thus a preventive mechanism against famine (Ram, 1990). Despite their urban middle-class milieu, most journalists had a sense of national development and a certain empathy for their fellow citizens – not just within the national territory but in the wider 'Third World'. The media operated within a quasi socialist framework, which encouraged a belief in a democratic and secular domestic agenda and a non-aligned policy in international affairs.

This attitude weakened as the state progressively lost its moral legitimacy as a growing number of politicians with besmirched reputations came to dominate public life. The partial privatization of airwaves started with the introduction of advertising onto the state broadcaster in the 1970s, followed by sponsored programmes. This process received a boost as India opened up to transnational infotainment corporations in the 1990s. In the initial years of this liberalization, India's own newspaper and publishing houses did not expand into broadcasting, although there was no regulation against private broadcasting – some newspaper groups, though, did get involved in television software: Living Media, Hindustan Times (Home TV), Business India (BiTV) and Eenadu were early converts to television. The gradual deregulation and privatization of television in the 1990s transformed the media landscape in a country which had one of the most regulated broadcasting environments among the world's democracies (Price and Verhulst, 1998; Page and Crawley, 2001).

Experiencing exponential growth in the number of television channels, India has emerged as one of the world's biggest television markets. At the beginning of the 1990s, there was no television industry worth the name in India: by 2007 more than 300 digital channels were operating, including some joint ventures with international broadcasters (Butcher, 2003; Rajan, 2005; Thussu, 2007b). This unprecedented growth has been spurred on by massive increases in advertising revenue as Western-based infotainment conglomerates tap into the growing market of 300 million increasingly Westernized, educated middle-class Indians with enhanced purchasing power and media-induced aspirations to a consumerist lifestyle. Cable and satellite television have increased substantially since their introduction in 1992, when only 1.2 million Indian homes had access to these facilities: growing annually at the rate of 10 per cent, television connectivity is set to touch 134 million households by 2010, of which 85 million are expected to be cable and satellite households. According to the trade press, in 2007 there were nearly 400 million television viewers in India. The media and entertainment business, one of the fastest growing industries in India, was estimated to be worth $10 billion in 2006 and was projected to more than double by 2011 to reach nearly $23 billion, according to the 2007 report *Indian Entertainment and Media Industry: A Growth Story Unfolds*, prepared by PricewaterHouseCoopers (PWC) for the Federation of Indian Chamber of Commerce and Industry (FICCI). In 2006, the Indian television broadcasting market stood at $4.3 billion and was projected to nearly treble in size to $11.8 billion by 2011 (Ali, 2006; FICCI, 2007). Television accounted for 46 per cent of the total advertising industry worth nearly $3.5 billion: although it is very small in comparison with US or Western Europe, infotainment conglomerates see huge potential for future growth: in 2006, nearly 400 million Indians did not own a television set, while only 42 per cent of the rural population had access to satellite and cable television (Kohli, 2003a; Ali, 2006; Credit Suisse, 2006).

Demonstrating a robust annual economic growth of eight per cent in the past few years, India is increasingly viewed internationally as an emerging economic and political power. One manifestation of this status is how India's popular culture is being perceived outside India, particularly within the metropolitan centres of the globe. 'The Rise of India' was the main theme of a 2006 issue of the influential journal *Foreign Affairs*, while *Time* magazine ran a cover story in July of the same year on 'India Inc.: Why the world's biggest democracy is the next great economic superpower – and what it means for the rest of us' (*Time*, 2006). According to the Confederation of Indian Industry estimates, international television revenues are expected to increase from 17 billion rupees in 2004 to 43 billion rupees in 2010. Liberalized policies have contributed to increased foreign investment in the media and entertainment sectors – over Rs 4 billion between 2003–2006. Indian entertainment corporations are even looking east for new markets beyond the diaspora: the success of the 2005 Chinese film *Perhaps Love* – the first musical since the 1950s and made with expertise from Bollywood – is indicative of the potential of collaborations among major non-Western cultures. Exploring such untapped potential by creating infotainment content that has international appeal can provide additional sources of revenue. The Indian infotainment sector is also benefiting from media outsourcing industries in such areas as animation and post-production services for Hollywood and other industries. The infotainment marriage between Hollywood and Bollywood is already on the global media agenda.

The globalization of Bollywood has ensured that Indian films are increasingly being watched by an international audience as well as a wider diasporic one: Hindi films are shown in more than 70 countries. Indian film exports witnessed a 20-fold increase in the period 1989–99. This has made it imperative for producers to invest in sub-titling to widen the reach of films, as well as privileging scripts which interest the overseas audience – by 2004 exports accounted for nearly 30 per cent of the industry earnings (FICCI, 2004; UNESCO, 2005). Plans for joint ventures between Indian film producers and Hollywood giants received a boost with the announcement in 2000 that the Indian government was to allow foreign companies to invest in the film industry.

A 2006 Credit Suisse report interestingly titled *Opportunities of Hollywood in Bollywood*, notes that the Indian media market is experiencing double-digit growth in advertising revenue, fuelled by growth in GDP and supported by the emergence of a strong consumer market, demonstrating significant opportunities for global infotainment conglomerates to develop new streams of income, attracted by the progressive easing of foreign ownership rules. Subscription revenue is widely expected to grow even faster than advertising, supported by government mandated transition to DTH satellite broadcasting, which the report predicts, could nearly double broadcasters' share of subscription revenue in the next four years (Credit Suisse, 2006: 4). Disney, which entered the Indian market with consumer products, books, magazines and TV broadcasting, has bought the children's channel Hungama and acquired a stake in Indian film and television production company UTV, while Sony has bought out Sab TV, a general entertainment channel.

As cross-media ownership rules are relaxed, there is greater trend towards concentration of media power: non-media groups such as Tata (India's largest industrial house), Adlabs and Bharti have invested heavily in DTH. Increasingly large companies are present across various segments of the media and entertainment world: new 'media conglomerates', drawing their inspiration from the US model, are in the making. The Credit Suisse report shows how a liberal regulatory environment has acted as a magnet for infotainment conglomerates: though the nearly $10 billion Chinese advertising market is more than double the size of India's, foreign companies receive merely 6 per cent of the total advertisement revenues, as against 30 per cent in India (Credit Suisse, 2006).

This expansion demanded new programme content, from news to game and chat shows, from soap operas to reality TV, which have been provided by a burgeoning television industry, catering to a huge Indian market as well as a large South Asian diaspora (Thussu, 2005a, 2007b). A combination of national and transnational factors, including the availability of new delivery and distribution mechanisms, as well as the growing corporatization of its film factories and television industry, have ensured that Indian television has entered the global infotainment arena, with the potential of pushing it in new directions. Since the transnational media conglomerates are the driving force behind marketization of cultural industries and growth of infotainment, and they are increasingly getting involved in India, what is happening to television in the world's largest democracy acquires international significance. As India integrates further into a globalized free-market economy, the Indian version of infotainment is likely to have a transnational reach, attracting new viewers beyond their traditional South Asian diasporic constituency. This interest has partly been generated by the growing visibility of Indian enterprise and its cultural products around the world.

The world's biggest TV news bazaar?

In the late 1990s and early 2000s India's news television sector demonstrated extraordinary growth in the number of dedicated news channels: from 1 in 1998 to nearly 40 in 2007, most of which were national, but many

Table 4.1 Indian 24/7 TV news channels

Channel name	*Language*	*Reach*
Star News	Hindi	International
NDTV 24 × 7	English	International
CNN/IBN	English	International
CNBC-TV18	English	International
Sun News	Tamil	International
Asianet News	Malayalam	International
TV9 News	Telugu	International
Tara Newz	Bangla	International
DD News	Hindi/English	International
Times Now	English	National
Aaj Tak	Hindi	National
NDTV India	Hindi	National
Zee News	Hindi	National
NDTV Profit	English	National
Sahara Samay	Hindi	National
Headlines Today	English	National
India TV	Hindi	National
Janmat	Hindi	National
Tez	Hindi	National
IBN7	Hindi	National
CNBC Awaaz	Hindi	National
Zee Business	Hindi	National
Teja News	Telugu	Regional
ETV2 News	Telugu	Regional
Udaya News	Kannada	Regional
Star Anand	Bangla	Regional

(Source: Data from news channel websites, 2007)

international in reach, some catered to the regional markets, as Table 4.1 shows.

Deregulation of the Indian television news sector (in which government allows up to 26 per cent foreign investment) has partly been responsible for this boom, as private investors – both national and transnational – have sensed new opportunities for revenue and influence by going into the television news business, making India the country with the largest number of

Table 4.2 Market share of TV news in India

Channel	*Language*	*Viewership share (%)*
Aaj Tak	Hindi	22
Star News	Hindi	16
Zee News	Hindi	12
NDTV India	Hindi	11
India TV	Hindi	7
IBN7	Hindi	7
TV9 Telugu News	Telugu	7
ETV2 Telugu News	Telugu	7
DD News	Hindi/English	6
Sun News	Tamil	5

(Source: Based on data from TAM, for April–June 2006, for satellite and cable households)

news channels in the world, and, what is more, most of these channels are profitable. Although the highly competitive news sector attracts only 4 per cent of national viewership, its share of television advertising revenue is nearer 11 per cent (Credit Suisse, 2006). According to the 2007 Indian Readership Survey, two of the top ten national television channels in terms of their reach and viewerships were dedicated news channels: Aaj Tak and DD News.

Bucking the trend in the US and Europe, in India there has been an increase in news viewership from 0.92 million households in 2001 to nearly 7 million households in 2005. This interest in news may reflect not only the low baseline from which it started but also popularity and diversity of debate in a complex political scene and the 'argumentative' nature of Indians (Sen, 2004). More and more groups – distinct in terms of language, region, politics and economic networks – have invested in television news. Given the multiplicity of languages and communities in India, the newsscape becomes all the more complicated. It is instructive to note that among the top ten news networks – none are English language news channels (see Table 4.2).

Another reason for the growth of news networks is the 24-million strong Indian diaspora, which is increasingly contributing to and benefiting from Indian economic growth: with an estimated net worth of $300 billion and their annual contribution to the Indian economy valued at up to $10 billion, tuning in to Indian news channels is an immediate and effective way of keeping abreast of developments in the home country. The market leader in the English language sector, NDTV 24×7 (part of New Delhi Television, which was founded in 1988 as India's first private news content provider for Doordarshan, the BBC and later for Murdoch's Star News), was available in 2007 to Indian diaspora in the US (via DirecTV), the UK (BSkyB), the Middle East (Arab Digital Distribution) and southern Africa (Multi-choice Africa). Star News and DD News, too, were available via Sky in the UK. NDTV has a strategic tie-up with Microsoft for marketing through MSN, including the sale of airtime on MSN portals and products through NDTV Media and has also entered a content partnership with Kuala Lumpur-based Astro Broadcast Corporation to set up two, 24-hour news channels in Indonesia and Malaysia.

NDTV 24×7 sees the potential of exploiting the synergies between entertainment and information and in 2007 announced the launch of an entertainment channel, NDTV Imagine, to be managed by the well-known Bollywood director Karan Johar (the opportunity in the Indian entertainment market is estimated to be worth $5.2 billion). Such diversification would need investment from overseas companies, and since, as a news broadcaster, it can only have a maximum 26 per cent foreign investment to comply with government regulations in the news broadcasting sector, the company set up a subsidiary, NDTV Networks, which will raise $150 million: NDTV is 'in the process of metamorphosis', according to the news network's CEO Vikram Chandra (quoted in Kohli-Khandekar, 2006a). Such a metamorphosis is likely to be on the basis of entertainment and lifestyle output, raising the concern that one of the most professional and politically liberal news networks may also be veering towards infotainment to retain its position – not only domestically but globally as an emerging powerhouse of English-language television.

Such synergies between film and the TV news and entertainment channels are common. The company that ran the Hindi news channel, Sahara Samay Rashtriya, is also involved in Bollywood film production and operated a film-based channel called 'Filmy'. Zee News was part of one of India's largest infotainment conglomerates with extensive interests in the entertainment industry: apart from general interest Zee Television, it also ran dedicated channels Zee Cinema and Zee Music, both excessively Bollywood oriented. TV-18, India's leading content provider and broadcaster of business, consumer and general news, operating since 1993, has made forays into film production with Studio 18. Star News regularly and unabashedly promotes the serials being shown on its sister channel Star Plus, with such spin-off programmes as *Saas, Bahu aur Saazish* (a magazine show about the 'lives' of the characters in the soap operas).

Global news organizations, such as CNN, though operating in India since 1992, rank very low in audience figures – less than 1 per cent, and therefore have entered into partnerships with Indian companies. CNN-IBN, an English general news and current affairs channel, launched in 2005, in association with TV-18 Group, is one key example. CNBC-TV18, an English business news channel, is another. A foreign presence is also to be noticed in another major news player *Times Now,* whose tagline 'Feel the news' – is indicative of the changes in news (it has been called the second generation news broadcast), owned by the *Times of India* Group and Reuters, and launched in 2006.

The Times-Reuters partnership points to an emerging synergy between different global media brands. With a history of more than 150 years in global journalism, Reuters is already a top brand, while the *Times of India* wants to be noticed as the most powerful Indian infotainment conglomerate, representing a big and dynamic nation. On New Year's Day in 2007, it inaugurated a campaign called *India Poised,* with a video featuring India's best-known actor Amitabh Bachchan, indicating this aspiration (Bose, 2007). Once a leader of the Brahminical press and an independent Third World voice in the world's press, *The Times of India* has become a major business – with leadership in newspaper publishing; magazines; music; retailing; FM Radio; Internet; interactive media; mobile services and television.

Murdochization of media in India

As in many other countries, the greatest contributor to the trend towards infotainment in India has been Murdoch, whose pan-Asian network Star, launched in 1991, pioneered satellite television in Asia, transforming TV news and entertainment (Butcher, 2003; Kohli, 2003b). Murdoch was responsible for introducing the first music television channel in India (Channel V); the first 24/7 news network (Star News); the first successful adaptation of an international game show *(Who Wants to be a Millionaire?)*, and the first reality TV series *(Lakme Fashion Show)* (Thussu, 2007b).

As noted in Chapter 2, Murdoch's extensive control of both information software (programme content) and hardware (delivery systems) has made him a hugely powerful player in the world of global infotainment, especially in Asia. Murdoch was able before many others to understand the potential of media in the world's largest continent, home to some of its fastest growing economies and he invested heavily in the Asian media scene. Starting with Hollywood-based programming aimed at the affluent but tiny English-speaking minority (less than 5 per cent of India's population), Murdoch recognized the limitations of this strategy and rapidly Indianized his television, including news operations in India. Though Murdoch's business interests in India are wider than television, his investment in television has been the most important feature of his strategies in India. The flagship of his operations

Table 4.3 Star TV in India

Entertainment	*Sports*	*Movies*	*Music*	*News/infotainment*
Star Plus	ESPN	Star Gold	Channel [V]	Star News
Star One	Star Sports	Star Movies		Star Ananda (Bengali)
Star Utsav				National Geographic
Star World (English)				History Channel
Vijay TV (Tamil)				

(Source: Star TV, 2007)

in India, the Hindi-language general entertainment channel Star Plus, is India's highest-rated private entertainment network. Star provides a comprehensive mixture of programming in all major genres of television: entertainment, movies, sport, music, news and documentaries.

News Corporation's interests in the Indian media industry are wide and growing (see Table 4.3). By 2007 Murdoch controlled directly or through joint ventures, a great deal of television in India. These included wholly owned channels (Star Plus, Star One, Star Gold, Star World, Channel V, Star Movies, Star Utsav, Star Vijay); joint ventures (ESPN, Star Sports, National Geographic, The History Channel, Star News, Star Ananda); distribution (Disney Channel, cable distributor Hathway, DTH Tata-Sky), and programming (Balaji telefilms, one of India's biggest makers of television serials).

The recent inclusion in the Star family of the southern Tamil language entertainment channel, Vijay TV and Star Ananda, a 24-hour Bengali news service, indicates Murdoch's interest of going beyond the Hindi-speaking parts of India, aiming at a mass audience and reflecting growing localization strategies. Almost from its entry into the volatile Indian broadcasting market in 1992, the localization of his operations in India was a unique characteristic of Murdoch's strategy in India. Unlike Disney or AOL-Time Warner, Murdoch did not see India as 'another syndication opportunity' and instead invested in local programming (Kohli, 2003b) and cooperation with local television companies. His control of the Zee network, India's largest television conglomerate, between 1993 and 2000, gave Murdoch a crucial insight into the Bollywood-driven Indian popular culture and Zee a platform to become a global broadcaster (Thussu, 2005a, 2007b). Having resourceful local partners remains crucial for infotainment conglomerates and Murdoch has shown uncanny knack at choosing these. Always investing in the future, the most significant of joint-ventures that Star signed in India was with Tata on DTH television for Tata-Sky, a pan-Indian, state-of-the-art digital infrastructure for pay television.

Murdoch's impact on television news in India has been far reaching: he was instrumental in introducing the idea of 24/7 news to India when, in 1998, he launched an English-language channel Star News, to coincide with the national elections that year, building on his success of Sky News in Britain and Fox News in the US. As with entertainment, having a strong local partner was a crucial component of Murdoch's strategy in entering the news arena and since Indian broadcasting regulation prohibited majority ownership of news channels by foreign companies, Star commissioned NDTV to provide all the news material including its presentation and packaging. This was a mutually beneficial partnership: NDTV could reach the homes of affluent Indians as well as diasporic audiences through the Star platform, while Star could benefit from gravitas of a serious news channel. However, the Star-NDTV contract came to an end in 2003 and NDTV decided to go it alone, launching two channels, the English-language, NDTV 24×7 and NDTV India, in Hindi. After the split, Star entered a joint venture with the Anand Bazaar Patrika group (a Calcutta-based Indian media company) to comply with government ownership regulations for news channels. In this new stage of its indigenization, Murdoch's news network transformed itself into a Hindi-only channel to widen its appeal, as the language spoken by the largest numbers of Indians. Before Star News was re-launched, its CEO Ravina Raj Kohli was sent to other Murdoch news operations including Fox News 'to see how news works, ... what clicks' (Kohli, 2003b). Within one week of the switch to Hindi, Star News ratings almost doubled. As if symbolizing the change in editorial focus of the news network, Star News headquarters also moved to India's commercial capital Mumbai.

As part of Murdoch's media empire, Star News has the resources to influence substantially the news market, with a team of anchors and reporters based in more than 20 bureaux across the country, providing live coverage. Star News is leading the way with a news agenda that thrives on infotainment, at the heart of which is the popularization of news, by making it accessible and entertaining, thus expanding the audience base for advertisers as well as promoting synergies among Murdoch's entertainment and news operations in India. In 2006 Star India – valued at about $3 billion – was aiming to move a significant part of its production activities, particularly relating to format shows and advertiser funded programming (AFP), in house and to achieve this Fox Entertainment Group set up a wholly owned subsidiary Fox Television Studios India (Kohli-Khandekar, 2006b). Star News had to operate within a crowded and fiercely competitive Hindi news market, with rivals including Zee News, the first Hindi 24/7 news aimed at a mass audience, and Aaj Tak, part of the India Today group, publisher of India's best known news magazine

India Today, and since its inception in 2000 almost the top news presence. Star News also faced stiff competition from Sahara Samay, part of the business group which owns one of the largest selling Hindi newspapers, *Rashtriya Sahara*.

The tabloidization of television news

Every day Star entertains 60 million Indians and much of what is available on its networks has given ammunition to Murdoch's critics to accuse Star of 'regressive' television and 'pandering to the lowest common denominator' (Kohli-Khandekar, 2006a). Particularly concerned by the tendency of tabloidization of television news are print journalists: the news weekly *Outlook*, which in 2005 examined the state of journalism in India, to mark ten years of the magazine's launch, noted: 'Subjectivity, inaccuracy, misquote; marketing men as editorial heads; sexing it up, dumbing it down, sting operations with methods and morals mixed up; "breaking news" dozen times a day on TV; TV studios as courtrooms; SMS voting on serious human rights issues; the PR industry as source; selling of editorial space' (Vasudev, 2005). This uncharitable view of the malaise afflicting broadcast journalism reflected the print media's pride in its editorial independence and professionalism. As elsewhere in the world, there are concerns that Murdoch's or Murdoch-inspired television news in India is going for the safety of the soft news option. The all-news channels in India are still in their infancy but even in their early formative years it is possible to detect emerging themes which reflect wider trends in broadcast journalism: competition is sharp and to win the ratings battles, they increasingly show a tendency towards infotainment.

Even Aaj Tak, the most serious of Hindi news channels, has been forced to broadcast 'exclusive' stories about the supernatural and the bizarre: in 2005 it ran a two-hour studio discussion about a man who claimed to have come back to life after having 'died'; while one news network let an anchor cover her own wedding, prompting a commentator to note that the news had gone 'crazy', with popular news channels altering 'the definition of news, and in the process, transformed their own fortunes'. 'Compelling TV' is the new phrase coined in newsrooms across channels. The story, packaging or the visuals have to be attention-grabbing and simply compelling. Siddhartha Gupta, director of Channel 7, told the *Times of India* 'The viewer, whether on the channel by appointment or by mere surfing, must be compelled to stop and absorb', (quoted in Sinha, 2005).

There is a noticeable change in style and content away from a considered, professional approach to a flashier and visually more dynamic presentation;

the emphasis seems to be not on the journalistic skills of news anchors and reporters but on how they look on camera, with style taking precedence over substance. Even serious news networks, such as NDTV 24×7, have increased their quota of talk and chat shows, and, since the launch of NDTV Profit in 2005, business stories have been given more prominence. An informal, entertaining schedule is being created to increase the audience base, with political satire becoming a regular feature: *The Great Indian Tamasha and Double Take* on NDTV 24×7; *Gustakhi Maaf* on NDTV India and *Pol Khol* on Star News, are a few prominent examples. Across the channels, ratings and revenues delivering programmes – sports, entertainment and lifestyle – have increased, while news and analysis have shown a corresponding decline.

The three Cs of Indian infotainment: cinema, crime and cricket

The three Cs – cinema, crime and cricket – encapsulate most of the content on Indian television news programmes. Prominent among these, and one which reflects infotainment trends elsewhere in the world, is the apparent obsession of almost all news channels with celebrity culture, which in India centres on Bollywood.

The showbiz syndrome: Bollywood in TV news

The power of Bollywood to sell television is perhaps most clearly demonstrated by the way Murdoch's Star Plus cleverly used the greatest Bollywood star ever as the host of *Kaun Banega Crorepati*, an Indian version of the successful British game show *Who Wants to be a Millionaire?*, giving its launch in 2000 extensive coverage on Star News. The show, hosted by the Bollywood superstar Amitabh Bachchan, dramatically changed Murdoch's fortunes in India, securing an average of 40 out of the top 50 shows every week for Star Plus. The third series of the programme, launched in January 2007 and hosted by the leading Bollywood star Shah Rukh Khan, has retained very high ratings, thanks to Khan's persona, his informal style and unprecedented publicity, including on Star News, making Star Plus the most popular private channel in the country.

Other networks too have realized the selling power of Bollywood and most now broadcast regular programmes about the glamour and glitz of Bollywood. Star News has a daily programme, *Khabar Filmi Hai* (The News about Cinema), full of film-based gossip and tabloid titbits. Such coverage also features in the main bulletins on news channels and it is not unusual, for example, to see Bollywood film music used as a backdrop for news stories. An increasing trend across the news channels to personalized reporting and a blatant intrusion of privacy is discernable: a taped private conversation between a hugely popular film star and his former girlfriend (later found to be a fake); the grainy video pictures intercepted through mobile telephones of a leading actress kissing her boyfriend also an actor; news crews following film stars on their holidays, are a few examples from recent celebrity-obsessed reporting. The tone of reporting is unabashedly promotional, the stories about private lives and public engagements of film stars: how they celebrate religious festivals, their holidays, their dress and eating habits, their likes and dislikes, are repeatedly given air time – across the board and on an almost daily basis. When a new big budget film is released, it is invariably headline news: television becomes the battle ground for marketing and promotion, with endless speculation about how a particular film might do at the box office, vox pops competing with experts. Most channels would also run interviews with stars of the film – and not just within the entertainment segment but as the main news item (Ninan, 2006b). Programmes such as 'The making of...' a particular (usually big-budget) film are routinely broadcast on news channels, and Zee News runs a daily bulletin called *Bollywood News.*

Such 'Bollywoodization' has even affected the political elite: even the sober former Indian Prime Minister Atal Bihari Vajpayee had a video of his poems telecast on television, sung and set to music by top composer and singer Jagjit Singh. The video, which had a Bollywood-style picturization, starring Shah Rukh Khan, was directed by Yash Chopra, one of India's most successful film-makers. In 2006, Amitabh Bachchan featured in a promotional video distributed by a political party. The Indian version of the History Channel in 2005 employed former Miss World Diana Hayden to front the series 'Biography', while since 2005, NDTV 24×7 has regularly run a spoof news bulletin fronted by film stars Abhishek Bachchan (son of Amitabh Bachchan) and Rani Mukherjee – 'Bunty and Babli do NDTV', as a promotion for their 2005 film *Bunty aur Babli.*

The lifestyle segment of news channels across the board is increasing – with such examples as *Nightout* (on NDTV 24×7) and *After Hours* (on Zee TV) – regularly broadcasting from the glitterati party scene. Since a large proportion of the private news network caters to the urban public, they have an unmistakable urban and metropolitan bias in their reporting – not just in the themes they cover but also the way they are framed. Star News leads with its programmes such as *City 60,* the daily hour of news and views from India's metropolitan centres, primarily from Mumbai and New Delhi, the centre of India's political power. Civic issues affecting the residents of India's largest cities are given regular airing on Star News, with more journalists working on metropolitan news stories than covering

India's regions and especially its huge rural hinterland. On other news channels too, the focus is on fashion shows, urban fads and frolics. Inevitably, a segment of news from the film industry is included in the daily package. The celebrity culture and what has been called the 'Page 3' world – gossip-laden reportage of the good times enjoyed by the metropolitan party-goers, dominates coverage.

As newspapers tend to follow the news agenda set by television news, such stories also receive front-page treatment even among quality newspapers such as *The Times of India*, which carries a Bollywood-related story on its cover page almost daily. Other newspapers also have a regular 'Page 3' quota about celebrities, mainly connected with the Bollywood lifestyle. Even serious news magazines such as *Outlook* and *India Today* have started 'lifestyle adjuncts to the main magazine, bursting with advertising' (Ninan, 2007). Most of this advertising is aimed at the increasingly Westernizing middle classes, consumers of a US-inspired infotainment-led media culture, helped by growing structural media links: *Outlook* has helped launch an Indian edition of *Marie Claire* while *India Today* has distribution agreements with *Time* and *Fortune* magazines. When in February 2007, India's two largest English language newspapers – The *Times of India* and the *Hindustan Times* launched *Metro Now*, Indian capital's first tabloid newspaper, a senior executive commented: 'Tabloidization is where the readership is going. Younger readers are less interested in deep analysis. They want more and more entertainment' (quoted in Ramesh and Jha, 2007: 24).

The media are obliging: the British film actress and model Liz Hurley's wedding in March 2007 received headline treatment among all news channels, while the Indian edition of *Hello!* magazine published a special 'exclusive' coverage of the celebrations. This was followed a month later by the wedding of popular Bollywood actors Abhishek Bachchan and Aishwarya Rai, a former Miss World, which received wall-to-wall coverage on national television. On the day of the wedding, the main news on Zee TV, available around the world, devoted almost the entire bulletin – 22 minutes out of 25 minutes – to the story about the elaborate ceremony, the guest lists, and the commotion. Rolling news networks vied with each other to provide as much trivia and tantrums as possible. Even NDTV 24×7 could not avoid the temptation to go for a ratings winner: a day after the wedding, the channel devoted its weekly *We the People* panel discussion programme to the wedding, under the broader theme of 'Media Mayhem' raising the question, 'Has tabloid journalism become the norm?' (NDTV 24/7 April 22, 2007).

Along with covering stories about celebrities, news networks focus on political sleaze and scandal, exposing bureaucratic mismanagement and corruption in public sector units and small private enterprises, but rarely if ever, the large corporate groups. Networks such as India TV claim 'sting journalism' as their speciality – one notorious example of this was when one of the channel's female reporters pretended to be an aspiring actress in Bollywood and tried to expose the 'casting couch' syndrome. Across the news channels, uncovering corruption of sexual or financial type is often done in a fast-paced and frivolous style, ostensibly preferred by younger viewers which incline towards a capsule version of TV news – 'Maximum news in minimum time', as one TV executive described it when Aaj Tak launched Tez (Fast) with its tag line of '*Khabarein Phataphat*' (quick news). At its launch in 2005, its chief executive Aroon Purie reportedly remarked that the channel would not indulge in 'long-winded discussions or unnecessary analysis' (quoted in *Satellite and Cable TV*, September 2005).

Crime as infotainment

Crime programmes such as action thrillers are another key constituent of television news channels, particularly among the Hindi-language networks, where crime journalists are becoming, in the words of one commentator, 'the news brahmins of television' (Sinha, 2005). As the ratings battle has intensified, news networks have rapidly moved towards reporting sensational stories, which are becoming progressively gruesome. Murder, gore and rape are recurring themes, with the tone and tenor of stories being inevitably populist. Exposés are routine, with a good deal of hidden camera work being deployed to give the stories a sensational edge. The presentation draws broadly on well-known and clichéd conventions of visualization of crime and corruption, inspired by B-grade Bollywood films, themselves a cloned copy of Hollywood originals. Star News, for example, runs two dedicated programmes daily on crime reporting: *Sansani* (Sensation in Hindi), usually about criminal gangs, about fraudsters and fixers. Although the channels claim to be presenting such stories with a public interest in mind, more often than not there is a tendency to titillate and shock. The other major tabloid-style crime programme on Star News, the half-hour long *Red Alert*, broadcast daily at prime time, is ostensibly about crime busting, in which intrepid reporters venture out often with police, looking for stories about criminals and crime syndicates. The rivals of Star News claim that the network deliberately covers crime stories from towns and cities where the audience measuring devices are located, thus enhancing interest in such places which translate into higher ratings (Ninan, 2005).

In the battle for ratings Zee News used the saga of a divorced woman named Gudiya, whose soldier husband had left her on suspicion of an extra-marital affair. This innocuous story was transformed into a live drama on the television screen, with audiences sending their views in SMS, emails as well as phone-ins, benefiting the telecom companies in the process (Ninan, 2004). NDTV India also regularly broadcasts such crime-centric programmes as *Dial 100*, and *Khabardar* (Beware). Although crime coverage has spiralled, especially on more populist Hindi channels, in the real India the crime rate has in fact fallen dramatically in the past ten years, especially the murder rate, which is the lowest in the past half century. Cases of the most common crime in India, theft, have dropped from 360,000 in 1991, to 270,000 in 2006, while robberies and burglaries have fallen by a third in this period (Kala, 2007).

Exposing crime and corruption is a legitimate role of journalism in a democracy and Indian journalists have a long and distinguished tradition of investigative journalism, though broadcast news is new to this genre. Indian newspapers have broken many stories in the public interest, even causing governments to fall: one notable example was the investigations undertaken by *The Hindu* to expose corruption in defence deals, contributing to the demise of the government of Prime Minster Rajiv Gandhi in the late 1980s (Verghese, 2003). However, 'Sections of the media earlier known for serious journalism have begun to dumb down,' lamented N. Ram, editor-in-chief of *The Hindu*, 'This is a disturbing trend. Investigative journalism has been given a bad name by the invasive spy camera. This keyhole journalism is rubbish' (quoted in Vasudev, 2005:). A defender of 'sting journalism', one of India's leading investigative reporters Aniruddha Bahal, reflected on the dilemmas for such journalism in an era of infotainment: 'You could have done an astounding investigation but if you are pitted against a snake chasing a kid on a rival channel you have no chance in hell in pulling in viewers. Even if you don't actually see the snake' (Bahal, 2006).

The business of televising cricket

The third C of Indian infotainment is one with which Murdoch's name is closely associated. As Andrews has argued, Murdoch has skilfully used sport television in his 'transnationalization' project, making it a core aspect of News Corporation's transnational market strategy to successfully penetrate national television markets in the US, Britain and Australia. He has not only deployed live coverage of sports to enter and manage local media markets but also redirected his corporation's organizational structure toward transnational sport (Andrews, 2003). As Murdoch experienced in Britain, having control over broadcasting rights to live sporting events is crucial for the success of a television channel. Sky has become one of the most profitable broadcasters in Europe, primarily because it owns broadcasting rights for key sporting events, including major football championships.

Murdoch's media recognizes the primacy of cricket in India's popular culture, the colonial game having become the most important sport among Indians, cutting across class, language and even gender barriers and second only to Bollywood in its popularity. Television has transformed cricket from a gentleman's game to a roaring business, dependent on corporate sponsorship. The live broadcast of cricket, especially the one-day matches, has been turned into a spectacle, a visual extravaganza. Television seems to have contributed even to changing the rules of one-day matches to 'ensure that the one-day cricket match is fast and furious, encouraging high scores and high drama' (Rowe, 1999: 154).

In India, through Star Sport, Murdoch has tried to replicate the British success story. Cricket-related stories appear almost daily on Star News as well as on other networks – and not just on sports news. These include details of private lives of cricketing stars as well as regular narratives on their expensive lifestyles. When international test matches are underway, Star News runs a regular hour-long programme titled *Match ke Mujarim* (The Guilty of the Match), where ex-cricketers and commentators dissect the day's sporting action, with active participation by audiences, naming and shaming the worst performing players on a particular day. As in the case of *Big Brother* discussed in the previous chapter, interactivity is central to such infotainment, as compelling coverage can lead to channel loyalty in the long run and at the same time provide a new revenue stream for privatized telecom networks, which obviously benefit from this convergence.

Cricket coverage also gets good play on elite channels: NDTV 24/7 runs two popular daily programmes: Sports 24/7 and Sports Unlimited, while CNN/IBN broadcasts *LoC – Love of Cricket*. The coverage reached a heightened pitch leading up to the 2007 World Cup, with Times Now running a daily show *The Game*, NDTV 24/7 broadcasting special episodes of 'India Questions' – an hour-long interactive interview with the former and current Indian cricket skippers; while Zee News aired a daily show called *Vishwayudh* (World War). Programmes including travelogues and contests that gave fans a chance to win World Cup tickets and celebrities to send across their messages to Indian players were regularly broadcast on all major channels. Comedians shared the screen space with cricket commentators, while a former Miss India was employed to bring the viewers the daily news segment (Sreedharan, 2007). During the 2003 World Cup, model Mandira Bedi anchored the cricket coverage and her glamorous presence not only led to 24 per cent growth for the channel but also brought 20 million women viewers to a male-dominated sport (Majumdar, 2006).

As cricket became bigger as an industry, largely triggered by satellite television, bookmakers, especially in South Asia, involved in the murky but lucrative world of sports betting and connected to organized crime syndicates, were alleged to have 'fixed' the results of matches as well as an individual cricketer's performance. Several cricketers, including former South African captain Hanse Cronje, were banned for life, forcing the International Cricket Council to establish an anti-corruption and security unit. During the 2007 World Cup the death of Pakistan's coach, Bob Woolmer, bought the issue of 'match-fixing' once again to the fore, and as news channels lost advertising revenue because of the early exit of the Indian team, in an unparalleled example of the alliance between crime, cricket and infotainment, Star News ran an hour-long whodunit programme with a dramatization of likely scenarios leading to Woolmer's death, and encouraged the viewers to vote by SMS.

The 'tamasha' of television news

The three Cs discussed above are indicative of a television news culture that is increasingly becoming hostage to infotainment. The growing tabloidization of television news indicates the influence of the Murdoch effect on news and current affairs television in India. I have characterized this 'Murdochization' of the media as 'a process which involves the shift of media power from the public to privately owned, transnational, multimedia corporations controlling both delivery systems and the content of global information networks' (Thussu, 1998: 7). It can be argued that the ideological imperatives of infotainment are debasing the quality of public deliberations in the world's largest democracy. By overwhelming public discourse with the three Cs, national and transnational infotainment conglomerates – some time in concert, sometime in competition – are 'colonizing the communication space' (Boyd-Barrett, 1998) in India at a time when it is integrating with the US-led neo-liberal economic and political system – both as a producer and consumer of commodity capitalism, a point that will be addressed in Chapter 6.

Where does this type of commercialism leave public broadcasting? Despite severe competition from private news networks, the state broadcaster still retains the highest number of audience in India: Doordarshan's main national channel, DD-1, reaches about 400 million viewers. In 2007, it was operating 27 channels, including DD News, the first and the only terrestrial news channel in the country with the highest reach into television households in India. However, in the affluent cable and satellite homes – mostly urban and exposed to the type of infotainment described above – the share of DD News was only 7 per cent.

The 'public' aspects of news seem to have been taken over by private corporate interests. The woeful lack of coverage of rural poverty, of regular suicides by small farmers (more than 100,000, in 1993–2003, the period of neo-liberal 'reform', according to government figures), and the negligible reporting of developmental issues: of health and hygiene, educational and employment equality (India has the world's largest population of child labour at the same time as having vast pool of unemployed young people), demonstrates that such grim stories do not translate into ratings for urban, Westernized viewers and are displaced by the diversion of infotainment. The lack of concern among television news networks for India's majority population is ironic in a country which was the first in the world to use satellite television for educational and developmental purposes, through its 1975 SITE (Satellite Instructional Television Experiment) programme (Thussu, 2007a). The generation of journalists who were intellectually rooted in the secular, socialist ideals of the Neruvian era have given way to a younger, brasher, MBA-type of journalist, in the field of 'business' of broadcast news. The concern for the poor and the dispossessed and for the broader questions of global equality and social justice appear to have been replaced by an admiration for business tycoons, charismatic and smooth-talking CEOs and American or Americanized celebrities.

In this endeavour, journalists have the support of the government, wedded to the notions of privatization and neo-liberal 'reform' and therefore keen to strengthen the Hollywood-Bollywood infotainment synergies. One example of this public-private convergence is 'Frames', an annual 'global convention' showcasing the Indian film and entertainment industry, organized since 2001 by FICCI. Another is the creation of the India Brand Equity Foundation – a public-private partnership between the Ministries of Commerce and Industry and the Confederation of Indian Industry with the primary objective, 'to build positive economic perceptions of India globally' (IBEF, 2005).

Paradoxically, as Indian corporations integrate into global capitalism and have aspirations to be taken more seriously on the world stage, its citizens are receiving only limited international news on television, despite the massive growth in news channels. As in other countries, international TV news does not appeal to most viewers, unless it concerns some major human or natural disaster, that can lend itself to dramatic pictures. It is not surprising then that in a competitive news market, broadcasters are increasingly focusing on the familiar and the saleable rather than the distant and the difficult, leading to the almost total disappearance of foreign news reports, especially on popular Hindi networks. To reflect the changing nature of news consumption, one particular segment in the Star News bulletin is appropriately titled *Duniya Do Minute* (the World in Two Minutes), which, in literally 120 seconds, trawls through happenings in the global village, often stories which may be termed as soft human interest rather than hard news.

Yet, when the US President George W. Bush visited India in March 2006, the television networks gave blanket coverage to his trip. In contrast, when Chinese President Hu Jintao was in India for three days in November of the same year, the first visit by a Chinese president in a decade, the coverage on television networks was shamefully scant: while DD News devoted 73 minutes to it, Zee News thought it merited only five minutes as against 53 minutes it gave to rumours about Amitabh Bachchan entering politics (Indiantelevision.com, 2006). Despite having the resources of infotainment conglomerates, most news networks have managed without any full-time foreign correspondents of their own, even in neighbouring countries: NDTV 24/7 being an exception. In Britain, a major diasporic market, Star News operates without even a continuity announcer. Part of the reason could be the assumption that foreign news does not interest the audience and therefore it does not make economic sense to invest in running foreign bureaux and hire time on expensive satellite networks for live transmission of news stories. It is much easier to use footage supplied by Murdoch's other international news networks: for its limited international coverage, Star News draws on material from Fox News Channel, from New York and Washington and Sky News (Europe's first 24-hour news network) from London. Star News also broadcasts everyday, news from Star News Asia, Murdoch's English language pan-Asian news operation, based in Hong Kong.

It is not surprising then that the Fox attitude to news may also be discernable in India, as was in evidence during the Iraq invasion of 2003 when Star News repeated often verbatim (though in Hindi translation) the Pentagon line on Operation Iraqi Freedom. The 'tamasha' of war which Fox News has raised to an art form, is the focus of the next chapter, which examines how conflict and war are presented on television news as high-tech infotainment spectacles.

5

WAR AS INFOTAINMENT

Television news, particularly 24/7 rolling news, reaches its apotheosis in times of war and conflict. The dramatic visual spectacle of violence and death grabs the attention and engages the audience like few other media subjects, whether its causes are human (wars, riots, killings), natural (floods, earthquakes, hurricane) or both (famines). The potential for constant twenty-four hour breaking news was most clearly demonstrated by the sudden rise to global fame of CNN during the 1991 Operation Desert Storm and similarly of Al-Jazeera during the US invasion of Afghanistan a decade later and of Iraq in 2003, as well as by the imitations that these have spawned. As noted in Chapter 3, CNN created a new paradigm of 24-hour news culture, which comes alive during conflict situation (Volkmer, 1999; Bennett, 2003a). According to the 2006 SIPRI Year Book, there have been 57 major armed conflicts since the end of the Cold War: in 2005, 17 were current in 16 locations around the world – almost all in the global South (SIPRI, 2006). Of course, not all conflicts receive such global coverage, but tend to be those in which the West is involved: the most mortal war is probably the least reported – more than three million have died in the Democratic Republic of Congo since the mid-1990s (Thussu, 2004).

It can be argued that such rolling news networks as Al-Jazeera have received international recognition precisely because of their coverage of conflict in one of the world's most geo-politically sensitive areas. Covering wars is inevitably a difficult journalistic endeavour but the demand for live 24/7 news, as well as competition among news providers, can lead to the sensationalization and trivialization of often complex situations and a temptation to highlight the entertainment value of news. Given the demand of television news for arresting and action-packed visuals and dramatic pictures, wars and civil conflicts are particularly susceptible to infotainment.

'Live from the battlefield'

Going 'live' to the site of breaking news is one of the defining characteristics of 24/7 news networks. The pressure to be first with the news can create a tendency among news channels to sacrifice depth in favour of the widest and quickest reach of live news to an increasingly heterogeneous audience. There is a danger that this aspect of news culture may be detrimental to the quality of news, as one commentator notes: 'By making the live and the exclusive into primary news values, accuracy and understanding will be lost' (MacGregor, 1997: 200). Television journalists work under the tremendous pressure of 'deadlines every minute', leaving them little time to thoroughly investigate and research a story before it is transmitted, a particularly problematic situation at the time of a conflict when disinformation/misinformation, rumours and half-truths are inevitably blended with accurate information. Reporters have to follow the instructions of their editors and producers to go 'live' and provide the most dramatic and engaging footage to beat rival news networks. CNN's Peter Arnett, one of the few Western journalists in Baghdad during the 1991 US invasion of Iraq, has written that because of its instantaneous coverage, CNN had become the world's 'most influential news organization' (Arnett, 1994: 359). Yet, this 'live' reporting was not often live, as two observers of US journalism later wrote: 'Television showed troops in preparation, convoys moving, artillery pieces firing on unseen targets, and fighter planes streaking down runways and dropping "smart" bombs on factories and buildings. Much of this action, however, had occurred hours earlier. Apart from the opening scenes in Baghdad and the later flashes of Scuds and Patriots missiles rising in attack, little live action appeared on television during the hundred hours of the ground war' (Donovan and Scherer, 1992: 313).

Given the demands of a 24-hour news cycle, reporters may find it difficult to obtain sufficient material to fill the airtime. In the absence of any new information on an unfolding event and tight control in the name of security, journalists may sometimes use unattributed sources, indulge in idle speculation or produce slanted reports influenced by rumour. During the events of 9/11, television networks had sometimes to resort to speculation and supposition rather than accurate reporting. In such situations, reporters tend to use almost any new information, even remotely connected to the story, in order to be first with the news. Often the elite media – such as CNN – may set the agenda while other networks more or less follow it. Such 'gang-reporting' is partly responsible for the generally similar editorial stance that television networks take on major international crisis situations (Thussu, 2003).

The 'embedded' reporter system of the 2003 Iraq invasion, an improvement on the press 'pool' developed during the 1991 Iraqi conflict, by the Pentagon was a mutually beneficial arrangement, providing direct use of their PR material and feeding the news channels' insatiable demand for footage:

> The Pentagon's embed strategy was ingenious because it increased rather than limited access to information. By giving broadcasters access to highly newsworthy action footage from the frontline, they were encouraging a focus on the actions of US and British troops, who would be seen fighting a short and successful war. The story was all about winning and losing, rather than a consideration of context in which the war was fought. (Lewis and Brookes, 2004: 298–9)

Paul Friedman noted that early embedded reports 'had a gee-whiz quality that overwhelmed the fact that very little information was being conveyed' and he further observes that, because the networks fetishized the use of live transmissions, embedded journalists spent much of their time with the technology, which was 'time that could not be spent on gathering pictures and information for more complete stories' (Friedman, 2003). One report in the *Guardian*, filed from Washington during first week of invasion, called embedding an 'astounding PR coup for the Pentagon'. The reporters used the words 'we' and 'us' profusely, 'identifying themselves with the military…', while another report on the same day from London observed that the perspective presented on British 24/7 news networks was 'determinedly Western' (The *Guardian*, March 27, 2003). The Pentagon's news management included barring 'negative' stories on television, such as the evacuation of victims of 'friendly fire'. Instead, broadcasters were encouraged to cover soft lifestyle features and 'reality' television shows about American soldiers in Afghanistan and Iraq: the Pentagon in one instance bypassed ABC news to collaborate with the network's entertainment section to produce a reality television show *Profiles from the Front Line*, broadcast in 2002 – based on the lives of US soldiers in Afghanistan.

Televising the spectacle of war

The representation of war on television has evolved in the past decade in parallel with the globalization of infotainment, demonstrating a tendency to use entertainment formats, including video/computer-game style images of surgical strikes by intelligent weaponry, arresting graphics and satellite pictures, and a 'chat-show'-style use of 'experts'. As a result of this homogenization of the coverage of conflicts – bloodless and largely devoid of any real sense of death and destruction – the audience can be desensitized to the tragedy and horror of war (Thussu, 2003). As the US 'Shock and Awe' campaign was declared, CNN headed up their 24/7 news and special 'Iraq War' programmes with, 'spectacular scenes of pyrotechnic explosions bursting across the night sky demonstrated for the benefit of coalition audiences the awesome power of the military bombardment, but did so in an aesthetized display that denied (and symbolically annihilated) the human carnage piling up beneath the lit-up night sky' (Cottle, 2006: 156).

Television news' obsession with high-tech war reporting has grown since the 1991 US war on Iraq. CNN's coverage of the Gulf War, for the first time in history, brought military conflict into living rooms across the globe. In the hi-tech, virtual presentation of war (Baudrillard, 1995), cockpit videos of 'precision bombings' of Iraqi targets were supplied to television networks by the Pentagon, thus presenting a major conflict, responsible for the huge destruction of life and property, 'as a painless Nintendo exercise, and the image of Americans as virtuous, clean warriors' (Said, 1993: 365). In this and subsequent US military adventures – in Somalia, Haiti, Bosnia, Kosovo, Afghanistan and Iraq – the humanitarian dimension of the military intervention was constantly promoted by the US media, often in high moral tones. The responsible behaviour of American forces in combat operations was underlined and the superiority of weaponry emphasized. When cockpit videos were first shown as part of news reports during Operation Desert Storm, broadcasters were careful to acknowledge that they were procured through the US Department of Defense. The process has been routinized to such an extent now that this admission is no longer considered necessary.

This kind of reporting was typical during the 2001 bombing of Afghanistan. Jamie McIntyre, CNN's military affairs correspondent, enthused about the types of munitions and aircraft being used in the bombing. In what appeared like a post-modern version of tele-shopping, a price tag ($2.1 billion) appeared on the screen with each aircraft. McIntyre described the bombers, B1 and B52s as 'extremely accurate' and mentioned how they were successfully used in Iraq and Kosovo for carpet-bombing. An extraordinarily ironic aspect of the coverage was that he also reported, with similar enthusiasm, the humanitarian relief being dropped by C-17s. This was a new development – delivering bombs and food at the same time. It is interesting to speculate whether the reporting of the raids would have been any different had the Pentagon had its own 24/7 news network (Thussu, 2003).

Another important source of visuals for reporting conflicts was satellite imagery, often used to illustrate the successes of aerial bombings, the pictures of sites of enemy defence installations and military barracks. As mentioned in Chapter 2, no one seems to question how these pictures were acquired (usually from military spy satellites) and the audience has to rely on 'expert' interpretations to 'see' what the often fuzzy and indeterminate images represent. In wartime, satellites become a vital source of images and news conglomerates are highly dependent, for example, on the US Department of Defense for visual material. During the 2001 Afghanistan invasion, the US government purchased all the satellite imagery of the area from commercial providers – themselves mostly US-based corporations, not only for its own use but to prevent its use by others. Satellite imagery was also extensively exploited by the US government to provide a justification for the 2003 invasion of Iraq. Colin Powell gave a multimedia presentation to the United Nations Security Council, broadcast live across the world, in which the Secretary of State presented compelling, graphic satellite evidence of Iraq's 'weapons of mass destruction' programme (US Government, 2003).

Both of the US military operations against Iraq were portrayed on television like simulations, a 'bloodless' version of conflict, with death and destruction minimized by the apparent surgical precision of bombardments (barring a few instances of 'collateral damage' and of 'friendly fire'). This highly sanitized war coverage championed by channels such as CNN simultaneously reached news broadcasters across the globe, reaffirming the 'awesome' superiority of US military power, as well as ignoring the ugly side of warfare. In addition to images from video clips and satellites, news programmes provided increasingly complicated maps, graphics and studio models to illustrate the progress of war. Mimicking war-gaming, miniature tanks and aircraft were used to re-create battlefields in the studio, where (mostly male) correspondents and experts enthusiastically discuss tactics and strategies, reinforcing the feminist critique of war as 'toys for the boys' (Thussu, 2003).

It is instructive to contrast the 24/7 news network's coverage of the efficiency of high-tech weapons with the death toll that these weapons actually caused. During bombing raids on Afghanistan in late 2001 some of the worst wartime atrocities were inflicted upon the Afghans: more than 300 were massacred in Qila-e-Jungi in November 2001 in a CIA-managed operation, as revealed in later reports (Channel 4 TV, 2002). This bloodless coverage, however, seemed to reflect the 'Pentagon's determination to control the flow of news from the front', as Neil Hickey, the editor of the *Columbia Journalism Review*, noted. 'Images and descriptions of civilian bomb casualties – people already the victims of famine, poverty, drought, oppression, and brutality – would erode public support in the US and elsewhere in the world' (Hickey, 2002).

Apart from constantly repeating recaps and summaries, 24/7 news networks have to fill their schedules with 'talk' and 'speculation' – discussion, analysis and phone-ins etc. – which have much in common with the genre of the 'chat show'. However, only certain categories of experts make it to 24/7 news screens. As Bourdieu wryly observed:

> ...if television rewards a certain number of fast-thinkers who offer cultural 'fast food' – pre-digested and pre-thought culture – it is not only because those who speak regularly on television are virtually on call (that, too, is tied to the sense of urgency in television news production). The list of commentators varies little (for Russia, call Mr. or Mrs. X, for Germany it's Mr. Y). These 'authorities' spare journalists the trouble of looking for people who really have something to say... (Bourdieu, 1998: 29–30)

Given the fiercely competitive ratings battle that television networks have to contend with, journalists are under tremendous pressure to make war reporting entertaining. After the initial excitement of a military campaign the audience tend to lose interest in wars, forcing reporters to bring in a human-interest element in their coverage. Boyd-Barrett writes:

> Classic warfare is the epitome of a 'good story', high in tension and drama, with complex main plots and sub-plots played out within traditional binary oppositions of aggressors and victim, winner and loser. While expensive to cover, warfare is commercially rewarding for the media, since its threat and unfolding ignite insatiable audience appetites for news. Advertisers may initially fear the risk of juxtaposing products with unsavoury and unsettling issues, but they soon benefit from higher audience numbers and from the potential for linking merchandise with the semiotics of patriotism. (Boyd-Barrett, 2004: 26)

Some enterprising television producers have used the 'war on terror' to make reality television programmes: one early example was MTV's *Military Diaries*, based on the daily life experiences of US soldiers in Afghanistan – the Pentagon being only too keen to provide access to such infotainment. 'Straight from the front lines in Iraq,' Deborah Scranton's 2006 documentary *The War Tapes* was 'the first war movie filmed by soldiers themselves', bringing a new dimension to this relationship. The documentary, based on videotaping of their everyday lives by five chosen soldiers for over one year, includes dramatic footage of full-scale gun battles between US soldiers and the Iraqi fighters in Falluja, filmed by a tiny camera strapped to a soldier's weapon.

The Foxification of war reporting

If televising Operation Desert Storm made CNN a household name around the world, the 'war on terror' catapulted Rupert Murdoch's television news networks into the international spotlight. As noted in Chapter 2, with Fox News in the United States, Sky News in Europe and Star News in Asia, Murdoch's media are relayed to television screens around the world. Fox News in particular is known as a right-wing network that tends to prefer live chat and an informal style of reporting, in which the boundary between straight news reports and opinion is constantly being crossed (Rampton and Stauber, 2004). A jingoistic, often xenophobic vocabulary, seems to characterize its coverage of conflict, witnessed by its 'aggressive cheerleading for the US armed forces' and 'hostile, even insulting portrayal of their opponents, described by Fox personnel as 'rats', 'terror goons' and 'psycho Arabs' (Hart and Naureckas, 2002). Hart and Naureckas recount how in November 2001, during the US invasion of Afghanistan, Fox News correspondent Geraldo Rivera reported: 'We've been in various conflicts, and we keep our chin up and keep focused on the fact that we want Osama bin Laden to end up either behind bars or six feet under or maybe just one foot under or maybe just as a pile of ash, you know. That's it.' To which Fox anchor Laurie Dhue replied: 'All right. Well said, Geraldo' (Hart and Naureckas, 2002).

Fox's approach of using the journalists' subjective comments seems to have hit a chord with broadcasters in Britain, too, as one senior executive of News and Current Affairs on Britain's Channel 5 noted: 'Fox News is striking because it feels passionate. I'd be interested to see for regulatory reasons whether we could get away with that because they do take sides. Their anchors engage – they call it like they think it' (quoted in Hargreaves and Thomas, 2002: 98).

Such a lack of impartiality in Fox News was also in evidence during the coverage of the US invasion of Iraq in March-April 2003, when networks tried to make their coverage distinct by 'branding' their news reports: while CNN preferred a neutral heading 'Strike on Iraq', Fox News did not hesitate to use 'Operation Iraqi Freedom', the Pentagon's official name for the invasion, as the tagline for its coverage. A Fox News directive instructed reporters to refer to the US Marines as 'sharp-shooters' rather than 'snipers'. This type of patriotism, part of the network's politically conservative agenda, and a strong belief in infotainment, seemed to attract new viewers: Fox News was able to score over its rivals in the ratings battle during the Iraq invasion.

Given the fact that Roger Ailes, the Head of Fox News, has extensive links with the right-wing Republicans, having worked on Presidential campaigns of Ronald Reagan and George Bush Senior, it is scarcely surprising that Murdoch's media acted as enthusiastic promoters of the US military action in Iraq. In line with other major US/UK news outlets, Murdoch's media played a central role in preparing and then retaining public opinion in favour of the invasion. Even before the US invasion, Murdoch himself appeared to be keen on the 'war', telling *Fortune* magazine that it could fuel an economic boom in the West. In an interview to an Australian news magazine *Bulletin* in February 2003, he expressed unconditional endorsement for the military actions proposed by the US leadership, praising George W. Bush as acting 'morally' and 'correctly.' Following their master's voice, virtually all of the 175 editors working for Murdoch's newspapers unequivocally supported the invasion of Iraq (Greenslade, 2003).

Fox News appeared to be keen to justify the invasion by repeatedly broadcasting the unfounded allegations that Iraq was linked to the 9/11 attacks; that it possessed vast 'weapons of mass destruction', and was ready and willing to use them. During the 'war', Fox News became little more than the mouthpiece of the round-the-clock, operational Office of Global Communications in the White House. Its flag-waving patriotism (with the US flag fluttering in the corner of the screens) and the description from its 'embedded' reporters of US soldiers as 'heroes' and 'liberators', was very well received among a large number of Americans. Even before the bombs started falling on Baghdad, one of the main presenters on Fox News, Bill O' Reilly, dismissed even mild scepticism about the desirability of military action or any disagreement on military tactics, telling viewers that the US should go in and 'splatter' the Iraqis. In this gung-ho approach, the network appeared to present the 'war' as a spectacle, with celebrity reporters, such as the Contra-scandal star Colonel Oliver North, filing live from Iraq.

The channel also clearly demonstrated its contempt of any dissent: when, for example, Michael Wolff, a regular contributor for *New York* magazine broke ranks at the daily press conference at the million-dollar press centre in Doha in Qatar, arguing that he was not covering the war but 'the news conference about the war', Fox News attacked him for his lack of patriotism, and one of its regular commentators, Rush Limbaugh, gave out Wolff's email address on air – in one day alone, according to Wolff, he received 3,000 hate emails (Wolff, 2003).

Moreover, in this version of televised 'regime change', military action was couched in the language of a war of liberation and presented in the form of an entertainment show, drawing on visual techniques borrowed from Hollywood. The rescue of Private Jessica Lynch, who became an icon of the conflict, provided a dramatic example of mixing entertainment and information (Kumar, 2004). One news network actually called her Jessica Ryan, no doubt influenced by the Hollywood film *Saving Private Ryan*. Lynch's 'capture' by the Iraqis and 'rescue' by US special forces, which became a major media story of the invasion was in fact a morale-boosting staged event for the cameras (Project for Excellence in Journalism, 2003). A BBC documentary later showed that the Iraqi doctors had actually looked after her well, with one of the doctors who treated Jessica recalling: 'It was like a Hollywood film. They cried, "Go, go, go", with guns and blanks and the sound of explosions. They made a show – an action movie like Sylvester Stallone or Jackie Chan, with jumping and shouting, breaking down the doors' (BBC, 2003). The Iraqi lawyer who risked his own life to save Lynch was hardly mentioned in the media (Al-Rehaief and Coplon, 2003). Having acquired the status of a minor celebrity, Lynch herself later insisted that the military had fabricated the 'event' – she had had a road accident and was treated by the Iraqi hospital. The televised toppling of a statue of Saddam Hussein in a square in central Baghdad, conveniently next to the hotel where the world's media were staying, was another example of a staged event, giving the impression that US troops were removing the statue at the behest of crowds of cheering Iraqis. In reality, it was the culmination of a well-orchestrated propaganda operation at the most crucial time of the invasion, highly symbolic in its significance, not just for Iraqis but the wider Arab world.

Given the reach of Murdoch's media, such an approach to news reporting is not confined to Fox News alone. In the market-driven broadcasting environment, it might justifiably be predicted that Fox's success could lead to the 'Foxification' of television news in other parts of the world; already other Murdoch networks, particularly in Asia, regularly use news reports and footage from Fox News. It appears that partisan reporting and commentary translates into ratings in the US, presumably this strategy could be equally successful in other countries. In the UK, Murdoch's Sky News has to operate within the remit of 'due impartiality', upheld by Ofcom, making it difficult for Sky News to openly pursue a political position. Given the cultural influence of the BBC and the public-service broadcasting ethos, Sky News has tended to follow the standards set up by the BBC news journalism. However, Sky is under pressure from its owner to treat news from conflict zones as drama and as an event. During the coverage of the invasion of Iraq, Sky News, though less belligerent than Fox, acted as a morale booster for the British troops in the theatre of war. Sky was also not beyond faking reports for dramatic impact. According to a BBC documentary *Fighting the War*, one Sky news correspondent reported a missile-launch exercise from a docked British submarine as if it were a launch from a vessel in action. It was actually an exercise conducted for the benefit of the camera crew. The news report, aired on Sky News between March 31 and April 2, 2003, ended with images of an underwater missile launch, but the Sky reporter had used archival footage of a different launch and the submarine in the report did not fire while the news crew was aboard. The report, part of a pool report made available to other news organizations, was also broadcast by Britain's ITV News.

Such instances reflect the pressure journalists are under to conform to a more entertainment-driven news agenda. Dissatisfied with what he perceives as its staid presentation and 'liberal bias', Murdoch wants Sky News to become more populist. 'Sky News is very popular and they are doing well but they don't have the entertaining talk shows – it is just a rolling half-hour of hard news all the time', Murdoch told the *New York Times*. Murdoch's approach to news presentation is also visible on Indian news operation, Star News, which used live coverage of the 'war' from Fox News and Sky News, relaying Pentagon briefings, sometimes in their entirety, as well as jingoistic studio discussions and live press conferences of US government officials and politicians.

War as entertainment

US popular culture, which is becoming increasingly global, is steeped in Hollywood spectacles on war, battles and conflict, as evidenced by the international success of films about war, conflict and battles between good and evil. As Table 5.1 shows, being able to mount a spectacle is crucial for the global success of war films. Fantasy and allegory, civilization vs. barbarism, alien invasion and intergalactic warfare are the recurring themes of these highest grossing war films, enacted by the 'special effects industry'.

Table 5.1 Highest grossing war films

Films	*Year released*	*Worldwide box office* ($ million)
The Lord of the Rings: The Return of the King	2003	1,129
Star Wars- Episode I: The Phantom Menace	1999	922
The Lord of the Rings: The Two Towers	2002	921
The Lord of the Rings: The Fellowship of the Ring	2001	860
Star Wars- Episode III: Revenge of the Sith	2005	848
Independence Day	1996	811
Star Wars	1977	797
Forest Gump	1994	679
Star Wars- Episode II: Attack of the Clones	2002	648
War of the Worlds	2005	591

(Source: Based on data from *Internet Movie Database* http://www.imdb.com/boxoffice/alltimegross?region=world-wide)

George W. Bush's declaration of an 'end to hostility' in Iraq in 2003 was a striking example of how film-fiction mashes with filmed facts. In what was described by one commentator as a '*Top Gun* act', Bush co-piloted a navy jet on to the deck of the *USS Abraham Lincoln* apparently somewhere in the Persian Gulf to cheering troops and television crew, pictures beamed around the world, and the coverage ranging 'from respectful to gushing'. In fact, as the Associated Press later reported, the ship was so close to the shore that officials 'acknowledged positioning the ship to provide the best angle for Bush's speech, with the sea as his background instead of the San Diego coastline' (Krugman, 2003: 31).

A regal declaration by a leader of 'mission accomplished' in a Hollywood-style military setting has an imperial subtext. Mega-hits of the Cold War era such as *Ben Hur* (1959), *Spartacus* (1960), *Cleopatra* (1964) and *Fall of the Roman Empire* (1964), can be interpreted as paeans to classical imperialism, a trend revived with recent films like *Gladiator* (2000), *Troy* (2004) and *Alexander* (2004) (Joshel et al., 2005; James, 2006). Hollywood blockbusters such as *Platoon* and *Full Metal Jacket* (on the Vietnam war), *Black Hawk Dawn* (on Somalia) and *Three Kings* and *Jarhead* (on Iraq) have provided the cultural context within which distant conflicts are romanticized and wars glorified as righteous, undertaken for moral purposes (Weber, 2006). The depiction of 'morally righteous violence', for example, as in the film *Behind Enemy Lines*, released soon after 9/11 and based on belated US military involvement in the civil war in the former Yugoslavia, champions US unilateralism (Ó Tuathail, 2005). Some have noted interesting parallels between the filmic narration of the Second World War and the staging of the Iraq invasion of 2003, presented as a virtuous endeavour in the contemporary geo-political space (Crampton and Power, 2005).

Collaboration between the US military and Hollywood has a long history, dating back to the First World War when the US government established the Committee of Public Information to support the war effort. By the time of the Second World War, a period when the visual image had become far more widespread and an integral part of propaganda, Hollywood studios liaised extensively with the US military, producing scores of films and documentaries, most notably Director Frank Capra's six-part documentary series *Why We Fight*, broadcast in 1943 and 1944. The Office of War Information – which operated between 1942 and 1945 – made sure that Hollywood movies could be used to legitimize allied propaganda (Koppes and Black, 1987).

This collaboration coalesced around the commercial success of Hollywood during the Cold War fight for freedom from communist dictatorships. In 1948, the Pentagon formally set up a special movie liaison office, as part of the Office of the Assistant Secretary of Defense for Public Affairs.

Filmmakers who wanted access to military equipment, locations, personnel, or Department of Defense archival footage, had to agree to their work being vetted by the Pentagon. Such international hits as *Top Gun, Pearl Harbour* and *Black Hawk Down* could not have been made without support from the US military. In a mutually beneficial arrangement, the Pentagon provided personnel, advice and equipment to filmmakers, creating a more authentic feel to the sets and therefore greater global success, while the Pentagon could make sure that in the name of entertainment, a particular version of conflicts in the world was being circulated across cinemas and on home videos and DVDs, and internalized. The trade-off between Pentagon interference in film production and Hollywood's acquiescence to soft propaganda in lieu of access to military hardware has been noted by former *Hollywood Reporter* staff member David Robb (2004). The website of the Air Force Entertainment Liaison Office, interestingly called *Wings over Hollywood,* states its purpose is to provide 'information and assistance to motion pictures and television programs with Air Force themes or segments' and candidly states that 'it has worked with a wealth of clients through its history of service. Motion picture studios, television networks, cable networks and more have relied upon our services to help them blend the US Air Force with Hollywood dream making' (www.airforcehollywood.af.mil)

Hollywood does not have a monopoly of providing war as entertainment. Russia's first film about its own war in Afghanistan, Fyodor Bondarchuk's *The 9th Company,* released in 2005, was a major box office success, while *Kabul Express*, a 2006 Bollywood film – the first foreign movie to be filmed in Afghanistan since the US invasion – ran successfully in India and among the South Asian diaspora. Glorification of combat is extremely strong in other countries too: the popularity of the French Foreign Legion in the Francophone world is indicative (Cooper, 2006). In Britain, the fascination with SAS and US Special Forces has spawned a publishing industry, with works by ex-SAS officers such as Andy McNab, who has become a best-selling author.

On television, in addition to Discovery Civilisation and The History Channel, for which war documentaries provide a staple diet, there are at least three cable channels devoted entirely to military and militarism. Discovery's Military Channel, launched in 2005, previously called Discovery Wings, competes with the Pentagon Channel and the Military History Channel, a spin-off of A & E's History Channel. As its website notes: The Military Channel salutes the 'sacrifices made by our men and women in uniform with real stories and unparalleled access to a world of human drama, strategic innovation and long-held traditions.' One of Military Channel's biggest specials was *Delta Company*, in which cameras filmed the Marines of Delta Company 1st Tank Battalion on their push to

Baghdad during Operation Iraqi Freedom. Such popular programmes as *Future Weapons* and *GI Factory* also glorify the Pentagon's killing machines.

In 1999, the BBC screened *Warriors*, a gritty drama about British soldiers trying to keep peace in the war-torn former Yugoslavia, while in 2007 Britain's Channel 4 broadcast *The Mark of Cain* which dramatized British troops in Iraq following the regime change in 2003, including graphic scenes of abuse of Iraqis. Many other war-related programmes were at the planning stage in 2007, including an HBO series called *Generation Kill* about being embedded with the US marines in Iraq. In the United States war stories were also central in the popularity of comics (Wright, 2001).

For the first time in 2005, a US TV drama set in wartime was produced and shown while it was still being fought, unlike the popular series in the past, such as *M*A*S*H* (Mobile Army Surgical Hospital – a 251-episode comedy set against the backdrop of the Korean war (1950–53) aired on CBS from 1972 to 1983), or *China Beach* (a 64-episode drama series about nurses set at a US-base in Vietnam during the Vietnam war, and broadcast on ABC from 1988 to 1991). *Over There*, screened on the cable channel FX, followed a fictional US military unit in Iraq and was graphically violent. It was created by Steven Bochco, responsible for such internationally popular police and law-and-order dramas as *Hill Street Blues*, *LA Law* and *NYPD Blue* (Peyser, 2005). FX's John Landgraf, who came up with the idea of setting the series against the war in Iraq – 'such a grand natural human drama' – reportedly said: 'The best purpose of television and film is to tell stories that are truthful and of the moment and dig into the human experience' (quoted in Soriano and Oldenburg, 2005). As Phil Strub, head of the Pentagon's film liaison office notes: 'These days, there is an unwillingness to criticize individual servicemen and women, which was quite common in the Vietnam era. Americans are very disinclined to do that now, and we're very glad this attitude tends to pervade all entertainment' (quoted in Soriano and Oldenburg, 2005). *M*A*S*H**, on the other hand, offered an anti-war message about the futility of the suffering caused by conflict and showed the Koreans – albeit in stereotypical roles – as fellow victims.

War as 'militainment'

The connection between US entertainment industries and the military is not new (Der Derian, 2001; Burston, 2003; The History Channel, 2004). What is new, however, notes one commentator, is 'the ubiquity, sophistication and complexity that has lately characterized this cooperation' (Burston, 2003: 168). During the late 1990s, Hollywood's ties to the US military-industrial complex deepened as the entertainment industry became the single largest employer in Southern California, prompting commentators to speak of the rise of Siliwood – the mixture of Silicon Valley and Hollywood (Hozic, 2001: 141). According to a US National Research Council report entitled *Modeling and Simulation: Linking Entertainment and Defense*:

> ... strong commonalities exist between defense and entertainment applications of modeling and simulation and in the technologies needed to support them. Whereas DOD [Department of Defense] has traditionally led the field and provided a significant portion of related funding, the entertainment industry has made rapid advances in 3D graphics generation, networked simulation, computer-generated characters, and immersive environments. Aligning the research agendas of these two communities to allow greater coordination of research developments, sharing of information, and collaborative research could provide an opportunity to more rapidly and economically achieve the goals of both the defense and entertainment industries. (National Research Council, 1996)

James Der Derian sees this cooperation as part of a 'Military-Industrial-Media-Entertainment Network' (Der Derian, 2001). By 2002, *Time* magazine had already coined the term 'militainment' (Poniewozik and Cagle, 2002). Academic centres such as the Institute for Creative Technology (ICT), affiliated with the University of Southern California, were set up in 1999 with assistance from the US Army to provide training simulators to prepare the army to deal with civil war and peacekeeping and peace-enforcing situations. It designs simulation programmes and games for US soldiers, many of whom carry personal DVD players and game consoles to combat camps (Burston, 2003). ICT also sells its video games: in 2004, it licensed *Full Spectrum Warrior*, an offshoot of its most successful training game, to the publisher THQ. Microsoft too has entered a deal with ICT to provide Xbox game stations to the US army (Virnini, 2005). Simulation games for training purposes have been used by the US military for many years: for equipment, communication networks in the battlefield, military logistics and war strategy, as well as how to respond to nuclear or terrorist threats. The *Guardian* reported that the Pentagon was hiring Arab-speakers to act in war games, dressed in traditional attire and set against a landscape simulating Afghanistan or Iraq. 'We are looking for more realism. The more actual culture we can inject into the exercise the better it is for our soldiers,' an officer in charge of the US Army's Joint Multinational Readiness Center, told the newspaper (Connolly, 2007: 16).

Hollywood spin-off games for computers and play-stations from war films such as those in Table 5.1 have also been very successful. As one commentator noted: 'Hollywood producers have helped to "naturalize digital combat", inaugurating a new infotainment sector that reflects a "confluence of economic and technological interests between the US defense industry and Hollywood mythmaking"' (Hozic, 2001: 139).

War games as infotainment

As video games became extensively used by young people around the world, infotainment conglomerates found an eager consumer audience for war and conflict entertainment. The interactive element, coupled with sophisticated and increasingly realistic 3D graphics, makes computer and video games a compulsive, even addictive leisure activity among a growing number of primarily boys and young men. Millions around the world – especially in the global North and middle-class children in the global South – are spending hours glued to their computers, playstations or television screens. Gaming is today a $35 billion global industry and as availability for broadband increases, the demand for games is likely to grow. Already such Second World War games as *Call of Duty: Finest Hour, Medal of Honor – Frontline* ('you don't play, you volunteer', to fight against the Nazi War Machine), and *Medal of Honor – Rising Sun* ('experience the powerful realities of war' and 'defeat the Japanese empire') are extremely popular. In 2002, the US military developed its own downloadable *Go Army* computer game: 'The Official Army Game' providing 'at once propaganda for the military, a recruitment tool, and participation in simulated military action' (Kellner, 2003: 10).

The political and ideological subtext is not hard to discern. The popular war game *Full Spectrum Warrior* encourages youngsters how to coordinate military missions in an urban guerrilla situation in a fictional Arab country. Covert military action in North Korea is the focus of another game called *Mercenaries: Operation Air Assault* which is about the 'war on terror', a theme developed further in *Tom Clancy's Rainbow Six 3*, released in 2004, a game about international terrorism and energy security for the US. The introduction of the game is worth quoting:

> The year is 2007, and the world stands on the brink of a terrifying global conflict. As the United States is caught in an embargo-induced oil crisis, terrorist attacks against American interests – and citizens – escalate. Venezuela, which still supplies the United States with oil, also becomes a target. As unrest grows in America, protests rock the streets of Caracas. And while the shadow of terror looms, madmen plot even greater acts of murder and destruction. No place is safe, no border secure in this hour of fear. Only one bulwark stands between the world and the threats that now face it: Rainbow, an international task force dedicated to combating terrorism in all

its forms. A top-secret organization consisting of the best field operatives the United Nations has to offer, Rainbow is the most potent weapon in the world's arsenal. Backed by the most sophisticated technology available and trained to the limits of human capability, they are our best hope in the war against terror. They may also be our only. (Rainbow Six 3, Ubisoft)

The Rainbow team is inevitably led by an American – with a post-modern name 'Domingo 'Ding' Chavez'; the other three members of the team are French, British and German. By 2004, some game companies such as the New York-based Kuma War were releasing computer video games, within weeks after the actual battle. *Al-Qaeda: the Battle for Mosul*, was for free download, using, as its website proclaims, 'advanced game tools, extensive research and satellite imagery' to provide 'an accurate replica of the area in which US Army troops repelled an al-Qaeda attack'. Other 'Reality Games', depicting unfolding events in a real war included *Uday and Qusay Hussein's last stand in Musul, Operation Anaconda in Afghanistan* and *Baghdad Mahdi Army Assault* (Soriano and Oldenburg, 2005).

The themes of the games reflect explicit geo-political concerns: *Conflict: Global Terror*, for example, released in 2005, focuses on the 'war on terror', while the on-line game *Battlefield 2 Modern Combat*, released in the same year, asks players to 'battle the enemy and the propaganda to decide the fate of oil-rich Kazakhstan'. The 2006 game *Big Oil* encourages players to 'build an oil empire, turn crude to ca$h', while *World in Conflict*, released in 2007, and set in a futuristic date when the Soviet Union has re-emerged, may indicate the concerns in Washington about the growing global clout of a resurgent Russia. This 'militainment' has redefined the 'war on terror' as an object of consumer play, deployed by the Pentagon in association with the gaming industry to train and recruit potential combatants, creating a 'third sphere' of militarized civic space where the young citizen interacts and idolizes the virtual citizen-soldier (Stahl, 2006). According to the US army research, about 90 per cent of recruits to the US army are 'casual' gamers, while 30 per cent are 'hard core' (Virnini, 2005). These digitally-designed wars are fought, Der Derian notes, 'in the same manner as they are represented, by military simulations and public dissimulations, by real-time surveillance and TV live-feeds' (Der Derian, 2001: xviii).

The 'immersive' nature of computer gameplay, in which the player can be transported into a 'simulated' world, can have profound effects on young minds: 'The challenges, thrills and threats are experienced and produced through intimate mental, emotional and physical engagement by the player with the game and the game technology' (Dovey and Kennedy, 2006: 8). It is clear that these games are much more than a leisure activity: they can leave a deep impression on young minds and have long-term cognitive and behavioural effects. These highly competitive and violent games 'provide allegories for life under corporate capitalism and Terror War militarism', observes Kellner, and are part of post-modern warfare. 'As military activity itself becomes increasingly dependent on computer simulation, the line between gaming and killing, simulation and military action, blurs, and military spectacle becomes a familiar part of everyday life' (Kellner, 2003: 10).

Macabre infotainment

Television, the Internet and other networked information technologies, have ensured that terrorism is visible everywhere in real-time, all the time. In turn, terrorism has taken on an iconic, fetishized and, most significantly, highly visual character (Der Derian, 2005). Websites are full of such macabre infotainment, with US soldiers posted in Iraq trading gruesome pictures of dead Iraqis for pornography. Videos of jihadi extremists beheading hostages in Chechnya and Iraq have been used for obtaining ransom payments as well as recruiting new members for terrorist groups (Lentini and Bakashmar, 2007). The video manifestos of suicide bombers have become an all too common sight on television news. Even more disturbing, in 2002, a photograph depicting a year-old Palestinian child from the West Bank town of Hebron, wearing the 'uniform' of a Hamas suicide bomber, complete with belts holding bullets and explosives, and with his forehead encircled by the red bandanna of the martyr reading *Al Qassam Brigades*, the name of the military wing of Hamas, was published and broadcast around the world, becoming 'part of the repertoire of the war on terror'. Condemning the photograph as a form of 'pornography' which is part of a 'celebration of death', a British tabloid, the *Daily Mirror* printed the image two days running. Following the claim in a Sky News interview by the family that the photograph was taken as a joke, the *Daily Mirror* ran the image again, this time titling the story 'It's a bit of fun' (Robson, 2004: 74). Another example of macabre infotainment was the popular comedy show about suicide bombings *Only in Israel* – on the Israeli commercial Channel 2, which made fun of a grim reality (Freedman, 2002).

Pictures of the abuse of Iraqi citizens in Abu Ghraib prison, among them the naked human pyramid of hooded and leashed men, became iconic only weeks after CBS's *60 Minutes II* made the photos public on 28 April 2004. One radio commentator Rush Limbaugh asserted that the photos showed nothing more than the 'need to blow some steam off among beleaguered soldiers' (quoted in Bennett et al., 2006: 470). A US study of the coverage of this outrage concluded:

> Even when provided with considerable photographic and documentary evidence and the critical statements of governmental and nongovernmental actors, the nation's leading media proved unable or unwilling to construct a coherent challenge to the administration's claims about its policies on torturing detainees. As it turned out in this case, the photos may have driven the story, but the White House communication staff ultimately wrote the captions. (ibid: 482)

According to Jean Seaton's analysis of carnage on the news, such portrayal of macabre reality appears to shock to a lesser degree than one would expect: 'viewer voyeurism' of spectacles of violence seems to be a 'social universal ... part of the mainstream of collective life'. 'The Romans watched lions eating Christians; modern audiences witness homicidal explosions and their macabre outcomes' (Seaton, 2005: 87). When Timothy McVeigh – accused of Oklahoma bombing – was executed in 2001, more than 200 media personnel were there to cover it live. The Executive Producer of *The Jerry Springer Show* told a Channel 4 documentary on reality TV: 'If I could execute someone on television, I would execute someone on television' (Channel 4 TV, 2005). The shooting of 32 students at Virginia Tech University in April 2007 showed how the genre of macabre infotainment was copied from the 'war on terror' by a US-Korean student who coolly posted a media package including video clips to NBC News during his killing spree. Within hours of receiving them, NBC News aired excerpts from his 'manifesto' despite much criticism. This was a significant lowering of the threshold of what was acceptable for broadcast – videos of the Columbine shootings were not shown on television eight years earlier. Audiences are not only becoming increasingly inured to violence but actively seeking it out as entertainment, especially on the unregulated Internet and through video games.

Taking the reality TV show to an extreme was one aired in Iraq in 2005 on the US-funded Al-Iraqiya television which ran *Terrorism in the Hands of Justice* in prime time, six days a week. In this version of macabre television, the Iraqi Ministry of Interior personnel interrogated prisoners accused of acts of terrorism on camera. An Iraqi doctor, Ali Fadhil, who filmed the programme for a special report for Britain's Channel 4 News, called it the Iraqi Big Brother – except that the participants were not volunteers but forced to take part, the aim presumably being to create an atmosphere of fear by showing it live on television, to frighten the population into subjugation to the American occupation (Channel 4 News, 2005).

Perhaps the most macabre form of infotainment was the global circulation of the last moments of the deposed Iraqi President, Saddam Hussein, a grainy video of whose hanging sent shockwaves across the world. The one-minute video was aired without sound by Arabic satellite channel

Al-Arabiya, and later shots of the execution taken by a witness from a mobile phone showing Saddam being taunted by his executioners in his final moments, were repeatedly shown on news channels across the world. The shots also recorded someone praising Muhammad Bakr al-Sadr, founder of the Shia Dawa party and an uncle of Shia cleric Muqtada al-Sadr, thus exacerbating tensions between Iraqi Sunnis and Shias. The *New York Times* called it 'a snuff reality show', in the process making a tyrant a martyr, ensuring that his name entered Arab folklore as a strong leader who gave his life for the Arab cause, facing death with dignity and standing up to US occupying forces and the client regime they created. The symbolic value of this was not lost on anyone: the execution before dawn on 30 December 2006 was carried out during the feast of *Eid al-Adha*, when traditional Muslims slaughter sheep, representing the innocent blood of Ishmael, offered for sacrifice by his father, Abraham.

The implications of war as infotainment

Despite occasional challenges by the media to the dominant 'framing' of the 'war on terror', sometimes as a result of 'elite discord' (Entman, 2003), there is little doubt that the majority of the US-led Western media have tended to operate within the basic terms of the terrorism discourse. As the liberal model of television has been globalized, as noted in Chapter 3, the US-influenced visualization of war and conflict is reproduced, with suitably adapted voice-overs, in television newsrooms across the world. Thus the 24/7 news networks help to promote the US foreign policy agenda to global audiences: when the US President George W. Bush addressed American citizens at the start of US invasion of Iraq in 2003, his message was simultaneously broadcast live on news channels around the world, reaching billions of viewers across time zones and continents. The ability for instantaneous media coverage of events across the globe has brought to the fore the role television can play in the conduct and implementation of foreign policy, and the US has been very successful in deploying 24/7 news networks in its image diplomacy to promote a televised version of its foreign invasions to international publics (Seib, 2004). The world's view of US military interventions has, to a large extent, been shaped by US-supplied images and the moralistic names that the invasions have been given by the US Government: *Operation Just Cause* in 1989 in Panama; *Operation Provide Comfort* (in Northern Iraq, following the Iraq invasion of 1991); *Operation Restore Hope* in Somalia in 1992; *Operation Uphold Democracy* in Haiti in 1994; *Operation Allied Force*, NATO's bombing of Yugoslavia in 1999; the 2001 *Operation Enduring Freedom*, the war on terrorism in Afghanistan and *Operation Iraqi Freedom*, launched in 2003.

Examining the mainstream news coverage of US military interventions, from the regime change in Panama in 1989, to the installation of a new puppet regime in Iraq in 2004, demonstrates that the representations of these invasions almost invariably deployed a language of humanitarianism and high moral rectitude (Thussu, 2000a, 2005b). These military actions were undertaken, in Pentagon-speak, primarily to promote peace, stability, and democracy across the world, pursuing what has been called the myth of democracy, exported via US television (Ferguson, 1992). However, under the cloak of exporting democracy and bringing peace to the world's hotspots, the US has advanced its geo-strategic and economic interests, whether it is in Kosovo (by changing the nature of NATO from a relic of the Cold War to a peace-enforcer whose remit now extends way beyond its traditional North Atlantic territory), or in Afghanistan (which has given the US government entry into an energy-rich Central Asian region) or Iraq (which has the world's second largest oil reserves). The dominant television news discourse does not seem to be interested in the deeper analysis of geo-political issues. Instead, in what amounts to an extremely skilful and generally successful diversion, wars are presented as high-tech infotainment spectacles, undertaken for just and moral causes and thus help to create a 'feel-good factor' among Western publics: the world's superpower is literally being shown doing something to make the world safer for them. The open-ended and global 'war on terrorism', with possibilities of 'pre-emptive strikes' is thus a vital component of the US agenda for renewed global hegemony. The 'force of freedom' is now central to US foreign policy rhetoric as Washington aims ostensibly to transplant freedom and liberty to 'outposts of tyranny'. Globalization of infotainment is crucial in this process, anchored as it is within the ideological tropes of 'neo-liberal imperialism', to which we turn our attention in the next chapter.

6
INFOTAINMENT AND 'NEO-LIBERAL IMPERIALISM'

'In a world increasingly saturated by information,' Castells notes, 'the most effective messages are the most simple, and the most ambivalent, so that they leave room for people's own projections. Images best fit into this characterization. Audiovisual media are the primary feeders of people's minds, as they relate to public affairs' (Castells, 2004: 372). The importance of the image and illusions in capitalist societies was emphasized by Daniel Boorstin way back in 1961 with the publication of his book, *The Image*. 'The making of the illusions which flood our experience has become the business of America,' he wrote, adding that Americans 'suffer primarily' not from their 'vices' or 'weaknesses', but from their 'illusions'; haunted, not by reality, but by those images they 'have put in place of reality' (Boorstin, 1971 [1961]: 5–6). This illusion of reality and what Boorstin called 'pseudo-events' have a particular purchase in the era of 24/7 globalized news. The convergence between information technologies and media products – films, games, on-line media – and their promotion by infotainment conglomerates, has profound implications for popular culture globally, helping to reinvigorate and re-inscribe the hegemony of the world's only hyper-power (Hozic, 1999; Nederveen Pieterse, 2004).

Has the ascendance of infotainment lulled the capacity for critical engagement among audiences – have they become merely consumers? The French situationist Guy DeBord in his famous 1967 book theorized about what he called the 'Society of the Spectacle', defining the spectacle as 'the existing order's uninterrupted discourse about itself, its laudatory monologue' (DeBord, 1977 [1967]: 24). The 'spectacle' and 'spectacle relations' are DeBord's substitutes for ideology and the Marxian notion of 'false consciousness'. He claimed that the imagery devised and shaped by television and the advertising industry masks social reality: 'the spectacle is capital to such a degree of accumulation that it becomes an image' (DeBord, 1977 [1967]: 34). Is infotainment a precursor for a global spectacle society?

While wars and conflicts are presented by infotainment conglomerates as high-octane spectacles of moral crusades to promote opaque notions of freedom and democracy across the world, real agendas may be more concerned with control and the consolidation of power on a global scale. And television as the global mass medium is central to this enterprise. Years before the globalization of television, critical scholars such as Herbert Schiller saw linkages between mass communications and US imperialism:

> Unavailable to expansionists of earlier times, modern mass communications perform a double service for their present-day controllers. At home, they help to overcome, by division in part, the lack of popular enthusiasm for the global role of imperial stewardship. Abroad, the antagonism to a renewed though perhaps less apparent colonial servitude has been quite successful ... deflected and confused by the images and messages which originate in the United States but which flow continuously over and through local information media. (Schiller, 1969: 2)

With the global circulation of Americana this capacity to divert and deflect has in fact increased many fold, despite appearances to the contrary – as I have documented elsewhere (Thussu, 2006a, 2007a). Global infotainment can be seen as part of a wider process of corporate colonization and thus it is essential to understand the political, economic, military and cultural vectors of neo-liberal imperialism. An assessment of global infotainment, it is argued, requires going beyond the debates about 'dumbing down' and examining it as a diversionary phenomenon, masking this ideological agenda. As David Harvey has recently argued, neo-liberalism has become a hegemonic discourse with pervasive effects on ways of thought and political-economic practices, making it part of the commonsense view of the world (Harvey, 2003, 2007).

Political context of neo-liberal imperialism

Is America leading a neo-liberal Empire? Is globalization an updated twenty-first century version of a nineteenth-century idea? Given the history of the United States, a country founded after an anti-colonial war and responsible, to a large extent, for the decline and fall of modern European imperial powers, many Americans and the mainstream US media resist thinking of their country as an empire. However, in the post-Cold War, post-Soviet world, the US global hegemony demonstrates elements of an imperial enterprise (Ali, 2003; Chomsky, 2003). As Andrew Bacevich has noted, the US mission is to create a seamless global market kept in place through overwhelming and permanent global military supremacy. This phenomenon is not new, argues Bacevich, as successive US governments, since around the time of the Spanish-American war at the end of the nineteenth century, have pursued a strategy of reshaping the world in its image, through free trade and military dominance (Bacevich, 2002). A recent longitudinal analysis of US imperial adventures in its historical context shows that the US has grown from regional and hemispheric to global hegemon (Go, 2007).

The US-led invasion and occupation of Iraq – the most blatant violation of international law and state sovereignty in recent history and in full public view on global 24/7 news networks – has rekindled debates about the return of imperialism. Proponents of the 'global pax-Americana', emphasize the importance of an 'empire of bases' scattered around the globe and the US control of 'the global commons' (Posen, 2003; Johnson, 2004). Historian Niall Ferguson has strongly argued that the US is an empire and it should admit as much and that its force for good in the world should be celebrated (Ferguson, 2004). Some prefer a soft-touch variety of Western imperialism – 'Empire Lite' – necessary to ensure peace and security in the world's conflict zones and for 'nation-building' (Ignatieff, 2003), while others see the US as the 'benign hegemon', which acts as 'the world's government' (Mandelbaum, 2006). Among the former imperial powers, such sentiments strike a nostalgic chord: Robert Cooper, sometime foreign policy advisor to British Prime Minister Tony Blair and later to the European Union Foreign Affairs Commissioner, championed the cause of the 'new imperialism' and the 'need for colonization' that would allow post-modern Western nations to impose order and stability around the globe, while Alfredo Valladão of the Institut d'études politiques de Paris observed the emergence of an 'American democratic empire', rising from the global informational and transportation revolution, which was fostering the development of 'a democratic hegemonism' (Cooper, 2003; Valladão, 2006).

In media and even academic discourses such arguments are generally associated with neo-conservatives, the 'neo-cons', whose ascendance in the foreign policy sphere has been steadily happening since the mid-1990s: its organization, the Project for the New American Century, was founded in 1997 in conjunction with the *Weekly Standard*, established two years earlier (Donnelly et al., 2000; Kristol and Kagan, 2000). Their influence on the Bush Presidency, especially in relation to the idea of 'pre-emptive strikes' and unilateralism, has been much commented on. However, the 'neo-libs', have also been promoting, in essence, the same arguments as indicated by think tanks such as the Progressive Policy Institute, which gained prominence under Bill Clinton's presidency (see, for example, Rieff, 2005; Marshall, 2006).

Since its inception in 2002, the so-called Bush Doctrine championed the idea of 'free market democracies', a blueprint for global freedom and prosperity. A crucial component of this doctrine is that military might could be used to 'enforce' democracy or to thwart attempts by 'rogue' states from acquiring weapons of mass destruction: this was first done under the fig leaf of the United Nations; followed by NATO in Kosovo in 1999 and, as witnessed in Iraq since 2003, by the US-led 'coalition of the willing'. At his second inauguration in January 2005, President George W. Bush exhorted: 'We are led by events and common sense to one conclusion: The survival of liberty in our land increasingly depends on the success of liberty in other lands. The best hope for peace in our world is the expansion of freedom in all the world... So it is the policy of the United States to seek and support the growth of democratic movements and institutions in every nation and culture, with the ultimate goal of ending tyranny in our world' (US Government, 2005b).

This missionary zeal to promote freedom worldwide complements the notion of 'global governance', despite the fact that 'global' institutional structures remain profoundly undemocratic: more than six decades after its inception, the United Nations Security Council still has no veto-wielding representation from Latin America, Africa or the Arab world. It is worth remembering that until 1972, Taiwan was a veto-wielding Security Council member, while China, representing one fourth of all humanity, was excluded from the UN. With occasional disagreements from Russia and China and sparingly by France, as during the 2002–3 Iraq debate, the US seems to set or manipulate the UN agenda and when it does not suit its political interests, to undermine the UN system – as it has repeatedly done, most unashamedly during the 2003 Iraq invasion.

In the post-Cold War world, the notion of state sovereignty, particularly with regard to 'weak' or 'failed' regimes, was altered in a manner that justified a 'right to intervene' by the 'international community' (the US) or even the right to 'regime-change' if a state's 'responsibility to protect' its citizens was not being respected. Increasingly powerful Western-sponsored international legal and human rights regimes were set in place to implement 'global governance', supported by an army of non-governmental organizations, operational around the globe to implement the US 'work for freedom's cause'. Information and ideas can act as 'strategic weapons', and US media aid to the South is funnelled through NGOs to avoid allegations of direct US intervention (Blinken, 2002). Though excluding political parties, the US government defines NGOs to include 'independent public policy advocacy organizations, non-profit organizations that defend human rights and promote democracy, humanitarian organizations, private foundations and funds, charitable trusts, societies, associations and non-profit corporations'. Its 'Guiding Principles on Non-Governmental Organizations', released in 2006, states: NGOs should be permitted to 'seek, receive, manage and administer for their peaceful activities financial support from domestic, foreign and international entities' and they should be 'free to seek, receive and impart information and ideas, including advocating their opinions to governments and the public within and outside the countries in which they are based' and that 'Governments should not interfere with NGOs' access to domestic – and foreign-based media' (US Government, 2007a).

Such activities fall into what Harvard political science professor Joseph Nye has called 'soft power': the 'power of attraction that is associated with ideas, cultures, and policies', a key imperative for strengthening US position in the world and for countering anti-Americanism (Nye, 2004: 87). Post-9/11, the main aim of US public diplomacy, under the guidance of a former advertising executive, Charlotte Beers, Undersecretary of State for Public Diplomacy and Public Affairs, was to understand the roots of anti-Americanism (Hoffman, 2002; Lennon, 2003; Ungar, 2005). One of her early initiatives was to broadcast *Shared Values*, a series of video messages from Muslims eulogizing life in the United States and shown around the world. Others included circulating more than a million copies of the brochure *The Network of Terrorism*, which was translated into 36 languages, the most widely distributed public diplomacy document (Thussu, 2005b).

In 2002, an Arabic-language popular music and news radio station, Radio Sawa, aimed at a younger Arab audience was launched and Radio Farda began transmitting into Iran. In 2004, Al-Hurra started broadcasting, funded by the Broadcasting Board of Governors (BBG), a US federal agency that supervises all non-military international broadcasting. The Pentagon, too, established a propaganda network: Al-Iraqiya, a radio and television station run by the California-based Science Applications International Corporation, one of the largest US companies, providing surveillance services for US intelligence agencies. According to Edward Kaufman, a former member of the BBG:

> Military power alone is often insufficient to resolve modern conflicts and will likely be unable to end this current war against terrorism. Effective broadcasting to 'win hearts and minds' strengthens the traditional triad of diplomacy, economic leverage, and military power and is the fourth dimension of foreign conflict resolution. Particularly in times of crisis, the United States must deliver clear, effective programming to foreign populations via the media. (2003: 299)

Senior US officials publicly admit that broadcasting is central to winning the battle for hearts and minds in the Muslim world. 'The real tug of war in the Middle East is about broadcasting,' Patricia Harrison, Assistant Secretary of State for Educational and Cultural Affairs told a House of Representative committee in 2004:

> Television and video products continue to be powerful strategic tools for bringing America's foreign policy message to worldwide audiences. ... We continue to produce "good news" stories on reconstruction in Iraq and Afghanistan that American and foreign news editors have incorporated in their programs, and we are distributing Department-oriented videos to foreign media outlets worldwide. (US Government, 2004a)

The US Government is interested in harnessing the expertise of infotainment conglomerates to improve the effectiveness of public diplomacy through the media. Peter Peterson, chairman of the Independent Task Force on Public Diplomacy sponsored by the Council on Foreign Relations, recommended in its 2002 report creation of a 'Corporation for Public Diplomacy' to encourage public-private involvement in public diplomacy with private-sector grants. Peterson has argued that 'the US leads the world in many industries crucial for winning hearts and minds abroad – television, digital technology, education and market research – and we must bring these to bear through reinvigorated public diplomacy' (Peterson, 2002). Such thinking is supported by BBG as indicated by its 2002–7 Strategic Plan, *Marrying the Mission to the Market*, which uses the language of infotainment conglomerates: of 'branding and positioning', of 'target audiences' and 'marketing and promotion' (US Government, 2002b: 23). Like infotainment conglomerates, the government is also keenly aware of the need for localization of content: 'Because every media market is different, a one-size-fits-all approach for US international broadcasting will not work. We must tailor everything we do for each of the more than 125 markets in which we operate. The news, information, and Americana we present; the language we speak; and the media we use must fully factor in local preferences and practices' (ibid: 10).

In the post-2003 Iraq situation, the public diplomacy remit seems to have been extended to include supporting 'US approaches to satisfying universal demands for human dignity; the rule of law; limits on the absolute power of the state; free speech; freedom of worship; equal justice; respect for women; religious and ethnic tolerance; and respect for private property' (US Government, 2007b). The public-private synergy received new impetus in January 2007 when the first Private Sector Summit on Public Diplomacy was convened in the US, co-sponsored by the Department of State and the Public Relations Coalition, to identify 'models for action for greater private sector involvement and support for US public diplomacy'. These models included 'developing business practices making public diplomacy a core element of international corporate public action' and 'become part of the local community through employee volunteerism, strategic philanthropy, and greater engagement with responsible NGOs' as well as to 'create "circles" of influence through relationships with organizations, chambers of commerce, journalists, and local business leaders' as well as 'support the creation of a corps of private sector "foreign service officers" made up of academics and business people with specialized expertise who could work abroad on short term assignments'. This was meant to 'create a new paradigm for public diplomacy in the 21st century which recognizes that public diplomacy is not the work of government alone'. As the US Secretary of State Condoleezza Rice emphasized at the summit, 'the solutions to the challenges of the 21st century are not going to be met by government alone. They come from all sectors of American society working together, and that means a close and vital partnership between government and the private sector' (US Government, 2007c).

Learning from the hegemon

Castells has observed in the context of the US, that 'politics is fundamentally framed, in its substance, organization, process, and leadership, by the inherent logic of the media system, particularly by the new electronic media' (Castells, 2004: 375). When in March 2007, the Iranian forces arrested 15 British sailors and marines on the charge of illegally entering Iranian territorial waters, the 'confessions' of the British sailors were broadcast on the government-run Arabic language satellite station, Al-Alam, obviously with an eye for propaganda in the region, showing the Arab constituency that Iran had the capability to resist Western military adventure in the region. Despite having an interview recorded with the captain of the mission by Sky News on March 13, days before their capture, in which he admitted that part of his mission was to gather information on Iran, the broadcast was held back and shown only after the release of British sailors on April 5. Within days of their release, the media were scrambling to buy the sailors' stories, with Faye Turney, the only woman in the crew, the first to sign a joint deal with *the Sun*, Britain's most popular newspaper as well as *Tonight With Trevor McDonald*, an infotainment programme on ITV. That the British Ministry of Defence allowed such blatant exploitation of personal experience (though it later imposed a ban), because of what it called 'exceptional media interest', may have something to do with the propaganda value of such information at a time when Iran is projected in the media as an Islamic 'threat' to Western geo-political and economic hegemony in the Middle East. The Iranian government responded in this propaganda battle by releasing footage of British sailors in captivity, apparently relaxed, playing table tennis and chess and watching football on TV, thus countering charges of mistreatment (Hodgson, 2007).

The role of television news as a political instrument is well attested in other contexts too: in Venezuela, for example, television played an important role in the April 2002 coup which briefly ousted President Hugo Chávez: the privately owned 'neo-liberal' news channels such as Globovisión barred his supporters from the airwaves and showed cartoons in place of the pro-Chávez demonstrations which helped restore him to power. On his part, Chávez hosts a regular Sunday programme on state-run television called *Alo Presidente* (Hello, President), a vehicle for state propaganda (Gott, 2006).

The globalization of US-style 'professional' political marketing, characterized by the employment of consultants from the United States and other leading industrialized states to manage electoral campaigns in other countries, including those in political transition, can act as agents for neo-liberal political-economic systems (Sussman and Galizio, 2003; Sussman, 2005). Their presence 'shifts the public gaze away from the question of how organized transnational interests, including media corporations, employ election events, symbolism, and public engagement to sustain their own legitimacy and reproduction' (Sussman and Galizio, 2003: 323).

The economics of the free market

As noted in Chapter 2, the US government has played a prominent role in creating the economic conditions for neo-liberal imperialism, helping to shape the economies of an increasing number of countries to fit into the neo-liberal, global free market system. Multilateral institutions such as the World Bank and the International Monetary Fund (IMF) – where the US possesses the largest bloc of votes – had an extremely important part in this enterprise through the 1980s and 1990s in forcing the countries of the former eastern bloc, as well as the developing world, to comply with the neo-liberal economic agenda, promoting the privatization of state enterprises. Under the Structural Adjustment Programmes, virtually dictated by the IMF and the World Bank (whose President during the second Bush presidency was Paul Wolfowitz, a prominent member of the neo-cons, and an architect of US invasion of Iraq), the economies of most of these countries were literally restructured to make them an easy target for transnational corporations. The creation of the World Trade Organization in 1995, with its clearly defined policies for liberalization and privatization, considerably strengthened the position of the free marketers, further eroding the already fragile economic sovereignty of many developing countries, whose economic policies were now largely being determined by the World Bank/IMF/WTO triumvirate.

As noted in Chapter 2, the combination of new communication technologies and WTO agreements to deregulate key sectors that benefited infotainment conglomerates, including telecommunications services and information technology products, accelerated the expansion of the mainly but not exclusively US-based corporations, some of which have incomes and assets bigger than the GDPs of several developing countries. In the deregulated, privatized and increasingly globalized market, these motors of 'digital capitalism' trade online across borders, unhindered by national regulations and dominate the emerging global electronic economy (Schiller, 1999). As Drezner has argued, the great powers remain 'the primary actors writing the rules that regulate the global economy'. The key variable affecting global regulatory outcomes is the distribution of interests among the great powers. A great power concert is a necessary and sufficient condition for effective global governance over any transnational issue. Without such a concert, government attempts at regulatory coordination will be incomplete, and non-state attempts will prove to be a poor substitute (2007: 5).

Veteran economist John Kenneth Galbraith, in one of his last treatises, noted that in a 'market system' the big corporations set the public discourse; private corporations have a crucial involvement even in such a public institution as the Pentagon. Yet mainstream economists, the policy elite and the media are party to what he termed as an 'innocent fraud' and since they had the 'respectability and authority' and little sense of 'guilt or responsibility', such fraud enters the public discourse, becoming public knowledge (Galbraith, 2004). The limited coverage in the media of the Enron scandal – the biggest fraud in US corporate history – is an indictment of limitations of such journalism. The media system, McChesney notes, 'is not only closely linked to the *ideological* dictates of the business-run society, it is also an integral element of the economy' (1999: 281, italics in original).

One of the world's biggest financial news operations, Bloomberg, for example, proudly claims: 'Our products drive investment decisions that affect millions of people – and billions of dollars worldwide' (Bloomberg website). Reporting corporate affairs and economic processes requires a special type of expertise and studies have shown that mainstream media's coverage is often incomplete or vague (Jensen, 1987). Others have observed that journalists involved in financial news coverage are, in a sense, 'captured' by corporate and pro-business agendas (Davis, 2002). Few financial journalists show the 'ambition to challenge or step outside the parameters of pro-market and pro-capitalist thinking' (Doyle, 2006: 446). Doyle's study of financial journalists in Britain found that 'the potential presence of "spin" in the interpretation given to economic events by players in the field is a widely recognized hazard' (ibid: 443). She noted: 'The claim that financial journalism is captured by business interests is not necessarily to do with the tenor of individual news items so much as about how coverage as a whole is framed and the sorts of values it serves to reinforce. For instance the weight given to "City opinion" may be seen as reinforcing norms such as "the market knows best"' (ibid: 446).

Researchers examining the constitution of the board members of ten major media organizations in the US found that there were 118 people who sit on 288 different American and international corporate boards, 'proving a close on-going interlock between big media and corporate America' (Thornton et al., 2005: 254). A media system which champions the cause of corporate globalization is likely to support private sector perspectives as against public concerns. A study which examined, for three years, 2001–3, the coverage of the annual World Economic Forum (WEF), which brings the world's financial elite to Davos, Switzerland, and contrasted it with the space given to protests against the organization's role in global economic policies, noted journalistic 'deference to the WEF communication agenda', which 'systematically managed the debate about globalization on terms that favoured elites over citizen-activists' (Bennett et al., 2004). Advertorials are a twentieth century phenomenon that from the start were dominated by corporations. A study of the op-ed page of *The New York Times* from 1985 – 98 showed an increasing presence of advertorials, including from such corporate giants as Mobil (oil), Northrop and Lockheed (defence) even in elite media outlets (Brown et al., 2001).

Some economists have vigorously defended the record of liberalized trading regimes – both in its historical version shaped by British colonialism and post-Second World War US economic hegemony – and have opposed statist attempts to regulate global markets (Lal, 2006). Others see a great future for developing countries within neo-liberalism, recommending the integration of the financial systems of developed and developing countries and creating effective 'corporate governance', necessary for attracting and managing investment (Mishkin, 2006). However, market-based globalization also has its downside (Stiglitz, 2002; Bardhan et al., 2006). One cumulative effect of the shift from a public to a private agenda is the increase in poverty among the world's poorest living in the countries on the receiving end of neo-liberal 'reforms' that have yet to deliver for a majority of the world's population.

The 2003 *Human Development Report* of the United Nations Development Programme noted that in the 1990s overall average income per head actually declined in 54 countries (UNDP, 2003). Market-based solutions and cuts to the public sector are having a devastating effect on employment, especially in the global South. According to the International Labour Organization, in 2004 half of the world's 1.38 billion workers lived on less than $2 a day and despite employment growth among some sectors, especially in Asia, the world's poorest got poorer in sub-Saharan Africa, for example, where the number of workers living on less than $1 a day increased by 28 million between 1994 and 2004, while in Latin America the number of working poor, earning as little as $1 a day, increased by 4.4 million between 1999 and 2003 (ILO, 2006)

The security scenario

The third pillar of neo-liberal imperialism is the military infrastructure; the neo-cons of the 'Project for the New American Century' argued for an expanded US military force, because, 'we need to accept responsibility for America's unique role in preserving and extending an international order friendly to our security, our prosperity, and our principles'. In 2000, just before George W. Bush became President, the PNAC published a report, *Rebuilding America's Defenses: Strategy, Forces and Resources for the New Century*, which called for the US 'to fight and decisively win multiple, simultaneous major theatre wars', to control the 'international commons' of space and cyberspace and to take on 'constabulary duties' around the world. (www.newamericancentury.org). The US is in a position to exercise such a globo-cop mission, with its extensive range of military installations: according to the US Department of Defense, 725 official overseas US military bases were dotted around the globe, from Australia to Japan, from Britain to Bahrain, from Kuwait to Kosovo and from Panama to Pakistan, controlled by the regional commanders in chief (C-in-C) – 'proconsuls to the empire' (Priest, 2003). Deployment of increasingly sophisticated and militarized space systems ensures US supremacy in the skies and gives the US 'full-spectrum dominance' for the collection of intelligence, communication and transmission of information, navigation and weapons delivery, operated by a new 'space cadre' with the purpose of establishing global vigilance and the ability to attack anywhere in the world. The US National Security Agency already operates an extensive international surveillance system *Echelon*, using a combination of spy satellites and sensitive listening stations, to eavesdrop on electronic communication around the world – from telephones to emails to radio signals, airline and maritime frequencies. According to the Defense Advanced Research Projects Agency, the Pentagon is planning a new generation of weapons under a programme code-named Falcon (Force

Application and Launch from the Continental US), aimed at total global reach and dominance.

Such policies provide succour to the great military industrial complex and keeps the world armament corporations revenues healthy: the SIPRI Annual Report on world armament for 2006 notes that global defence expenditure has seen an upturn of 34 per cent over the past decade (1996–2005). World military expenditure in 2005 was estimated to have exceeded one trillion dollars, which corresponds to 2.5 per cent of world GDP. As the world's hyper-power, the US was responsible for 48 per cent of the world total defence spending, distantly followed by Britain, France, Japan and China, with 4–5 per cent each (SIPRI, 2006).

During the same period, the North Atlantic Treaty Organization (NATO) – a relic of the Cold War – has been reinvented as 'global NATO', whose rapid reaction units can be airlifted anywhere on the globe to defend Western interests. It is now operating in Kabul with a new mandate. 'Creating a global NATO is not about saving the alliance from obsolescence,' wrote two leading commentators, 'the issue is not whether NATO goes out of area or out of business. The issue is how the world's premier international military organization should adapt to the demands of the times in a way that advances the interests not just of the transatlantic community but of a global community of democracies dependent on global stability' (Daalder and Goldgeier, 2006). The European Union, too, has indicated that it wants to present itself as peacekeeper, resolving humanitarian operations and regional crises when it deployed its rapid reaction force without the US-dominated NATO to war-torn Democratic Republic of Congo in 2003: the so-called *Operation Artemis*.

Public-private partnerships are becoming increasingly prominent in creating a global security environment, noticeable in the mushrooming of what are called 'Private Military Firms' and the annual revenues of the global private security market are expected to reach $200 billion by 2010. The privatized military industry represents 'alternative patterns of power and authority' linked to the global market rather than limited to the territorial state and can act as 'investment enablers' (Singer, 2003). Singer classifies these firms into three categories: 'providers' (of military power for use on the battlefield), 'consultants' (in military training programmes) or 'support' firms (offering logistics and maintenance support but not fighting on behalf of the client). The invasion and occupation of Iraq has provided private security firms with an excellent opportunity to enhance their revenues. According to Singer, Halliburton subsidiary Kellogg, Brown and Root won an estimated $13 billion contract to provide supplies for US troops and maintenance for equipment in Iraq – a figure Singer notes is two and a half times what the United States paid for the 1991

Operation Desert Storm (Singer, 2005). The excesses committed by private firms in Iraq have also received some academic and media attention. Blackwater Security, one of the biggest private security firms operating in Iraq, had an electronic newsletter purported to have come from the firm's President Gary Jackson sent to its staff in March 2005 saying that 'actually it is "fun" to shoot some people'. It added that terrorists 'need to get creamed, and it's fun, meaning satisfying, to do the shooting of such folk' (quoted in Townsend, 2005).

In parts of Africa, especially in the Great Lakes region, international 'entrepreneurs of insecurity', have been a key component in the conflict which has inflicted horrendous damage on the Democratic Republic of Congo (Reyntjens, 2005). In many other regions in Africa, transnational corporations have introduced their own forms of community development, known as 'strategic philanthropy', to protect and police oil and other resource-rich installations (Barnes, 2005). Some have cautioned against using corporate mercenaries for peacekeeping operations in the developing world (Renou, 2005).

The US invasion of Iraq was an example of how, by deploying small number of troops and targeted weaponry for a short sharp media spectacle of a war, much broader geo-political and economic aims could be achieved. Despite belated criticism, even in the mainstream media, of President Bush's policies in Iraq and the mythologies associated with the 'war on terror', the invasion has given far-reaching powers to the imperial project (Thussu, 2006b). Castells has noted that the most apparent consequence of the Iraq invasion was the 'confirmation of the possibilities and success of unilateralism based on technological-military superiority' (Castells, 2004: 351). It also demonstrated the distinct nature of American imperialism: an 'empire of indifference', which works on a finance-based logic of 'risk control' (Martin, 2007). It has been argued that the invasion of Iraq was, at least, partly dictated by the need to protect the dominance of the dollar by ensuring that oil-exporting nations do not start denominating their trade in Euros, as Baathist Iraq had dared to do. Now that Iraq is firmly within the dollar zone, the 'dollarization' of other oil rich economies can move apace. In central Asia, the US has already expanded its energy interests – at stake are the rich oil and gas resources in the Caspian Sea basin.

Framing the 'war on terror'

Television's framing of wars as the consequence of inadequate governance by corrupt and inefficient elites in the developing world or of ethnic rivalries and transnational terrorism, creates an ideological space within which a moral discourse about humanitarianism and compassion can be constructed. This presentation of civil wars and state failures as a threat to international security thus legitimizes supposedly benign Western interventionist policy, which is ostensibly aimed at modernizing traditional societies as well as contributing to peace-enforcement and even 'nation-building', in an imposed neo-liberal framework. Joseph Nye has recently observed that 'television news has come to play a crucial role in world affairs'. 'In 1990 and 1991,' he notes, 'after Saddam Hussein invaded Kuwait, the dominance of CNN and the BBC allowed the issue to be presented as cross-border aggression. If the dominant world TV news service had been based in Baghdad, it might have been successfully presented as Iraq's recovery of a lost province' (Nye, 2007: 36).

The clearest example of framing is perhaps the one of the 'war on terror', a contraction of the official Global War on Terrorism (GWOT), announced by President Bush on 20 September 2001, barely ten days after the attacks on New York and Washington: 'Our war on terror begins with al-Qaeda, but it does not end there, it will not end until every terrorist group of global reach has been found, stopped, and defeated.' Calling it a 'civilization's fight' and asking 'every nation to join us', in a barely concealed threat to the rest of the world, the President intoned: 'Every nation, in every region, now has a decision to make: either you are with us, or you are with the terrorists' (quoted in US Government, 2004b: 337). The phrase 'war on terror' was snapped up by the US media and through its global circulation gained worldwide currency, legitimizing the phenomenon, though how a state can wage a war against 'terror', which is neither an organization nor a state, remains an open question. Despite flimsy, not to say false evidence, the US government was able to justify its invasion of Iraq as part of this global and open-ended 'war on terror', a conflict which could be used as a pretext for military intervention in perpetuity. Former Central Intelligence Agency director James Woolsey, member of the Project for the New American Century, described the invasion of Iraq as the onset of the 'Fourth World War' (the third being the Cold War).

The naming of a conflict is itself a 'geo-political act' and the 'politics of naming' can provide a useful marker in the mediated discourse of wars and conflicts and how they are framed by the global media (Bhatia, 2005). The phrase 'Gulf War II' to denote the 2003 invasion of Iraq has become fashionable in media, policy and academic discourses. Even if the two major US military campaigns in Iraq – in 1991 and 2003 – are accepted as 'wars', though invasion is a more accurate description of what happened in 2003, this was not the second but the third Gulf War; the first was the nearly forgotten decade-long Iran-Iraq war, which claimed more than a million lives and was initiated by Saddam Hussein with the firm backing of the West, to contain revolutionary Islam emanating from Iran.

International political terrorism has a long history, going back in modern times to anarchists who killed Tsar Alexander II in 1881, and later in 1914, Archduke Ferdinand of Austria, triggering the First World War. Germany's Baader-Meinhoff (1968–92), Italy's Red Brigade, which kidnapped and killed former Prime Minister Aldo Moro, as well as the Irish Republican Army and Spain's Basque terrorist organization ETA are other prominent European terrorist groups. From the Shining Path in Peru (largely secular) to the Lord's Salvation Army in Uganda (Christian) to Sri Lanka's Tamil Tigers, the pioneers of suicide bombing, who killed former Indian Prime Minister Rajiv Gandhi in 1991, and Nepal's Maoists (both Hindus), there is a long list of non-Muslim 'terrorist' groups. Yet none of these are identified as a religious terrorist group: one rarely finds the IRA or ETA discussed as Catholic terrorism, or Sri Lankan Tamil separatists described as a Hindu terrorist group. However, the myth persists about the ubiquity and danger of 'Islamic' terrorism, exemplified by shadowy networks with their alleged links to 'rogue' states (BBC, 2004b; Burke, 2004). This view of Islamic militancy is undifferentiated: Islamist groups in different parts of the world – al-Qaeda (reputedly led by Saudi fugitive Osama bin Laden – himself a creation of the CIA) in Afghanistan/Pakistan, Hezbollah in Lebanon, Hamas in Palestine, Jemaah Islamiyah in Indonesia – are all presented in the mainstream media as part of a seamless transnational terror network (Thussu, 2006b).

In such a polarized framing of issues in the media, the distinction between 'political Islam' and 'Islamic fundamentalism' is collapsed, ignoring the long history of the US government harnessing and cultivating radical Islamic groups to fight godless communism in Afghanistan during the 1980s: the 'freedom fighters' of Cold War years have mutated into enemies of freedom, creating and feeding into 'the politics of fear' (BBC, 2004b; Khalidi, 2004; Mamdani, 2004). Islamic militant groups – in Palestine, Chechnya, Afghanistan, India – have used terrorist activities as an extreme manifestation of political protest and some 'Islamist' groups have descended into extortion, blackmailing rackets and criminal syndicates, but, as evident in occupied Iraq, the vast majority of the world's one billion Muslims have nothing to do with terrorism. As Desai has argued, the roots of the new terrorism are not in religion but in a political ideology of 'global Islamism' which uses religious language, and that its purpose is like any other political ideology, to win power (Desai, 2006).

Television can be very effective at framing conflicts within a context of binary opposition, an us-versus-them dichotomy, in which Islamist opposition is projected as irrational and fanatical, pitted against a firm, rational, and reasonable US leadership. The demonization of Islamic leadership is also facilitated by television's preference for the exotic and the unusual. A turbaned, bearded, one-eyed Mullah Omar, the former leader of Taliban in Afghanistan, or a gun-wielding Osama bin Laden fits the image of a villain in the popular Western imagination, influenced by a stereotyping of the Islamic East that has deep cultural and historical roots (Said, 1997). A 2007 report published by the UK-based Islamic Human Rights Commission expressed concerns about Hollywood's representation of 'crude and exaggerated' stereotypes of Muslims, which, the report claimed, was perpetuating Islamophobia. Among the examples included were from such popular Hollywood films as *Executive Decision* (1996), which shows Palestinian terrorists reciting prayers before and after murdering innocent passengers in a hijacked plane, 'almost defining terrorism as an Islamic ritual', and the repeated juxtaposition of Islamic ritual practices, in the 1998 film *The Siege*, with scenes of exploding bombs and indiscriminate killing, implying that 'terrorist acts are intrinsic to Islamic beliefs and practices' (IHRC, 2007).

The myths of Islamic terrorism were used to construct a media discourse about the dangers posed by Iraq. A study of the coverage of the 2003 Iraq invasion by the *New York Times*, showed that the editorial page of the newspaper did not once mention the words 'UN Charter' or 'international law' in any of its 70 editorials on Iraq from September 11, 2001, to March 20, 2003 (Friel and Falk, 2004), while another study of the reporting of the Weapons of Mass Destruction (WMD) in the US and UK media called it 'classic scandal coverage', emphasizing 'breaking news' and 'partisan contests' rather than 'technological or scientific debates or the policy ramifications – especially the international ramifications' (Moeller, 2004: 20). In 2004, the Carnegie Endowment for International Peace released a detailed report based on 'pre-war intelligence, the official presentation of that intelligence, and what is now known about Iraq's programs'. Analysing the pre-war evidence that was available to the US and international intelligence communities about Iraq's weapons programmes and comparing that data to the claims that were made by the Bush administration, the report concluded that there had been no immediate threat of WMDs from Iraq: its nuclear programme had been 'suspended for many years' (Grincione et al., 2004).

The heavy reliance on official sources by the major US television news networks during the invasion of Iraq was documented in a study conducted by the media watchdog, Fairness and Accuracy in Reporting (FAIR). The study covered news programmes about Iraq during a three-week period following the first day of bombing in Iraq (March 20, 2003) on six television networks and news channels: ABC *World News Tonight*, CBS *Evening News*, NBC *Nightly News*, CNN's *Wolf Blitzer Reports*, Fox's *Special Report with Brit Hume, and*

PBS's *NewsHour with Jim Leher.* It concluded that 63 per cent of all sources were current and former US government employees, and a vast majority of these expressed pro-war opinions, while only one anti-war group leader appeared as a source. Anti-war sources 'were almost universally allowed one-sentence soundbites taken from interviews conducted on the street. Not a single show in the study conducted a sit-down interview with a person identified as being against the war' (Rendall and Broughel, 2003).

This was not official censorship: ratings-driven market pressures were the key factor for the commercial media not to appear 'unpatriotic', as one commentator noted: 'Commercial advertisers generally do not wish to be associated with a programme that presents, much less advocates, a minority political viewpoint on a matter as controversial as war, let alone a view that runs counter to moneyed interests. The consequence of this condition is that those who dissent find it difficult to make their voices heard. But the censorship they face is not that of the government, at least not directly. Rather, it is market censorship. American commercial television provides a near-perfect form of repression because it does so by touting the seemingly wholesome principle that it responds to what the audience wants' (Calabrese, 2005b: 171). Such was the cheerleading for military action that attempts by peace groups to purchase airtime to broadcast advertisements for peace were refused by all major television networks (Rendall and Broughel, 2003).

Cultural contours of neo-liberal imperialism

More than the Pentagon's high-tech weaponry, it is the US cultural hegemony, represented globally by infotainment conglomerates, as noted in Chapter 2, which effectively legitimizes neo-liberal ideology as a precursor to a post-modern free-market utopia. Neo-liberal imperialism cannot sustain itself by hard military power alone; creating, reinforcing and reinvigorating its ideology of economic, political, technological and cultural superiority, is essential for its survival: US culture – 'from Hollywood to Harvard – has greater global reach than any other' notes Nye (2004: 7). Television, with its semiotic and symbolic power, is a crucial element in propagating this ideology, as publicity is 'the golden ring of infotainment society' (Dean, 2002: 14). New digital technologies are likely to strengthen this cultural power: Jean-Noël Jeanneney, president of France's Bibliothèque Nationale, has expressed concerns about the plans by Google to digitize works written mostly in English; arguing that such acts of selection can only extend US cultural hegemony (Jeanneney, 2006). Elsewhere, I have discussed how strong US presence is in the world's visual landscape, despite the steady increase in volume and value of media 'contra-flow' from such countries as India, Japan and Brazil (Thussu, 2007a). As one analyst wrote: 'If the United States intends to exercise its power effectively, even against the wishes of its allies, it should do so with a bland smile, not boastful words' (Cohen, 2004: 59). In cultural terms, it faces few obstacles in spreading that smile. As Jürgen Habermas notes:

> Global markets, mass consumption, mass communication, and mass tourism disseminate the standardized products of a mass culture (overwhelmingly shaped by the United States). The same consumer goods and fashions, the same films, television programmes, and bestselling music and books spread across the globe; the same fashions in pop, techno or jeans seize and shape the mentalities of young people in even the most far-flung places; the same language, English, assimilated in a variety of ways, serves as a medium for understanding between the most radically different dialects. The clocks of Western civilization keep the tempo for the compulsory simultaneity of the non-simultaneous. This commodified, homogenous culture doesn't just impose itself on distant lands, of course; in the West too, it levels out even the strongest national differences, and weakens even the strongest local traditions. (2001: 75)

In his well-known book on propaganda, Jacques Ellul distinguishes between an overtly political and a more subtle conception of propaganda – a propaganda of 'integration' which unconsciously moulds individuals and makes them conform to the dominant ideas in a society. In the long run, popular cinema, television, advertising and public relations, can be more effective in reinforcing the official political agenda than control or manipulation of news (Ellul, 1965 [1962]). In advanced capitalist societies, the 'relative autonomy' of the political and ideological from the economic, as Althusser contended, helps in the legitimization of elite social and political discourses (Althusser, 1971). The transnational articulations of neo-liberal ideology – through such mechanisms as intergovernmental and international non-governmental organizations, corporate synergies, business news and marketing networks, training and seminars, academic and professional consultancy – has revitalised what Jameson has called 'the world space of multinational capital' (Jameson, 1991: 54). Given the extension of mainly US-based infotainment conglomerates across the world, as noted in Chapter 2, the notion of 'the culture industry', enunciated by Max Horkheimer and Theodor Adorno in a specific historical juncture of the evolution of Western capitalism, is in the process of globalization, heightened in the era of global branding under neo-liberalism, resulting in what Lash and Lury call a 'global culture industry' (Lash and Lury, 2007). Peters (2003) has observed that the culture industry argument is still valid in the era of globalization. Its sense of 'the interlocking of culture industries with others (banking, electricity); the push to product differentiation (the narcissism of petty differences); the micro-adjustment of production (pseudo-individuality) to audience tastes.' Horkheimer and Adorno, he notes, never say that 'the culture industry simply produces trash; many of its wares are calculated perfection, corrupted by slickness, a rationalized signature meant to please and to soothe' (Peters, 2003: 70).

Karl Marx famously called religion 'the opium of the people ... the illusory happiness of men'. Can global infotainment be the twenty-first century version of such acts of cultural sedation? Does it provide parallels with what Marx called the 'fetishism of commodities', a type of popular irrationality where commodities acquired 'mystical', 'mysterious' and 'fantastic' value, way beyond their real worth? In his essay, 'How to Look at Television', originally published in the 1960s, Adorno wrote: 'Mass culture, if not sophisticated, must at least be up to date – that is to say, "realistic", or posing as realistic – in order to meet the expectations of a supposedly disillusioned, alert, and hard-boiled audience. Middle-class requirements bound up with internalization – such as concentration, intellectual effort, and erudition – have to be continuously lowered. This does not hold only for the United States, where historical memories are scarcer than in Europe, but it is universal, applying to England and Continental Europe as well' (Adorno, 1991: 162).

Had Adorno witnessed the globalization of media, he would have noticed how much standards have been compromised to reach the widest possible audience base. In the name of bringing down political and cultural barriers to transnational interactions and democratizing global communication, infotainment conglomerates have promoted a certain version of freedom which chimes with Isaiah Berlin's notion of 'negative liberty' – an argument for the defence of individual liberty as against a defence of democratic government – leaving individuals alone to do what they want, provided that their actions did not interfere with the liberty of others. Such a utilitarian formulation of liberty was in contrast with a more progressive view of liberty – 'positive liberty', rooted in the emancipatory potential of European enlightenment which suggests that humans could be free from bigotry and ignorance and choose the path of reason and rationality. Berlin argued that in this idealised form – which was exploited by socialist and communist governments – liberty was trampled by authoritarian regimes (Berlin, 1969). This *laissez-faire* individualism, central to the idea of 'negative liberty', has been an ideological constituent of neo-liberal imperialism.

'Soft news' selling neo-liberal imperialism

When Disney, traditionally dominant in entertainment, entered the global television news arena by taking over ABC in 1995, its chief executive officer,

Michael Eisner commented: 'There are many places in the world, like China, India and other places, that do not want to accept programming that has any political content. But they have no problem with sports, and they have no problem with Disney kind of programming' (quoted in Utley, 1997: 8). Although 'Disney kind of programming' and its local clones dominate television schedules, with the globalization of 24/7 news culture, political programming, too, is now circulating even in countries such as China, where the state and the ruling party continues to control news and current affairs networks. Yet governments across the globe are less perturbed by the growth of infotainment, as it can keep the masses diverted with various versions of 'reality TV' and consumerist and entertaining information, displacing serious news and documentaries, which might focus on the excesses of neo-liberal imperialism. In this context, it is extremely important to understand the role of the national elites – part of a transnational class which largely benefits from neo-liberal economic activities – in the establishment and popularity of global infotainment. As Sklair has observed: 'The transnational capitalist class is not identified with any foreign country in particular, or even necessarily with the First World, or the White world, or the Western world. Its members identify with the capitalist globalization and reconceptualize their several local and other interests in terms of the capitalist global system. Their political project is to transform the imagined national interests of their countrymen and women in terms of capitalist globalization' (Sklair, 2002: 156).

This transnational elite imbibes the ideas emanating from the intellectual centre of the empire. Nye notes that US 'soft power' is not confined to the global circulation of American popular culture but also includes 'the high cultural ideas' which the US 'exports in the minds of the half-a-million foreign students who study every year in American universities, or in the minds of the Asian entrepreneurs who return home after succeeding in Silicon Valley, and are more closely related to elites with power. Most of China's leaders have a son or a daughter educated in the United States who portray a realistic view of the US that is often at odds with the caricatures in official Chinese propaganda' (Nye, 2004: 93). That class is central to such communality of interests has been somehow neglected in contemporary analyses of social realities, with their focus on identities, based on ethnicities, gender or sexuality. It is useful to remind ourselves what Marx had to say about the importance of class in shaping dominant ideology: 'The ideas of the ruling class are, in every age, the ruling ideas: i.e. the class which is the dominant material force in society is at the same time its dominant intellectual force. The class which has the means of material production at its disposal, has the control at the same time over the means of mental production, so that in consequence the ideas of those who lack the means of production are, in general, subject to it' (Marx, 1970: 93).

Infotainment conglomerates are part of the dominant economic force in neo-liberal societies and, it could be argued, operate within what Ellul refers to as a 'total' and 'constant' propaganda 'environment', which can render the influence of propaganda virtually unnoticed (1965 [1962]). The transnational capitalist class – in its infancy in many developing countries and in transition economies – is susceptible to the charms of neo-liberalism, as it benefits from having closer ties with the powerful core of this tiny minority, largely based in the West, as the annual *Fortune 500* listings amply attests. In this sense the Gramscian idea of hegemony – often discussed in the national setting – can be deployed in a wider context to assess how far neo-liberalism has been embraced, almost universalized by dominant sections of the global elites, who have come to regard its basic tenets – private (efficient and therefore preferable) vs. public (corrupt and inefficient); individualism (to be applauded) vs. community (to be decried); market (good) vs. state (bad), as undisputed opposites which fall within the rubric of 'commonsense'.

Though the primary constituency for such ideas are the elites – the agents of neo-liberal modernity, global 'knowledge systems' perform the interpretive work for their wider consumption. There exists, Vinay Lal suggests,

> an empire of knowledge, perhaps far more considerable than the empires we associate with Euro-American imperialism or with the large corporate undertakings that have divided much of the world among themselves, and it has shaped the categories through which we view the world; and since many of these categories are largely invisible, or bathed in the language of kindness, good intentions, and progress, they are more insidious in their operations than the forces and agents through which naked domination is exercised. (Lal, 2002: 4)

A 1964 report from US Committee on Foreign Affairs, *Winning the Cold War: The US Ideological Offensive* stated:

> In foreign affairs, certain objectives can be better achieved through direct contact with the people of foreign countries than with their governments. Through the intermediary of the techniques and instruments of communications, it is possible today to reach important and influential sectors of the population of other countries, to inform them, to influence their attitudes, and may be to succeed in motivating them to certain determined actions. These groups, in turn, are capable of exercising considerable pressure on their governments. (cited in Sklair, 2002: 171)

The globalization of neo-liberal ideology and the near global reach and circulation of televised infotainment has provided neo-liberal imperialism with a powerful opportunity to communicate directly with the world's populace, as more and more global infotainment conglomerates are localizing their content to reach beyond the 'Westernised' elites. Ellul (1965 [1962]) noted that although the educated classes believed that they are not affected by propaganda, in fact, they were more vulnerable as they consumed a greater quantity of news than the general population, and engaged regularly with processes of political communication. In the context of globalization of infotainment, it is the Westernized, mostly young and middle-class social groups, with aspirations to a consumerist and hedonistic lifestyle, which engage with neo-liberal media. The contestants on the Indian version of the reality television show *Big Brother*, for example, belonged mostly to Hinglish-speaking urban India, exposed to the Western reality television culture. The success of Murdoch's TV channels in India, as noted in Chapter 4, has primarily been predicated on infotainment, blending the Hollywood style, Bollywood-generated spectacle in ways that refigure neo-liberal ideology in Indianized forms (Thussu, 2007b). The growing presence of 'glocal Americana' is feeding into and creating a media culture in which neo-liberalism is taking deep roots. And the United States, the fount of such an ideology receiving acceptance bordering on admiration: a 2005 survey by the Pew Global Attitudes Project found that US image was strongest in India, with 71 per cent of Indians expressing a positive opinion of the United States, compared with 54 per cent in 2002 (Pew Research Center, 2005). A Pew survey conducted a year later reported that support for the US 'war on terror' in India had increased significantly – from 52 per cent in 2005 to 65 per cent in 2006 (Pew Research Center, 2006).

As noted in Chapter 4, the changing pattern of employment among middle-class youth in India, favouring corporate jobs to public sector positions, may also be part of the explanation for such attitudinal preference. A cognitive and behavioural shift has been seen among the educated youth working for transnational call centres and 'programmed' to implement globalization of the networked 24/7 electronic marketplace (Aneesh, 2006; Biao, 2006). Though physically located in India, these workers operate in a 'transnational virtual space'– lending their expertise and skills to first world corporations while based in a 'third world' setting (Aneesh, 2006). To make this 'virtual migration' effective, they are trained and coached by the medium of US television programmes such as *Friends* and *Sex and the City*, thus acquiring the requisite cultural capital to operate successfully within the neo-liberal imperium. Some call centres insist that their workers acquire a different persona, a new hybrid identity and even a 'Western' name.

Similar trends are discernable in other developing and transition societies; it is not unusual to find Chinese students studying outside their country to have a Western name. Infotainment is more conducive to this new generation with its individualistic worldview, social and geographical mobility and transnational working environment. The 'negative liberty' that Berlin spoke of in the context of Cold War Europe, is now being celebrated around the world, thanks to the infotainment conglomerates, whose 'soft news' is masking the hard realities of neo-liberal imperialism. Their pro-business bias is well attested, as we have chronicled in this book. As infotainment becomes entrenched in news conventions around the world, the US experience of what Jeffrey Scheuer has termed 'Sound Bite Society', is likely to become widely acceptable and thus benefit the right-wing political agenda, one predicated on the supremacy of the market (Scheuer, 2001). Luhmann, who saw the mass media as one of the key cognitive systems of modern society, posed a crucial question: '*How* is it possible to accept information about the world and about society as information about reality when one knows *how* it is produced?' (Luhmann, 2000: 122, italics in original).

Yet amid the welter of information overload, the myth of freedom and liberty is played out on a regular basis on 24/7 news networks. The borderless 'war on terror' continues apace while state sovereignty is constantly threatened under the new political, economic and military dispensations of neo-liberal imperialism. Galbraith's 'innocent fraud' is relentlessly and regularly publicised, often in a spectacular fashion. One US commentator candidly summed up the situation: 'To legitimize colonial rule by some other name, and to create institutions that can conduct it, has become one of the great challenges of contemporary statecraft – necessary not only to ease the misery of anarchy, but also to avert the dangers posed by anarchy in the age of weapons of mass destruction and suicide bombers' (Cohen, 2004: 61–2). However, as witnessed in Iraq, the resistance to such thinking has been the concomitant to the implementation of neo-liberal imperialism. The possibilities and opportunities that new digital media provide in creating what I have termed a 'global infotainment sphere' is the theme of the final chapter.

7

A GLOBAL INFOTAINMENT SPHERE?

Despite the unprecedented growth of infotainment programming on a global scale and its capacity to help legitimize neo-liberal media and communication regimes, disjunctures and dissonances are appearing which offer possibilities for resistance to the new version of Western imperialism, discussed in the previous chapter. In both economic and geo-political terms, new configurations of power are emerging. The economic recovery and upturn in Russia under President Vladimir Putin and the resultant assertiveness from the Kremlin has global reverberations; China's double-digit economic growth and the extension of its influence in parts of the developing world, especially Africa, once the preserve of Western-based corporations, is reorienting the global economy. The globalization of service industries is changing the 'geographies of global trade' and benefiting countries such as India. Based on the IMF's purchasing power parity, India was set to overtake Japan as the world's third largest economy by 2007, with a GDP of $4 trillion, while China was predicted to surpass in the near future the US as the world's largest economy: China's GDP in 2007 was just over $10 trillion, compared to $13 trillion of the United States. The trend towards social democracy in Latin America is giving new hope to progressive constituencies elsewhere in the developing world. The European Union is strengthened with the extension of its membership to countries of eastern Europe, while in the Middle East anti-Western sentiments among the populations – if not among the ruling elites – are on the ascendant (Kohut and Stokes, 2006).

These political-economic changes at a macro level could place a limit on the influence of the world's hyper-power. A 'second superpower' – world public opinion – has started to assert itself, although the scale and scope of its impact and imaginings is much smaller than that mounted by infotainment conglomerates and market ideologists. A 2007 international opinion poll conducted for the BBC World Service by the international polling firm GlobeScan, together with the Program on International Policy Attitudes at the University of Maryland, found that people thought the United States had a 'mostly negative influence in the world' (51 per cent of those polled). The only two countries to beat the US were Israel (56 per cent) and Iran (54 per cent) (GlobeScan website). Even in Europe, the alleged 'inauthenticity' of American culture has been part of European elite opinion for well over two hundred years. It is often overlooked that in cultural terms, the United States is the world's biggest and most powerful European country, and yet 'anti-Americanism as a European lingua franca' has been in existence for a long time, as noted in a new study of the roots of anti-Americanism (Markovits, 2007).

A Pew Global Attitudes survey in 2006 highlighted fundamental differences that divide Islam from the West: Westerners see Muslims, it observed, as 'fanatical, violent', and 'intolerant', while Muslims see Westerners 'as selfish, immoral and greedy - as well as violent and fanatical'. The US invasion of Iraq and its aftermath has made the 'world a more dangerous place'. 'These disapproving opinions do not arise simply out of inattention or naïve anti-Americanism', the survey notes, 'Instead, they are a reaction to US foreign policy, especially the war in Iraq. News accounts of US prisoner abuses at Abu Ghraib and Guantanamo shape these negative views of the US' (Pew Research centre, 2006: vii).

Why might this be the case? Has the arsenal of its hard military and soft cultural power failed to convince the world at large about the virtues of American freedom? Has its seductive and subversive infotainment spectacles ceased to attract? What of its public diplomacy and private infotainment conglomerates, with all their PR skills, resources and professional expertise? Have they failed to sell neo-liberal imperialism?

One factor which has helped to create and sustain these disjunctures in the mainstream neo-imperial narrative is the availability and adoption of new information and communication technologies and their diffusion not only among the elites but to the wider population, enhancing the global news and information landscape. The proliferation of 24/7 news networks, as discussed in Chapter 3, coupled with the rapid growth in the penetration of broadband, has contributed to the creation and circulation of media content from around the world, sometimes challenging, sometimes being co-opted by the dominant infotainment conglomerates. The Internet has profoundly influenced media, providing new and personalized platforms for news content to a global constituency of potential consumers and also changing the time-frame of news production and distribution. In an era of real-time news, while journalists are under constant pressure to provide up-to-the-minute information, ordinary citizens now can access the content of the world's top news agencies, 24-hour news channels and news portals, once available only to journalists, without being mediated by the editorial gate-keeping of news organizations (Berger, 2000). Most news outlets provide backgrounders and archival material on their websites, linked to many other useful information resources.

Journalists can now find their material, in most cases for free or for a nominal fee, in a virtual global library, stacked with newspapers, television channels, information data bases, archives of news photographs and moving pictures, from across the world. They do not have to depend on PR handouts about a corporate annual report or a government policy document to write their stories; they can go straight to the original source, unimpeded by governmental or corporate spin. The Internet has also been a key resource for the civic sector: for example, the US-based project Iraq Body Count (www.iraqbodycount.org) – the 'world's only independent and comprehensive public database of media-reported civilian deaths in Iraq' – has emerged as a credible source for information about casualties in Iraq. Given the global nature of the Internet, journalists can incorporate various viewpoints in their reports: in foreign reporting such access can be particularly useful to provide a more balanced coverage on contentious international issues. In addition, the Internet also provides opportunities for developing and strengthening a transnational network of journalists and information activists to cooperate and exchange ideas and information.

Though still a largely elite operation, the Internet has transformed transnational communication: according to Internetworldstats in 1995 it had just 20 million users, by 2000 it had 400 million, rising to 1,114 million by early 2007, covering 17 per cent of the world's population, though mostly concentrated in the more industrialized countries. As communication technologies become cheaper and more sophisticated, their diffusion has occurred with unprecedented speed and geographical reach, contributing to a more democratic, many-to-many, global communication model. In April 2007, China had more than 137 million Internet users (just over 10 per cent of its population of 1.3 billion); while India had 40 million (less than four per cent of its population). The two giants with huge and yet largely under-explored markets have become key sites for the attention of transnational corporations, with India having emerged as a creative software hub in their global operations.

It is worth reflecting how on-line traffic will change in the coming years and decades – already China has the second largest blogger population in the world. It is little wonder that transnational corporations are bending over backwards to partake of the world's potentially largest on-line market: Yahoo! launched a Chinese site in 1998; Murdoch was involved in developing ChinaByte and CSeek, Goldman Sachs supported the popular portal Sina; Intel and Dow Jones backed Sohu; AOL supported China.com, while Google inaugurated a China-specific search engine in 2006. By 2006, China had also emerged as the world's largest mobile telephone market and its biggest exporter of information technology products.

The convergence of mobile technologies and broadband will provide Internet access at high speeds, ensuring that television news will increasingly circulate within a package which will be dominated by entertainment material: music, games, gambling, adult content, video and personalization services. As more mobile handsets become capable of playing broadcast quality video, TV news will migrate to what has been called the 'fourth screen' – after cinema, TV and PC. Murdoch's Fox was the first network to recognize the potential for this smaller screen when in 2005 it launched *24: Conspiracy* 'mobisodes' – a 24-part series of one-minute episodes linked to the hit drama shown on Fox and other Murdoch networks. The Apple Ipod has given a new term to broadcasting – the podcast – embraced by broadcasters such as the BBC, which since 2006 has been podcasting its radio and television programmes, while ITN rolled out a package specifically for mobile telephones in early 2007. CNN produces the *Briefing Room,* a daily news-in-a-nutshell service for email, mobile and Internet.

As broadband access is broadened, and more and more tele-visual content moves on-line, new peer-to-peer television communities will grow around such file-sharing services as Joost, which will be able to provide DVD quality pictures and give the viewers a chance to construct their own channels, with their own schedules. In such a personalized convergence of television and the Internet, a viewer will be able to converse with other users watching the same channel, while simultaneously being able to access online content provided by the broadcaster. Al Gore, the former US Vice-President was claiming to be 'democratizing television' through his 'Current TV', the channel made of clips created by viewers and producers, and in operation since 2005. Such multimodal communication – from anywhere to anywhere at any time – is creating a 'mobile network society' (Castells et al., 2006). Though much of the connectivity has been colonized for e-commerce, activists and information mavericks have also enriched the transnational public discourse by providing alternative voices and perspectives on contemporary issues (Downing, 2001; Atton, 2005; Hackett and Zhao, 2005). 'The synthesis of global corporate capitalism and information and entertainment technologies', Kellner has argued, 'is constructing novel forms of society and culture, controlled by capital and with global reach' and creating what he has called 'networked infotainment society' (Kellner, 2003: 14).

Media multitude

In an informational society, Castells has argued, the main agency of social movements is 'networking'. And these networks – anti-globalization movements or religious fundamentalist groups – do more than organizing activity and sharing information: 'They are the actual producers, and distributors, of cultural codes' (Castells, 2004: 427). One successful example of such activism was the use of the Internet to mobilize international support against the US-sponsored Multilateral Agreement on Investment (MAI) – though the fact that some European governments, such as France, were opposed to an agreement which would have given unfettered powers to transnational corporations to move capital from one country to another, may have contributed to thwarting the MAI. In India, the New Delhi-based news portal Tehalka.com (Sensation) almost cost the government of Prime Minster Atal Bihari Vajpayee, when in 2001, in an undercover operation it exposed the corruption in procuring international defence deals. Salam Pax, the so-called Baghdad blogger, who chronicled the 2003 US invasion of Iraq and its bloody aftermath, became a minor media celebrity: besides writing a regular column for the *Guardian*, later published as a book, he also produced video diaries for the BBC. As blogs bourgeoned in cyberspace, some like the US-based Blogspot, a blog hosting service, receiving a larger audience of unique users across its million-plus blogs collectively than the NYTimes.com, the mainstream media had to start taking note of a phenomenon which could undermine traditional journalism.

In South Korea, OhmyNews, an 'independent internet newspaper' that hybridizes features of commercial and 'alternative' media, has been in operation since 2000 and has enriched journalism (Kim and Hamilton, 2006). 'Blog for America' became a major source of campaigning by Howard Dean in 2004 US presidential elections, demonstrating that the Internet was emerging as a vehicle for enhanced civic involvement with the potential to counteract the negative effects of television on the political process (Kerbel and Bloom, 2005). For some the development of the blogosphere was a diversionary virtual space for disenchanted citizens (Keren, 2006), while for others the blogosphere and its 'citizen journalists' and activists, were challenging the notion of editorial gate-keeping and professionalization of journalism (Hachten and Scotton, 2006).

Reflecting these changes, *Time* magazine announced that its famed 'Person of the Year' for 2006 was 'YOU', its readers, for seizing 'the reins of the global media, for founding and framing the new digital democracy' (*Time*, December 13, 2006). By 2007, editor-in-chief of the influential journal *Foreign Policy* was speaking of 'The YouTube Effect'. Most of the videos on the popular video-sharing website were frivolous, produced by and for teenagers, he wrote. However, the serious clips can either 'reveal truths' or spread 'disinformation, propaganda, and outright lies'. This phenomenon, he notes, is amplified by a double echo chamber: 'One is produced when content first posted on the Web is re-aired by mainstream TV networks. The second occurs when television moments, even the most fleeting, gain a permanent presence thanks to bloggers or activists who redistribute them through websites like YouTube' (Naím, 2007). That there is potential for business in this new and constantly mutating media world was indicated when YouTube was purchased by Google and MySpace by Murdoch. New digital media segments – including online video games, films, music, video-on-demand, satellite, radio and electronic books – generated $160 million globally in 2000; this figure had climbed to $11.4 billion in 2004, and was estimated to touch $73 billion by 2009, according to a Pricewaterhouse-Coopers report (2005: 15).

The trillion-dollar global entertainment and media market was predicted in 2007 to show maximum growth in the Asia-Pacific region, annually averaging about 12 per cent. Blogging is big in South Korea (the country with the world's highest broadband connectivity) and in China, where it is growing at a rapid pace. As search engines become increasingly sophisticated, multilingual and simpler to navigate, 'social computing' will be globalized with a myriad 'citizen journalists', net-activists and bloggers trying to compete for attention to produce and distribute media content, creating what might be termed as a 'global infotainment sphere'. Such a space will be predicated on providing entertaining information in an interactive and innovative manner. YouTube, Facebook and MySpace are harbingers of what is to come. The 'rise of the moving image' and the emerging computer-edited and -distributed 'new video' culture, it has been suggested, could transform global communication (Stephens, 1998).

In the new global infotainment sphere, multiple messages, voices and images can be transmitted instantaneously, from the many-to-the-many as well as one-to-one, informing and entertaining, with identifiable social and political effects. US marines can transmit pictures of abused Iraqis via email and mobile phones; the Chinese government has to admit that it had a health epidemic on its hands as millions of text messages are circulated by Chinese citizens, as happened during the 2002 SARS crisis; the Tsunami in 2004 and the bombing in London in 2005 also provide examples of citizen journalism; while *Loose Change*, a documentary film about 9/11 has become the most downloaded film on the Internet, and Jihadi beheadings are circulated as political pornography around the world. For McNair such 'cultural chaos' is undermining authority and dominant ideologies. 'The ideological environment comprises a chaotic whirl of competing ideas and belief-systems, sitting atop a crowded cultural-commodity marketplace of unprecedented depth, diversity and adversarialism towards elites in all walks of life' (McNair, 2006: 204).

However, is this marketplace a level playing field? Can one realistically equate a few renegade extremist groups posting propaganda on the net with the systematic, structural and seductive domination by the world's most powerful producer of cultural signs and symbols? Will on-line communication be a largely US-led and managed operation, as it controls both hardware and software of the Internet? Eli Noam thinks so:

> The United States has a large Internet community with entrepreneurial energy, big content producing companies with worldwide distribution and experience in reaching popular audiences, creative and technological talent from all over the world, and efficient production clusters; it also benefits from the *lingua franca* advantages of the English language and the cultural prowess of being the world's superpower. There are also leading computer hardware, components, and telecom industries, a pro-competition push, and a financial system that provides risk capital. Some of these factors are also available elsewhere, but nowhere in such combination. Thus, the medium of Internet TV combines the strengths of the US economy and society in entertainment content, in Internet, and in e-transactions. Add to that economies of scale, and there is nothing on the horizon that can match it. And, therefore, Internet TV will be strongly American. (2004: 241–2)

Good infotainment?

The notion of infotainment is closely associated with the idea of 'dumbing down'. Rather than fulfilling intellectual curiosity and promoting rational discourse, infotainment thrives on emotional appeal and irrational human impulses (Bourdieu, 1998; Gitlin, 2002). In 'the Anglo-American heartland', media are plagued by a 'chronic democratic deficit', a recent study observes. 'The deficit is multifaceted, it derives not only from media's failures in constituting a democratic public sphere, in sustaining healthy communities and political cultures, and in stimulating diversity in public communication, but also from media's complicity in maintaining inequality, in diminishing the public commons of knowledge and in excluding the public from shaping the mandates of cultural industries' (Hackett and Carroll, 2006: 199).

Such criticism stems from an idealised view of journalism. The traditional model of what James Carey called 'high modern' journalism (Carey, 1993), was applicable to an elitist conception of public communication with a rather limited popular purchase. By making political communication appealing, those who are not politically informed could be made more interested in civic affairs, contributing to a more democratic and inclusive media environment (Brants, 1998; McNair, 2006). The notion of a single public sphere based on universal rationality, with a 'common normative dimension' (Garnham, 1996: 369) is seen as part of a paternalist approach, one that belongs to the era of broadcasting, not narrowcasting and webcasting. Such a conception is hard to sustain in the twenty-first century television landscape and a 'globalized public sphere' (McNair, 2006: 143). Proponents of popular media democratization have argued that the binary opposition between information and entertainment is not sustainable in the post-modern hybridized television ecology and that digital broadcasting can encourage rather than erode serious coverage of politics (Hartely, 1999). Media spectacles and the dramatization of news can be attractive, as noted by Graber: 'Dramatic framing does attract viewers who might otherwise ignore newscasts, it increases their emotional involvement with significant political issues, and it stimulates them to care and think about these issues' (Graber, 1994: 505). Defenders maintain that those who denigrate infotainment base their criticisms on idealized notions of what news should be rather than what it is. The current level of infotainment, they contend, is adequate for the informational needs of citizens in a democracy and therefore we should settle for less demanding standards of quality (Zaller, 2003).

Baum argues that the rise of what he refers to as the 'soft news media' – entertainment-oriented, quasi-news and information programmes – has had the unintended effect of increasing the likelihood that a foreign policy crisis will receive public attention, particularly among demographics of the population not typically interested in politics or foreign policy (Baum, 2003, 2005). Such 'news lite' programmes as *The Daily Show* with Jon Stewart have been popular among young Americans and its influence during the 2000 and 2004 presidential elections was 'exceptional' (Baumgartner and Morris, 2006). Others caution against treating such shows as 'fake news' and applaud their hybrid nature, borrowing techniques drawn from genres of news, comedy and talk-shows as a post-modern 'experiment in political journalism', as 'an alternative journalism, one that uses satire to interrogate power, parody to critique contemporary news, and dialogue to enact a model of deliberative democracy' (Baym, 2005: 261).

Such infotainment programming may attract more young people to civic engagement: Mindich, who studied why young Americans are not watching news, notes 'the evidence for the long-term decline in news interest is overwhelming' (Mindich, 2005: 19). This may be part of what political scientist Cass Sunstein has called the tendency towards 'Daily Me', a self-selected diet of news and information that reinforces opinions already held (Sunstein, 2002). While some studies have concluded that positive consequences of soft news for the political process remain to be demonstrated (Prior, 2003), others have argued that 'softer' sources of political information – such as late-night comedy and daytime talk shows – can enhance political engagement (Moy et al., 2005).

In Britain, BBC's excellent comedy series *Yes Minister* and *Yes Prime Minister*, broadcast in the 1980s and repeated and enjoyed globally ever since, demonstrated that good political satire has international currency.

Programmes mocking 24/7 news culture, notably BBC's *The Day Today* (1994) and *Broken News* (2005), have been very popular, while accomplished impressionists such as Rory Bremner through their biting satire and intelligent critical comments have enriched political discourse on British television. Such programmes as *Pol Khol* (Exposure) fronted by Shekhar Suman on Star News, launched in 2004, and the *Sabse Politically Incorrect Kaun?* (Who is the Most Politically Incorrect?), launched in 2007 on NDTV India, have been able to make important political points in a lighter vein.

In a television world where fact and fiction regularly intersect, it has been suggested that the didactic potential of such fictional television dramas as NBC's *The West Wing* can contribute to the process of political education: a special episode of the acclaimed political series devoted to the issue of terrorism attracted more than 25 million viewers, nearly three times the viewership for the NBC News (Crawley, 2006). The woman-as-President drama, *Commander-in-Chief*, starring Geena Davis may have brightened up the chances of Senator Hilary Clinton to reach the White House in 2008. The US government has also 'recognized the power and potential benefits in circumventing traditional channels of communication (namely, journalists and news networks) to speak directly to American and global citizens through a variety of entertainment programming' (Jones, 2004: 7). After 9/11, the FBI sought leads or tips on terrorist suspects via a special edition of *America's Most Wanted*, the programme dedicated to catching criminals by enlisting the viewing audience's assistance, while the US Secretary of State Colin Powell appeared in a live 'town hall' meeting on MTV's *Be Heard*, fielding questions from young adults in seven countries (ibid: 7).

Such developments, argues Jones, are part of wider changes in politics, making it entertaining and therefore 'pleasurable'. This so-called 'new political television' has 'begun to explore multiple avenues for presenting politics in imaginative ways, treatments that can offer voices, positions, and perspectives not found in traditional television presentations of politics. It also suggests that audiences are receptive to (if not hungry for) political programming that is meaningful and engaging to them, programming that connects with their interests and concerns, provides new ways of thinking about politics, and speaks to them through accessible and pleasurable means' (ibid: 9.) The 'spectacular success' and global visibility of chat-show host Oprah Winfrey is part of such 'touchy-feely' infotainment (Illouz, 2003). In Europe, where symptoms of disengagement with democracy and diminishing levels of confidence in political institutions is leading to political disaffection (Torcal and Montero, 2006), the idea of pleasurable politics and enriching citizenship through infotainment has found many followers (van Zoonen, 2004). On British television, such charity 'telethons', as *Live Aid, Children in Need* and *Comic Relief*, have helped amass millions of pounds for non-governmental organizations both within Britain and internationally.

In South Korea, the two main political parties *Min-Joo Dang* (Millennium Democratic Party) *Hannara Dang* (Great National Party) used Internet broadcasting sites to put substantial resources into 'infotainment', in order to attract the younger generation, whose orientation is presumed to be towards entertainment and games. They put considerable effort into building virtual communities, in which web users 'share relatively non-political information but which are also intended to provide supportive messages for the party's line' (Hague and Uhm, 2003: 202–3).

In India the 2006 Bollywood film *Lage Raho Munnabhai* (Carry on Brother Munna) used imaginative ways to bring back the ideas of Mahatma Gandhi into popular discourse, even coining and popularizing the phrase 'Gandhigiri' (the force of Gandhian ideas). If, in the US, commentators mourn the distorted network news coverage of Presidential elections as 'Nightly News Nightmare' (Farnsworth and Lichter, 2006), in India networks such as NDTV have excelled in providing a comprehensive electoral coverage in general elections in the world's largest democratic exercise. Wrote Barkha Dutt, Managing Editor of NDTV 24x7, and one of India's best-known television journalists who hosts a popular weekly discussion programme *We the People*: 'I shudder at the outsourcing of journalism to private detectives and their hidden cameras…I am bored by the banality of breaking news, and I am ashamed when television converts suicide into a spectacle. Yet, every once in a way, something happens to do us proud. Most recently, the wave of Indian middle-class activism has sprung from the shores of television studios. Campaigns for justice or for the right to information have all used television as their launch pad' (Dutt, 2006).

Television coverage of communal clashes in the western Indian state of Gujarat in 2002 – the first major riots of the 24/7 television news era – demonstrated that large sections of the television networks were able to provide serious coverage and commentary, accelerating action from national government (Mehta, 2006). Pakistan's Geo TV, known for its campaigning journalism, has brought into the public sphere such taboo subjects as Islamic *Shari'a* law in its talk show *Zara Sochiye* (Think for a Moment) (Subramanian, 2006). In a media ecology like that of China, where state censorship is still dominant, commercialism may have widened the public discourse, as McCormick and Liu note:

> the commercialization of Chinese media means that private issues occupy an increasing portion of China's public sphere while the public discussion of public issues is in relative decline. This could be a first step toward reconstituting a more autonomous and diverse discussion of public affairs. The increasing emphasis on producing news and other media products that make

ordinary people's experiences a prime source of value is a welcome replacement to a public sphere denominated in terms imposed by elite bureaucrats. (2003: 155)

Critical investigative programmes such as *Jiaodian Fangtan* (Focus) on China's CCTV have widened the public debate, albeit within a framework set up by the state and the communist party (Li, 2002).

The tradition of telenovelas in Latin America has been to highlight socially relevant messages about health and hygiene, civic responsibility and gender and ethnic equality, weaving them into the storylines of these popular soap operas. In India the government has used 'social advertisements' on television to increase awareness of the environment and health. African road-shows of celebrities such as musicians Bono and Bob Geldof accompanied by television cameras may not have eradicated poverty but at least they have helped bring the issue of debt relief and scourge of the HIV/AIDS epidemic in Africa into the global consciousness. Feature films such as *Blood Diamond*, set in Sierra Leone, created popular awareness about the problems of diamond trade in Africa, while the *Constant Gardener* focused on the corruption of pharmaceutical conglomerates operating in Africa.

Edutainment

Television's potential for education has sadly been not fully harnessed, although a majority of its consumers belong to low education groups. John Lloyd has observed that 'in most countries, rich and sophisticated people are often mass media poor: they don't watch much TV. Most of the poor, and certainly the lesser educated... are mass media rich: they usually watch a lot of television. Conversely – a problem at the heart of our modern societies – the people who watch a lot of TV tend to be information poor, and the people who don't are often information rich' (Lloyd, 2004: 27). How can the power of the visual medium be used to enhance the learning experience? Neil Postman (1985) believed that the problem of television was epistemological in nature: it encouraged entertaining distractions rather than cerebral atonement. Making learning a leisure-time pursuit and 'fun' has led to the emergence of edutainment, 'a hybrid mix of education and entertainment that relies heavily on visual material, on narrative or game-like formats, and on more informal, less didactic styles of address' (Buckingham and Scanlon, 2005: 46).

Making education entertaining without sacrificing quality is rare: the US children's programme *Sesame Street* – produced by Children's Television Trust, a not-for-profit organization – and broadcast around the world, is one striking example of how this can be done. The 'entertainment-education paradigm' defined as 'the process of purposely designing and implementing a media message to both entertain and educate, in order to increase audience members' knowledge about an educational issue, create favourable attitudes, shift social norms and change overt behaviour' (Singhal and Rogers, 2004: 5).

The globalization of edutainment networks is exemplified by The History Channel, partly owned by Murdoch, which has expanded vastly across the globe, from 12 million subscribers in 1995 to 195 million in 2005, growing at an average rate of 32 per cent per year, reflecting the popularity of televised history. In the globalized television economy, documentary has become a transnational 'popular televisual commodity' through localization, exports and joint-ventures by such corporations as Discovery Network International and the National Geographic Channel, through a hybrid mixing of genres taken from conventional documentary, reality TV and docudramas to make it accessible to a heterogeneous global audience (Hogarth, 2006).

Historian Simon Schama wrote and presented the very successful big-budget BBC series, *The History of Britain*, while Niall Ferguson presented his history of the British Empire for Channel 4. In Britain, televising history created media celebrities of otherwise aloof academics and has had a major role in educating the general public. Historians such as A.J.P. Taylor and Kenneth Clark pioneered the presentation of history on television, especially the latter's epic series *Civilization* (shown in 1969 and rebroadcast in 23 countries) and, in a similar vein, Jacob Bronowski presented the great achievements of science and technology in *The Ascent of Man* (1973). Such programming was part of Reith's legacy. English philosopher Roger Scruton wrote about the Reithian BBC as being 'decorous, civilized, reserved, with a meticulous respect for truth, a consciousness of authority and an acknowledgement of standards'. Its freedom from advertising and all commercial pressures enabled it to offer to 'ordinary listeners (and subsequently viewers) not the things they wanted to hear or see, but the things that they ought to hear or see, on the understanding that, in a civilised society, these would be one and the same' (Scruton, 2000: 232).

Former US vice-president Al Gore's Oscar winning documentary about global warming, *An Inconvenient Truth*, released in 2006 to commercial and critical success, is a striking example of how serious scientific issues can be made accessible to a wide range of audiences. In the US, free copies of the documentary have been distributed among schools. Michael Moore's 2004 *Fahrenheit 9/11* (which earned $220 million – the highest for any documentary, according to the Internet Movie Data Base) or Morgan Spurlock's *Super Size Me* about the dangers of MacDonald fast-food, are other prominent examples of this. Robert Greenwald's *Outfoxed: Rupert Murdoch's War on Journalism*, exposing the right-wing bias of Fox News, was sold online as 'guerrilla' DVD, made on a shoestring budget and largely funded by campaigning organizations, such as Moveon.org, which screened the film at around 3,500 'house parties' across the US. Greenwald's *Iraq For Sale: The War Profiteers*, about the privatization of Iraq under US occupation, focused on those corporations which have benefited most from outsourcing of neo-liberal imperial adventures. *Enron: The Smartest Guys in the Room* as well as *The Corporation* are other key examples of documentaries exposing corporate corruption. *The Control Room*, an intimate portrait of Al-Jazeera during the 2003 Iraq invasion is another edutainment candidate. Other recent hits include Errol Morris' *The Fog of War*, a biography of Robert McNamara and the Antarctic docu-drama *March of the Penguins*. Many of these films have been released in theatres. Infotainment conglomerates have seen commercial potential in serious documentaries: *When the Levees Broke*, Spike Lee's four-hour documentary about New Orleans coping with the after effects of Hurricane Katrina, released in 2006 was first shown on HBO TV. *Iraq for Sale* and *Iraq in Fragments* also won critical acclaim and were screened in homes via DVDs and on-line downloads. Adam Curtis's award-winning *The Power of Nightmares*, a BBC three-part series, screened in 2004, about the 'war on terror' was also released in selected cinemas. The spate of such politically charged edutainment has been made possible with the advent of the digital revolution, enabling independent film makers to produce and distribute films within relatively small budgets. The growth of dedicated documentary channels has provided potential funding as well as distribution possibilities. There is also a growing audience interested in such critical examinations of contemporary issues, which feels let down by a commercially-oriented news industry: the percentage of Americans who say they regularly listen to National Public Radio has approximately doubled since 1994 (from 9 per cent to 17 per cent) (Project for Excellence in Journalism, 2006).

Global on-line education, too, has been mediatized, as Internet offers a new market for educational services internationally, via distance learning provided by multimedia universities which may become more powerful if and when education becomes a service industry under GATS. Already many universities, notably Britain's Open University, offer courses through the Internet. However, if opened to the market forces, a commercialized system of edutainment is likely to be privileged at the expense of more didactic traditional learning. Companies such as McGraw-Hill produce, through Cisco Systems Global Learning Network, course specific articles and websites for Personal Digital Assistants (PDAs). Professor Google and Dr Wikipedia have become indispensable tools for an increasing number of school and university students, prompting fears about plagiarism and intellectual laziness in an era when students can purchase made-to-order essays and other academic assignments over the Internet.

Is the unprecedented growth of infotainment outlets and their globalization leading to an information overload responsible for civic disengagement bordering on cynicism? Or on the contrary, is the Internet revitalizing and reinvigorating a diverse, deliberative global political discourse, engaging citizens at a transnational level to debate on issue of global significance? The globalization of news media has prompted scholars to extend the Habermasian idea of a public sphere into a global arena. The growth in transnational satellite news networks and on-line journalism have contributed to the creation of a global public sphere (Volkmer, 2003; McNair, 2006). With its very European roots, the concept of the public sphere has been expanded to include the world – in his later writings, Habermas has spoken of a globalized 'post-national' constellation world of numerous debating publics less constrained by nationalism (Habermas, 2001). Thomas Meyer has argued that party-based democracy is now changed into 'media democracy' (Meyer and Hinchman, 2002). With the growth of 'counter publics' (Asen and Brouwer, 2001) there is need to discuss the global public sphere within a pluralist perspective, notwithstanding the concerns about institutional power relations between different spheres (Sparks, 2001).

A global public sphere remains an abstract notion and for some an unrealisable one (Sparks, 1998). Even a pan-European public sphere in its infancy is fraught with difficulties, despite political and economic structures in place with a common currency and a semblance of common defence and foreign policies (Splichal, 2006). Studies show that in most EU countries preference for public television goes hand-in-hand with greater knowledge of EU political matters (Holtz-Bacha and Norris, 2001). A cross-national comparative content analysis of the coverage of European Union politics in British, Danish, Dutch, French, and German television news found that it was more prominent in public-broadcasting news programmes. Coverage of the EU itself was of limited visibility and without protagonists and the Europeanization of television news coverage is more an illusion than a reality (Peter and de Vreese, 2004). A meta-analysis of 17 studies on European media between 1994 and 2003, examining works in three major European languages – English, German and French – showed that EU topics accounted for 'an extremely small proportion of reporting in the particular national media. Compared with national protagonists, the players at EU level also only feature in minor roles' (Machill et al., 2006: 78).

Given the linguistic diversity of Europe – the continent has 34 official languages – a multi-language news network could be desirable, yet public-service

EuroNews, the only pan-European news channel to broadcast simultaneously in more than two languages, has hardly made a dent in news broadcasting on the continent or indeed internationally. That Britain is not part of this news-exchange programme is indicative of the British media's attitude towards Europe (though between 1997–2003 ITN had a 49 per cent managing stake in Euronews). The audience share of the pan-European culture channel ARTE, on air since 1992 via satellite and cable, a joint venture of ARD, ZDF, and the French ARTE Corporation, is minimal.

Dahlgren notes that the 'Internet extends and pluralizes the public sphere' (2005: 148) but it is less clear as to the extent to which it is enhancing democracy (Jenkins and Thornburn, 2003). What Dahlgren has called the 'journalism domain' within the net, is important for our discussion as 'the online journalism sector is a core element of the public sphere on the Internet' (Dahlgren, 2005: 153). Internet-based civic activist organizations such as Indymedia, it is claimed, are 'extending radical democratic practice' (Pickard, 2006: 334), and their citizen-generated news content is seen as a response to corporate media consolidation (Stengrim, 2005). Lance Bennett has argued that new technologies and anti-globalization movements have enabled what he calls 'lifestyle politics' which form part of a 'collective individualism' in which 'ideology, party loyalties, and elections are replaced with issue networks that offer more personal and often activist solutions to the problems' (Bennett, 2003b: 27). This kind of analysis is not atypical and emanates from a rather narrow, middle-class view of politics. Much more robust opposition is originating from quarters directly affected by neo-liberal imperialism, as Chomsky observes:

> The harmful effects of corporate globalization project have led to mass popular protest and activism in the South, later joined by major sectors of the rich industrial societies, hence becoming harder to ignore. For the first time, concrete alliances have been taking shape at the grassroots level. These are impressive developments, rich in opportunity. And they have had effects, in rhetorical and sometimes policy changes. (2003: 236)

Towards global public media

As this book has argued, market-led journalism is undermining public media internationally but in some quarters the demise of state-controlled media has been celebrated as a victory for freedom of expression and pluralism. It is certainly the case that the dynamism of the market has in many instances made for better television news, especially in countries where broadcasting was in the stranglehold of information bureaucracies, where audiences scarcely mattered and apathy and incompetence reigned. Among Western European nations, as state broadcasting monopolies ended, a perceptible shift in television news culture from public-service to profit-oriented programming was in evidence, as noted in Chapter 1. This shift raises a contradiction identified by Schiller: 'Publicly unaccountable media-cultural power today constitutes the ultimate Catch-22 situation. The public interest, locally and globally, demands honest messages and images. These, however, are dependent on private media providers, whose own interests are often incompatible with the public's' (Schiller, 1996: 126).

How is this public interest – with all its attendant ambiguities and contradictions (whose public; public or publics?) – to be protected and promoted? Beyond the infotainment spectacle and above the din of digital media cacophony, it is possible that there is an unmet global demand for what Baker called 'edification', which includes 'education, exposure to wisely selected information, or wise opinion and good argument' (2002: 12). Roger Silverstone's conception of a mediapolis – a moral space 'of connection and compassion', based on 'representational ethics', is a good starting point for a discussion of global public media. Silverstone defines the mediapolis as the 'mediated public space where contemporary political life increasingly finds its place, both at national and global levels, and where the materiality of the world is constructed through (principally) electronically communicated public speech and action' (Silverstone, 2007: 24).

Unlike Habermas' conception of the public sphere with its rational debate and argument – a singular and narrow kind of reason, the mediapolis, Silverstone notes, is more inclusive, 'because within it communication is multiple and multiply inflected: there is no rationality in an image, and no singular reason in a narrative. Both rhetoric and performance subvert the simple order of logic. The political, civic space of mediated representation, globally, nationally, locally, depends on both the capacity to encode and to decipher more complex sets of communications than mere reason enables' (ibid: 34).

Such an inclusive formulation may provide a positive dimension to the global infotainment sphere. Is there a role for journalism education in training journalists to treat serious issues with panache and attractive framing? In the United States, where the media are commodified to an advanced degree, as outlined in Chapters 1 and 2, the scrutiny of media is also one of the highest in the world, from blogs to advocacy groups and media monitoring organizations. In the absence of a public-service tradition in television news, coupled with a perceived erosion in the quality of civic communication and political participation, and declining news audiences in the early 1990s, some journalists and journalism scholars had proposed the idea of 'public journalism' (Rosen, 2001). The activities of such media reform and

Table 7.1 Most trusted global news brands

Company	*Country*	*%*
BBC	UK	48
CNN	US	44
Google	US	30
Yahoo!	US	28
Microsoft/MSN	US	27
Newsweek	US	25
Time	US	24
Al-Jazeera	Qatar	23

(Source: GlobeScan, 2007)

campaigning organizations as Media Channel (www.mediachannel.org) established in 2000 and Free Press (www.freepress.net) in operation since 2002, have provided an invaluable resource and advocacy for media reform in the US.

The London-based openDemocracy (www.openDemocracy.net) launched in 2001, has evolved from a fledging website to a global on-line magazine (Curran, 2003). It can be argued that there is an urgent need for a global media education and reform organization, embodying the growing sense of unease among a number of journalists, academics and activists for a public media, not constrained by governmental or corporate propaganda. Some have made the case for a greater degree of engagement from academia in political affairs in the wake of 9/11 and for progressive social change, utilizing their material and considerable intellectual resources (Jensen, 2004). James Curran has argued for the extension of the BBC- style public service to reinvent itself by developing specialised channels such as a European or a global film channel. The 'public service tradition,' he notes, 'cannot afford to be boxed into a one-nation tradition, allowing its market rivals to present themselves as the principal agents of globalism and pluralism' (Curran, 2002: 213).

In praise of public television

Despite the influence of infotainment, the BBC still ranks as the world's most trusted global news brand (see Table 7.1). According to a 2006 international opinion poll conducted in Britain, US, Brazil, Egypt, Germany, India, Indonesia, Nigeria, Russia and South Korea, more people trust the media than their governments, especially in developing countries. The poll for GlobeScan, in conjunction with the BBC and Reuters, as well as the

Media Centre, a non-profit think tank, found that media is trusted by an average of 61 per cent compared to 52 per cent for governments across the countries polled. In Nigeria, 88 per cent of those polled trusted the media, as against 34 per cent who had trust in their government.

Such trust in the media is rooted in its public role: a belief that the airwaves can be used to inform and enlighten, to raise the level of social and political conversation to achieve higher intellectual and aesthetic quality (Price and Raboy, 2001; Lowe and Per, 2005; Banerjee and Seneviratne, 2006). It is fashionable, not to say customary, in these post-modern times of reality television and populist scholarship to dismiss such arguments as elitist and even arrogant. Nicholas Garnham makes an important defence of high-brow programming in referring to the BBC's annual Reith Lectures, which he notes:

> ...supremely symbolize a vision of broadcasting as an 'intellectual' enterprise in the sense of recognising the social importance of broadcasting's pedagogic role. They grant an accredited intellectual largely unmediated access to the means of modern mass communication to talk to a general audience, using a classic mode of academic address, on an issue of contemporary intellectual importance. The test of worth, both of the speaker and of the subject, is not that of popularity, the normal currency of the mass media, but of peer recognition within the intellectual milieu itself, now largely concentrated within universities and specialized publishing. The value of thus allowing the general public to participate in the discourse of an intelligentsia, and by so doing legitimating that intelligentsia's role of national life and culture, is seen as self-evident. (2000: 87)

It may be instructive to note that private broadcasters have rarely ventured into such intellectual territory. The BBC has also excelled in producing internationally distributed quality documentary series: notably *The Second Russian Revolution* (1991); *The Death of Yugoslavia* (1995); *The People's Century* (1996–1997) and *The 50 Years War: Israel and the Arabs* (1998). These and other programmes enrich the public discourse about important international events. Public television has also been instrumental in covering sombre historical events: perhaps one of the most important such programme was *Shoah*, Claude Lanzmann's 9 1/2-hour documentary about the Holocaust, broadcast first in France in 1985. Innovative and intelligent television series which challenge conventional thinking – for example, Adam Curtis's *Pandora's Box* (1992); *The Century of the Self* (2002); *The Power of Nightmares* (2004) and *The Trap* (2007) – all broadcast on the BBC – are the kinds of programmes which nourish intellectual faculties and enhance citizenship – both nationally and globally.

Even in the US, where public broadcasters have an audience figure of less than two per cent, such pre-eminent programmes as the pre-school *Sesame*

Street, created by the Children's Television Workshop and shown repeatedly around the world, as well as the 11-part 1991 series, *The Civil War*, have been produced by the not-for-profit public broadcaster. In fiction programming too, the public-service broadcasters have an impeccable record: notable examples include: Edgar Reitz's outstanding trilogy of German history from the First World War to German reunification, *Heimat* (broadcast on German public service television in 1984), *Heimat 2* (1992) and *Heimat 3* (2004); Chandra Prakash Dwivedi's historical saga *Chanakya*, set in the third century BC, about the life and times of the intellectual force behind Mauryan Empire who was a scholar at the University of Takshashila (the ruins of which are a UNESCO World Heritage site in Pakistan;) shown on Doordarshan in 1990 and rebroadcast on the BBC; and the nine-part 'state of the nation' drama *Our Friends in the North*, broadcast on the BBC in 1996. It is unlikely that in the infotainment era of broadcasting commercial networks would invest in such high-quality programming. A global public media would ensure that the circulation of such televisual nourishment is as wide as possible. Some have argued for a balance between private and the public media interests, 'utilizing the market-oriented mechanisms of competition where appropriate but resorting without shame or hesitation to citizen-oriented public interest interventions when necessary' (Feintuck and Varney, 2006: 269).

Socially and politically significant stories such as minimum wage 'are hard to convert into riveting news stories because they take too long to set up, well over the 2-minute maximum imposed by broadcasters. In the time it would take for a reporter to explain the rationale for the different positions people take on the minimum wage, you could be well on your way to switching to Turner Movie Classics' (Kerbel, 2000: 79). One study of international factual programming on British terrestrial television found 'the continuing low proportion of "harder" factual international programmes: conflict and disaster; politics; development, environment and human rights, together accounted for 10 per cent of total output.' Among the mass channels, 'soft' programmes, such as on travel and wildlife dominated: accounting for as much as 90 per cent of factual international programming on ITV1, Britain's most popular channel, and 72 per cent on the BBC (Seymour and Barnett, 2006: 10).

In the past there seems to have been less of a contradiction between what was popular and what was good, with a tradition of progressive popular journalism by great writers. In France, journalists saw their role as men (usually) of letters, with many famous literary figures such as Balzac and Emile Zola using popular newspapers to reach a wider audience. In Britain, Charles Dickens worked as a journalist and read his novels at public performances (Campbell, 2000). One of India's best-known writers Premchand spent much of his life writing newspaper articles. Such pan-African magazines as *Drum* played an important role in creating a pan-African transnationalism (Odhiambo, 2006). From Gandhi to Sun Yat Sen; from Lenin to Mao and Marx to Mark Twain, political journalism has been at the heart of human progress and there is no reason to believe that in the era of multimedia, multimodal and multi-vocal communication it will cease to exist and exert its force on the public discourse. There are reasons for optimism: in the middle of the nineteenth century only about 10 ten per cent of the world's adults could read or write; by 2000, more than 80 per cent had minimal reading and writing skills, according to UNESCO: the global literacy rate increased from 56 per cent in 1950 to 82 per cent in 2000 and is expected to reach 86 per cent by 2015. Yet, more than 700 million people in the world were still illiterate (UNESCO, 2006b).

According to the BBC: 'Broadcasting can create collective value in the world precisely because it is a public good. But public goods like broadcasting or national defence or clean air are not handled well by conventional markets. To be delivered efficiently to those who would benefit from them – which, by definition, is the whole population – they require public intervention' (BBC, 2004b: 7). In the late 1990s a high-profile international gathering of intellectuals and policy-makers came up with the idea of 'global public goods' (Kaul et al., 1999). Their report divided the global commons into three classes: natural global commons, such as the ozone layer or climate stability; human-made global commons: scientific and practical knowledge, principles and norms, the world's common cultural heritage and transnational infrastructure such as the Internet; and global policy outcomes, which include peace, health and financial stability. Though it has potential for global public good, in its present form Infotainment would appear to be one of what has been called 'global public bads', such as disease, environmental degradation, violence. Global bads seem to be more visible than global goods, which may 'explain why policy agendas nationally and internationally are often focused just on reducing bads rather than producing goods' (ibid: 456).

Some have campaigned for the creation of a global 'creative commons', where access to knowledge is guaranteed free of cost (Lessig, 2004). UNESCO's 2005 'Convention on the protection and promotion of the diversity of cultural expressions', recommended the establishment of an International Fund for Cultural Diversity. However, how are these great initiatives to be funded? UNESCO's World Commission on Culture and Development recommended that the airwaves and space should be part of 'the global commons', a collective asset that belongs to all humankind and therefore regional or international commercial satellite interests which use the global commons, should pay 'property rights' and thus 'contribute to the financing of a more plural media system. New revenue could be invested in alternative programming for international distribution' (UNESCO, 1995: 278). The UNDP suggested a 'bit tax' on data sent through the Internet: a tax of one US cent on every 100 lengthy e-mails, according to its estimates, would generate more than $70 billion a year (UNDP, 1999). Global civil society groups have proposed the introduction of the so-called Tobin Tax, which would tax short-term speculation on currencies and would be administered by the UN.

On a more modest basis, a report on the coverage of the developing world in British television by Britain's Department for International Development (DFID) recommended that senior commissioning editors should create experimental strands for films with a global perspective and encourage training seminars and cross-channel initiatives, in which commissioners from various channels address a global agenda, as well as a bursary to enable British programme makers to work in the television or film industry of a developing country (DFID, 2000, 176). Versions of such bland media reform proposals, which do not in any way question or redress the power of global infotainment conglomerates, are replicated by media aid programmes of many other Western governments, as well as those of multilateral organizations and non-governmental sector, where professional seminarists jet around the world to teach and train journalists how to operate neo-liberal media. The remit of such training courses and workshops are such that the fundamental structural issues about media ownership and control are conveniently sidelined in favour of rather narrowly defined journalistic conventions. Ultimately, who owns the means of communication matters. As Baker has shown in the US context, media concentration can be harmful to a democracy which will thrive only within a more democratic distribution of communicative power within the public sphere and a structure that provides safeguards against the abuse of media power. He writes: 'This is a *democratic distribution principle* for communicative power – a claim that democracy implies as wide as practical a dispersal of power within public discourse. As applied to media ownership, this principle can be plausibly interpreted structurally as requiring, possibly among other things, a maximum dispersal of media ownership' (Baker, 2007: 7, italics in the original).

The changing global television newsscape

Media ownership may be concentrated but television news has certainly diversified. Al-Jazeera English boldly claims to be 'setting the global news agenda', an agenda which ostensibly aims to privilege news from the global South. The launch in 2007 of its documentary channel is likely to bring more Southern voices and views on to the global television and computer screens. Telesur – the first pan-Latin American public broadcaster, too, seems to have a similar news agenda, though more stridently anti-US. France 24 has helped circulate more news on Africa and the Arab world onto the global agenda, while, despite their emphasis on 'protocol news', Russia Today and CCTV-9 have provided alternative viewpoints on global issues. The growing number of joint ventures between transnational media corporations and Indian television news operations – Times Now and CNN-IBN – as indicated in Chapter 4, will also bring in these multiple perspectives into the emerging global infotainment sphere.

These developments could reduce the imbalances in global news flow, which were part of the UNESCO-sponsored debates and demand for the New World Information and Communication Order (NWICO) in the 1970s and 1980s (Boyd-Barrett and Thussu, 1992). In the new neo-liberal media environment the so-called 'development journalism', investigating the process behind a story rather than merely reporting the news event itself, has all but disappeared from the news as it is accurately perceived as not marketable. UNESCO-led initiatives to promote Southern regional exchange mechanisms, established in the late 1970s, largely failed to make much difference to global, or even regional news agendas. Such arrangements as the Non-aligned News Agencies Pool, designed to promote news among non-aligned countries, were perceived as lacking journalistic credibility, while an international news agency with an explicit Southern focus such as the Rome-based Inter Press Service (IPS) has not been able to make itself commercially viable and is dependent on funds from multilateral and UN organizations (Boyd-Barrett and Thussu, 1992; Thussu, 2000b).

Yet issues relating to development remain as pressing today as during the NWICO debates. 'In the face of avoidable violence, disease, inequality, oppression, poisoning and other global afflictions,' writes Gitlin, 'it makes sense to worry about the public cost of media bounty, to fear that it distracts from civic obligations, induces complacency and anaesthesia, and works to the advantage of the oligarchs' (Gitlin, 2002: 120). Does this anaesthesia and illusion of the contemporary infotainment world reflect the type of experience that was made famous by the 1998 Hollywood film *The Truman Show*, an allegory of false consciousness – where the hero does not realise he is the central character in a reality TV show? While the West wallows in consumerist fetishism, in the global South – at the receiving end of neo-liberal imperialism – the media multitude is creating new levels of awareness. Jon Snow, one of Britain's best-known broadcast journalists and anchor of Channel 4 News, notes the paradox: 'The North's media are providing a deft counterpoint to the terrorist endeavour by keeping our "developed" populations in ignorance of the world beyond Pop Idol, ER and EastEnders.

As our technological capacity to reach and inform grows, so our horizon shrinks to the stuff of soaps, sports and scandal. Our world is narrowing just as theirs is expanding. The cocktail is truly explosive' (Snow, 2004: 377). Away from news flashes, celebrity banter and reality television, the real world has witnessed the carnage of death and destruction, most notably in post-2003 Iraq, thus far the most serious adventure of neo-liberal imperialism. Besides the death of more than half a million people since the 2003 invasion, Iraq has plummeted from a commendable rank of 50 on the United Nations Human Development Index in 1990 to 126 in 2002, a slide unmatched by any other country; since then it does not even figure in the index; as the daily massacre of innocent Iraqis has been routinized to such an extent that it is not news anymore.

Television news has a strong performative component, as it draws from the conventions of the world of the moving image, which can evoke strong emotions and feelings, sometimes false, often fleeting. The 2003 German feature film *Goodbye Lenin*, a black comedy co-written and directed by Wolfgang Becker, very cleverly shows how moving pictures can fundamentally change their meanings when the voice-over is altered to suit a particular reading of an event – in this case the end of East Germany as a separate nation. This makes the problems of television news phenomenological. The image it projects does not necessarily conform with social reality. Globalization of a consumerist culture, based on individualism and crass commercialism is creating a 'global feel good factor' with little thought being given to its sustainability at a time of rapidly depleting global resources.

The future of the planet will be bleak if every citizen in China and India started copying the profligate consumerist American way of life, driving their own cars and consuming gallons of Coca Cola. The 2006 *Human Development Report* of the UN makes sobering reading: 2.6 billion people – half the developing world's population – do not have access to basic sanitation and 1.1 billion people do not have access to a minimal amount of clean water – about 5 litres a day – one tenth of the average daily amount used in rich countries to flush toilets: on average, people in Europe use more than 200 litres, and in the US more than 400 litres, of water every day. Every year some 1.8 million children die as a result of diarrhoea and other diseases caused by unclean water and poor sanitation (UNDP, 2006: 5–6). Juxtapose this against the annual spending on pets in the US, which in 2006 crossed $38 billion, more than the total cost of providing clean drinking water and basic sanitation for every citizen on the planet.

Water shortage and sanitation do not make marketable infotainment; pets do, they are cuddly and evoke touchy-feely reactions, and most important, look pretty on television. Global infotainment, a mask for neo-liberal imperialism led by the United States, is transforming television news around the world. One of the most striking examples of why the US model of television has become so popular perhaps belongs to the hugely successful and delightfully subversive cartoon series *The Simpsons*, produced by Fox Network and which regularly mocks the network and sometimes even its owner Rupert Murdoch. In one of its more interesting episodes, Lisa Simpson is tasked to produce a television news bulletin as part of her school project and, true to her character, she tries to put together a programme brimming with serious and earnest reports, to the chagrin of others working with her, including her teachers. Bart Simpson, her younger sibling and one who is characteristically down-to-earth and has mastered at an early age the essence of infotainment, comes up with a totally different set of stories – sleazy and sensational. The spectre of spectacles is a resounding success, not unlike global infotainment.

REFERENCES

Adorno, Theodor (1991) *The Cultural Industry: Selected Essays on Mass Culture.* London: Routledge.

AFP (2005) France enters 'battle of the images' with 'French CNN', Agence France-Presse: Paris, November 30.

Al-Rehaief, Mohammed Odeh and Coplon, Jeff (2003) *Because Each Life is Precious.* New York: HarperCollins.

Ali, Saadat (2006) It's Getting Crowded in Here, *BusinessWorld,* May 22.

Ali, Tariq (2003) *Bush in Babylon: The Recolonization of Iraq.* London: Verso.

Althusser, Louis (1971) *Lenin and Philosophy and Other Essays.* London: New Left Books.

Anderson, Bonnie (2004) *News Flash: Journalism, Infotainment and the Bottom-Line Business of Broadcast News.* New York: Jossey-Bass.

Andrews, David (2003) Sport and the Transnationalizing Media Corporation, *Journal of Media Economics,* 16(4): 235–252.

Andrejevic, Mark (2003) *Reality TV: The Work of Being Watched.* Maryland, MA: Rowman & Littlefield.

Aneesh, Aneesh (2006) *Virtual Migration: The Programming of Globalization.* Durham, NC: Duke University Press.

APTN website (2007) http://www.aptn.com

Arden, John Boghosian (2003) *America's Meltdown: The Lowest-Common-Denominator Society.* Westport, CT: Praeger/Greenwood.

Arnett, Peter (1994) *Live from the Battlefield.* London: Bloomsbury.

Arvidsson, Adam (2003) *Marketing Modernity: Italian Advertising from Fascism to Postmodernity.* New York: Routledge.

Asen, Robert and Brouwer, Daniel (eds) (2001) *Counterpublics and the State.* Albany, NY: State University Press of New York.

Atton, Chris (2005) *An Alternative Internet: Radical Media, Politics and Creativity.* Edinburgh: Edinburgh University Press.

Auletta, Ken (2003) *Backstory: Inside the Business of News.* New York: Penguin.

Ayish, Mohammed (2002) Political Communication on Arab World Television: Evolving Patterns, *Political Communication,* 19:137–154.

Bacevich, Andrew (2002) *American Empire: The Realities and Consequences of US Diplomacy.* Cambridge, MA: Harvard University Press.

Bagdikian, Ben (2004) *The New Media Monopoly,* seventh edition. Boston, MA: Beacon Press.

Bahal, Aniruddha (2006) The lens with bite, *Outlook,* 16 October.

Baker, C. Edwin (2002) *Media, Markets, and Democracy.* Cambridge: Cambridge University Press.
Baker, C. Edwin (2007) *Media Concentration and Democracy: Why Ownership Matters.* Cambridge: Cambridge University Press.
Bandurski, David (2006) China's Yellow Journalism, *Far Eastern Economic Review,* June.
Banerjee, Indrajit and Seneviratne, Kalinga (eds) (2006) *Public Service Broadcasting in the Age of Globalization.* Singapore: Asian Media Information and Communication Centre.
Bardhan, Pranab, Bowles, Samuel and Wallerstein, Michael (eds) (2006) *Globalization and Egalitarian Redistribution.* Princeton, NJ: Princeton University Press.
Barker, Chris (1997) *Global Television.* Oxford: Blackwell.
Barkin, Steve (2002) *American Television News: The Media Marketplace and the Public Interest.* New York: M.E. Sharpe.
Barnes, Sandra (2005) Global Flows: Terror, Oil, and Strategic Philanthropy, *African Studies Review,* 48(1): 1–22.
Baudrillard, Jean (1994) *The Illusion of the End.* Cambridge: Polity.
Baudrillard, Jean (1995) *The Gulf War Did Not Take Place.* Bloomington: Indiana University Press.
Baum, Matthew (2003) *Soft News Goes to War: Public Opinion and American Foreign Policy in the New Media Age.* Princeton, NJ: Princeton University Press.
Baum, Matthew (2005) Talking the vote: Why presidential candidates hit the talk show circuit, *American Journal of Political Science,* 49: 213–234.
Baumgartner, Jody and Morris, Jonathan (2006) *The Daily Show* Effect: Candidate Evaluations, Efficacy, and American Youth, *American Politics Research,* 34(3): 341–367.
Baym, Geoffrey (2005) *The Daily Show:* Discursive Integration and the Reinvention of Political Journalism, *Political Communication,* 22(3): 259–276.
Bazalgette, Peter (2005) *Billion Dollar Game.* London: Time Warner Books.
BBC (2003) War Spin, BBC 2, *Correspondent,* May 18.
BBC (2004a) *The Power of Nightmares,* BBC October 2, 20, 27 and November 3.
BBC (2004b) *Building Public Value: Renewing the BBC for a Digital World.* London: British Broadcasting Corporation.
Bek, Mine Gencel (2004) Tabloidization of News Media: An Analysis of Television News in Turkey, *European Journal of Communication,* 19(3): 371–386.
Bellos, Alex (2001) Real Life TV Drama Enthrals Brazil, the *Guardian,* August 31, p.13.
Bennett, Lance (2003a) *News: The Politics of Illusion,* fifth edition. New York: Addison Wesley Longman.
Bennett, Lance (2003b) New Media Power: the Internet and Global Activism, in Nick Couldry and James Curran (eds) *Contesting Media Power: Alternative Media in a Networked World.* Lanham, MA: Rowman & Littlefield. pp.
Bennett, Lance, Pickard, Victor, Iozzi, David, Schroeder Carl, Lagos, Taso and Caswell, Evans (2004) Managing the Public Sphere: Journalistic Construction of the Great Globalization Debate, *Journal of Communication,* 54(3): 437–455.
Bennett, Lance, Lawrence, Regina and Livingston, Steven (2006) None Dare Call It Torture: Indexing and the Limits of Press Independence in the Abu Ghraib Scandal, *Journal of Communication,* 56: 467–485.
Berger, Guy (2000) Grave New World? Democratic Journalism Enters the Global Twenty-first Century, *Journalism Studies* 1(1): 81–100.

Berlin, Isaiah (1969) *Four Essays on Liberty.* Oxford: Oxford University Press.
Bernhard, Nancy (1999) *US Television News and Cold War Propaganda 1947–1960.* Cambridge: Cambridge University Press.
Bernstein, Carl (1992) The Idiot Culture, *The New Republic,* June 8, 22–28.
Bernstein, Paula (2001) TV Veteran Takes First Steps to Revive CNN, *Variety,* July 1.
Berridge, Victoria (1978) Popular Sunday Papers and Mid-Victorian Society in G. Boyce, J. Curran and P. Wingate (eds) *Newspaper History from the Seventeenth Century to the Present Day.* London: Constable.
Betting, Ronald and Hall, Jeanne Lynn (2003) *Big Media, Big Money.* Lanham, MA: Rowman & Littlefield.
Bhatia, Michael (2005) Fighting Words: Naming Terrorists, Bandits, Rebels and Other Violent Actors, *Third World Quarterly,* 26(1): 5–22.
Biao, Xiang (2006) *Global 'Body Shopping': An Indian Labor System in the Information Technology Industry.* Princeton, NJ: Princeton University Press.
Bignell, Jonathan (2005) *Big Brother: Reality TV in the Twenty-first Century.* London: Palgrave.
Bishop, Ronald (2004) The Accidental Journalist: Shifting Professional Boundaries in the Wake of Leonardo DiCaprio's Interview with Former President Clinton, *Journalism Studies,* 5(1): 31–43.
Blinken, Antony (2002) Winning the War of Ideas, *The Washington Quarterly,* 25(2): 101–114.
Bloomberg website (2007) www.bloomberg.com
Blumler, Jay and Kavanagh, Dennis (1999) The Third Age of Political Communication: Influences and Features, *Political Communication,* 16: 209–230.
Bonnell, Victoria and Freidin, Gregory (1995) *Televorot* – the role of television coverage in Russia's August 1991 coup, in Nancy Condee (ed.) *Soviet Hieroglyphics: Visual Culture in Late-twentieth Century Russia.* Bloomington: Indiana University Press.
Boorstin, Daniel (1971 [1961]) *The Image: A Guide to Pseudo-events in America.* New York: Atheneum.
Born, Georgina (2004) *Uncertain Vision: Birt, Dyke and the Reinvention of the BBC.* London: Secker and Warburg.
Bose, Jaideep (2007) India Poised: Make 2007 the year of India. *Times of India,* January 1.
Bourdieu, Pierre (1998) *On Television and Journalism.* London: Pluto Press.
Boyd-Barrett, Oliver (1998) Media Imperialism Reformulated, in Daya Kishan Thussu (ed.) *Electronic Empires: Global Media and Local Resistance.* London: Arnold.
Boyd-Barrett, Oliver (2004) Understanding the Second Casualty, in Stuart Allan and Barbie Zelizer (eds) *Reporting War.* London: Routledge.
Boyd-Barrett, Oliver and Rantanen, Terhi (eds) (1998) *The Globalization of News.* London: Sage.
Boyd-Barrett, Oliver and Thussu, Daya Kishan (1992) *ContraFlow in Global News.* London: John Libbey/UNESCO.
Braman, Sandra (ed.) (2004) *The Emergent Global Information Policy Regime.* Basingstoke: Palgrave.
Braman, Sandra (2006) *Change of State: Information, Policy and Power.* New Haven, CT: Yale University Press.

Brantlinger, Patrick (1985) *Bread & Circuses: Theories of Mass Culture as Social Decay.* London: Cornell University Press.
Brants, Kees (1998) Who's Afraid of Infotainment?, *European Journal of Communication,* 13(3): 315–336.
Brenton, Sam and Cohen, Reuben (2003) *Shooting People: Adventures in Reality TV.* London: Verso.
Bresnahan, Rosalind (2003) The Media and the Neoliberal Transition in Chile Democratic Promise Unfulfilled, *Latin American Perspectives,* 30(6): 39–68.
Brown, Clyde, Waltzer, Herbert and Waltzer, Miriam (2001) Daring to Be Heard: Advertorials by Organized Interests on the Op-Ed Page of *The New York Times,* 1985–1998, *Political Communication,* 18: 23–50.
Bruce, Iain (2005) Venezuela sets up 'CNN rival', *BBC News,* 28 June.
Buckingham, David and Scanlon, Margaret (2005) Selling Learning: Towards a Political Economy of Edutainment Media, *Media, Culture & Society* 27(1): 41–58.
Burke, Jason (2004) *Al-Qaeda: The True Story of Radical Islam.* London: Penguin.
Burston, Jonathan (2003) War and the Entertainment Industries: New Research Priorities in an Era of Cyber-Patriotism, in Daya Kishan Thussu and Des Freedman (eds) *War and the Media: Reporting Conflict 24/7.* London: Sage.
Butcher, Melissa (2003) *Transnational Television, Cultural Identity and Change: When STAR Came to India.* New Delhi: Sage.
Calabrese, Andrew (2005a) The Trade in Television News, in Janet Wasko (ed.) *A Companion to Television.* Oxford: Blackwell.
Calabrese, Andrew (2005b) Casus Belli: US Media and the Justification of the Iraq War, *Television & New Media,* 6(2): 153–175.
Campbell, Kate (ed.) (2000) *Journalism, Literature and Modernity: From Hazlitt to Modernism.* Edinburgh: Edinburgh University Press.
Cappella, Joseph and Jamieson, Kathleen Hall (1997) *The Spiral of Cynicism: The Press and the Public Good.* New York: Oxford University Press.
Carey, James (1992) *The Intellectuals and the Masses.* London: Penguin.
Carey, James (1993) The Mass Media and Democracy: Between the Modern and Post-Modern, *Journal of International Affairs,* 47:1–21.
Carlin, Dan (2006) CNN, BBC, Al Jazeera ... and France 24?, *BusinessWeek,* December 4.
Carroll, Rory (2002) Newsnight Italian Style, the *Guardian,* February 25, Media section, p.6.
Castells, Manuel (2004) *The Information Age: Economy, Society and Culture,* vol. 2: *The Power of Identity,* second edition. Oxford: Blackwell.
Castells, Manuel, Qiu, Jack Linchuan, Fernandez-Ardevol, Mireia and Sey, Araba (2006) *Mobile Communication and Society: A Global Perspective.* New Haven, CT: Yale University Press.
Caves, Richard (2005) *Switching Channels: Organization and Change in TV Broadcasting.* Cambridge, MA: Harvard University Press.
Center for Media and Democracy (2006) *Fake TV News: Widespread and Undisclosed.* April 6, Center for Media and Democracy, Madison. Available at www.prwatch.org
Chakravartty, Paula and Sarikakis, Katharine (2006) *Media Policy and Globalization.* Edinburgh: Edinburgh University Press.
Chalaby, Jean (ed.) (2005) *Transnational Television Worldwide: Towards a New Media Order.* London: I. B. Tauris.

Chan, Joseph Man (2003) Administrative Boundaries and Media Marketization: A Comparative Analysis of the Newspaper, TV and Internet Markets in China, in C.C. Lee (ed.) *Chinese Media, Global Contexts.* London: Routledge. pp. 159–76

Channel 4 News (2005) Special report on Iraq by Dr Ali Fadhil, May 11.

Channel 4 TV (2002) 'The House of War', *True Stories.* London: Channel 4 Television, 4 July.

Channel 4 TV (2005) I'll Do Anything to Get on TV. April.

Chapman, Jane (2005) *Comparative Media History.* Oxford: Polity.

Chomsky, Noam (2003) *Hegemony or Survival: America's Quest for Global Dominance.* New York: Metropolitan Books.

Chrisafis, Angelique (2006) The News Through French Eyes: Chirac TV Takes on 'Anglo-Saxon Imperialism', the *Guardian,* December 6.

Cirincione, Joseph, Tuchman Mathews, Jessica and Perkovich, George, with Orton, Alexis (2004) *WMD in Iraq: Evidence and Implications.* Wasingdon: Carnegie Endowment for International Peace.

Clausen, Lisbeth (2004) Localizing the Global: 'Domestication' Processes in International News Production, *Media, Culture & Society,* 26(1): 25–44.

CNN website (2007) http://www.cnn.com.

Cohen, Eliot (2004) History and the Hyperpower, *Foreign Affairs,* 83(4): 49–63.

Cohen-Almagor, Raphael (2002) Responsibility and Ethics in the Canadian Media: Some Basic Concerns, *Journal of Mass Media Ethics,* 17(1): 35–52.

Collins, Scott (2004) *Crazy Like a Fox: The Inside Story of How Fox News Beat CNN.* New York: Portfolio.

Columbia Journalism Review (1998) The Erosion of Values: A Debate among Journalists over how to cope, *Columbia Journalism Review,* March/April, 44–47.

Connolly, Kate (2007) It's Only a Wargame! Arabs Reject US Army Bit-part, the *Guardian,* March 5, p.16.

Cooper, Nicola J. (2006) The French Foreign Legion: Forging Transnational Identities and Meanings, *French Cultural Studies,* 17(3): 269–284.

Cooper, Robert (2003) *The Breaking of Nations: Order and Chaos in the Twenty-First Century.* New York: Atlantic Books.

Corner, John (2002) Performing the Real: Documentary Diversions, *Television and New Media,* 3(3): 283–293.

Corner, John and Pels, Dick (eds) (2003) *Media and the Restyling of Politics: Consumerism, Celebrity and Cynicism.* London: Sage.

Cottle, Simon (2006) *Mediatized Conflict.* Maidenhead: Open University Press.

Council of Europe (2004) *Transnational Media Concentrations in Europe.* Report prepared for the Council of Europe Steering Committee on the Mass Media. Media Division, Directorate General of Human Rights: Strasbourg, November.

Crampton, Andrew and Power, Marcus (2005) Frames of Reference on the Geopolitical Stage: *Saving Private Ryan* and the Second World War/Second Gulf War Intertext, *Geopolitics,* 10(2): 244–265.

Crawley, Melissa (2006) *Mr Sorkin Goes to Washington: Shaping the President on Television's the 'West Wing'.* Jefferson, NC: McFarland & Company.

Credit Suisse (2006) *Opportunities for Hollywood in Bollywood: India Media and Entertainment Tour,* Equity Research December 1.

Croteau, David and Hynes, William (2005) *The Business of Media: Corporate Media and the Public Interest,* second edition. London: Sage.

Crumley, Bruce (2000) Full-Screen Press: French Television Program *Arrêt sur Images* Entertains Audiences by Taking the Media to Task, *Time,* December 4.
Culf, Andrew (1997) Here is the News: Read by Vic Reeves, the *Guardian,* July 22 p. 1.
Curran, James (2002) *Media and Power.* London: Routledge.
Curran, James (2003) Global Journalism: A Case Study of the Internet, in Nick Couldry and James Curran (eds) *Contesting Media Power: Alternative Media in a Networked World.* Lanham, MA: Rowman & Littlefield.
Curran, James (2004) The rise of the Westminster School, in Andrew Calabrese and Colin Sparks (eds) *Towards a Political Economy of Culture.* Lanham, MA: Rowman & Littlefield.
Curtis, Perry (2001) *Jack the Ripper and the London Press.* New Haven, CT: Yale University Press.
Daalder, Ivo and Goldgeier, James (2006) Global NATO, *Foreign Affairs,* September/October.
Dahlgren, Peter (2005) The Internet, Public Spheres, and Political Communication: Dispersion and Deliberation, *Political Communication,* 22:147–162.
Davis, Aeron (2002) *Public Relations Democracy: Public Relations, Politics and the Mass Media in Britain.* Manchester: Manchester University Press.
Dean, Jodi (2002) *Publicity's Secret: How Technoculture Capitalizes on Democracy.* Ithaca, NY: Cornell University Press.
DeBord, Guy (1977) *The Society of the Spectacle.* Detroit: Red and Black. First published in 1967 as *La societe du spetacle* by Buchet-Chastel, Paris.
Delli Carpini, Michael and Williams, Bruce (2001) Let us Infotain You: Politics in the New Media Environment, in W. Lance Bennett and Robert Entman (eds) *Mediated Politics: Communication in the Future of Democracy.* Cambridge: Cambridge University Press.
Der Derian, James (2001) *Virtuous War: Mapping the military-industrial-media entertainment network.* Boulder, CO: Westview.
Der Derian, James (2005) Imaging Terror: Logos, Pathos and Ethos, *Third World Quarterly,* 26(1): 23–37.
Desai, Meghnad (2006) *Rethinking Islamism: The Ideology of the New Terror.* London: I.B. Taurus.
Devine, Marie (2002) Case against Fortuyn Suspect Unfolds on Live TV, The *Independent,* August 10, p.10.
DFID (2000) *Viewing the World: A Study of British Television Coverage of Developing Countries.* London: The Department for International Development.
Dicken, Peter (1998) *Global Shift: Transforming the World Economy,* third edition, London: Sage.
Donnelly, Thomas; Kagan, Donald and Schmitt, Gary (2000) *Rebuilding America's Defenses.* Washington, DC: The Project for a New American Century.
Donovan, Robert and Scherer, Ray (1992) *Unsilent Revolution: Television News and American Public Life, 1948-1991.* New York: Cambridge University Press.
Dorner, Andreas (2001) *Politainment.* Frankfurt: Suhrkamp.
Dovey, Jon and Kennedy, Helen (2006) *Game Cultures: Computer Games as New Media.* Maidenhead: Open University Press.
Downie, Leonard and Kaiser, Robert (2002) *The News About the News: American Journalism in Peril.* New York: Knopf.
Downing, John (2001) *Radical Media: Rebellious Communication and Social Movements.* Thousand Oaks, CA: Sage.

Doyle, Gillian (2006) Financial News Journalism: A Post-Enron Analysis of Approaches Towards Economic and Financial News Production in the UK, *Journalism,* 7(4): 433–452.

Drezner, Daniel (2007) *All Politics is Global: Explaining International Regulatory Regimes.* Princeton, NJ: Princeton University Press.

Dutt, Barkha (2006) 24/7 Channels: India, in a Minute, *Outlook,* 16 October.

Ellul, Jacques (1965) *Propaganda: The Formation of Men's Attitudes. New York:* Knopf. Originally published in French as *Propagandes* in 1962.

Engel, Matthew (1996) *Tickle the Public: One Hundred Years of the Popular Press.* London: Gollancz.

Entman, Robert M. (1998) *Democracy Without Citizen: Media and the Decay of American Politics.* New York: Oxford University Press.

Entman, Robert (2003) *Projections of Power: Framing News, Public Opinion, and US Foreign Policy.* Chicago: University of Chicago Press.

Esser, Frank and Pfetsch, Barbara (eds) (2004) *Comparing Political Communication: Theories, Cases and Challenges.* Cambridge: Cambridge University Press.

Farnsworth, Stephen and Lichter, Robert (2006) *The Nightly News Nightmare Television's Coverage of US Presidential Elections, 1988–2004,* second edition. Lanham, MA: Rowman & Littlefield.

Feintuck, Mike and Varney, Mike (2006) *Media Regulation, Public Interest and the Law,* second edition. Edinburgh: Edinburgh University Press.

Fenton, Tom (2005) *Bad News: The Decline of Reporting, the Business of News, and the Danger to us All.* New York: HarperCollins.

Ferguson, Marjorie (1992) The Mythologies about Globalization, *European Journal of Communication,* (7): 69–93.

Ferguson, Niall (2004) *Colossus: The Price of America's Empire.* London: Penguin.

FICCI (2004) *The Indian Entertainment Industry: Emerging Trends and Opportunities.* Federation of Indian Chambers of Commerce and Industry in association with Mumbai: Ernst & Young.

FICCI (2007) *Indian Entertainement and Media Industry: a Growth Story Unfolds,* prepared by PricewaterhouseCoopers. Mumbai: Federation of Indian Chamber of Commerce and Industry.

Flournoy, Don and Stewart, Robert (1997) *CNN: Making News in the Global Market.* Luton: University of Luton Press.

Franklin, Bob (1997) *Newszak and News Media.* London: Arnold.

Franklin, Bob (2004) *Packaging Politics: Political Communication in Britain's Media Democracy,* second edition. London: Arnold.

Frau-Meigs, Divina (2006) *Big Brother* and Reality TV in Europe: Towards a Theory of Situated Acculturation by the Media, *European Journal of Communication,* 21(1): 33–56.

Freedman, Des (2006) Dynamics of Power in Contemporary Media Policy-making, *Media, Culture & Society,* 28(6): 907–923.

Freedman, Samuel (2002) A Cork Pops, People Duck and Israel Laughs, *The New York Times,* June 30.

Friedman, James (ed.) (2002) *Reality Squared: Televisual Discourse on the Real.* New Brunswick, NJ: Rutgers University Press.

Friedman, Paul (2003) The War on TV: A Missed Opportunity, *Columbia Journalism Review* 3: May/June. Available at: www.cjr.org

Friel, Howard and Falk, Richard (2004) *The Record of the Paper: How the* New York Times *Misreports US Foreign Policy.* London: Verso.

Fürsich, Elfriede (2003) Between Credibility and Commodification: Nonfiction Entertainment as a Global Media Genre, *International Journal of Cultural Studies*, 6(2): 131–153.
Galbraith, John Kenneth (2004) *The Economics of Innocent Fraud: Truth For Our Time*. New York: Houghton Mifflin.
Galperin, Hernan (2004) *New Television, Old Politics: The Transition to Digital TV in the United States and Britain*. Cambridge: Cambridge University Press.
Garcia Canclini, Nestor (2001) *Citizens and Consumers*. Minneapolis: University of Minnesota Press.
Garnham, Nicholas (1996) The Media and the Public Sphere, in Craig Calhoun (ed.) *Habermas and the Public Sphere*. Cambridge, MA: MIT Press.
Garnham, Nicholas (2000) *Emancipation, the Media and Modernity*. Oxford: Oxford University Press.
Geradin, Damien and Luff, David (eds) (2004) *The WTO and Global Convergence in Telecommunications and Audio-visual Services*. Cambridge: Cambridge University Press.
Gershon, Richard (1997) *The Transnational Media Corporation: Global Messages and Free Market Competition*. Mahwah, NJ: Lawrence Erlbaum.
Gershon, Richard (2005) The Transnationals: Media Corporations, International TV Trade and Entertainment Flows, in Anne Cooper-Chen (ed.) *Global Entertainment Media: Content, Audiences, Issues*. Mahwah, NJ: Lawrence Erlbaum.
Gibson, Owen (2005) Fans Mourn End of Ozzy's Family TV Triumph, the *Guardian*, April 18.
Ginsborg, Paul (2004) *Silvio Berlusconi: Television, Power, and Patrimony*. New York: Verso.
Gitlin, Todd (2002) *Media Unlimited: How the Torrents of Images and Sounds Overwhelms Our Lives*. New York: Metropolitan Books.
GlobeScan website (2007) http://www.globescan.com
Go, Julian (2007) Waves of Empire: US Hegemony and Imperialistic Activity from the Shores of Tripoli to Iraq, 1787–2003, *International Sociology*, 22(1): 5–40.
Goddard, Peter, Corner, John and Richardson, Kay (2001) The Formation of *World in Action:* A Case Study in the History of Current Affairs Journalism, *Journalism* 2(1): 73–90.
Gott, Richard (2006) *Hugo Châvez and the Bolivarian Revolution*. London: Verso.
Graber, Doris (1994) The Infotainment Quotient in Routine Television News: A Director's Perspective, *Discourse & Society*, 5(4): 483–508.
Greenslade, Roy (2003) Their Master's Voice, the *Guardian*, 17 February,Media section, pp.1–3.
Habermas, Jürgen (2001) *The Postnational Constellation: Political Essays*. Cambridge: Polity.
Hachten, William and Scotton, James (2006) *the World News Prism: Global Information in a Satellite Age*, seventh edition. Oxford: Blackwell.
Hackett, Robert and Carroll, William (2006) *Remaking Media: The Struggle to Democratize Public Communication*. New York: Routledge.
Hackett, Robert and Zhao, Yuezhi (eds) (2005) *Democratizing Global Media: One World Many Struggles*. Lanham: Rowman & Littlefield.
Hague, Rod and Uhm, Seung-Yong (2003) Online Groups and Offline Parties Korean Politics and the Internet, in Rachel Gibson, Paul Nixon and Stephen Ward (eds) *Political Parties and the Internet: Net Gain?* New York: Routledge.

Hallin, Daniel (2000) *La nota roja:* Popular Journalism and the Transition to Democracy in Mexico, in Colin Sparks and John Tulloch (eds) *Tabloid Tales: Global Debates over Media Standards.* New York: Routledge.
Hallin, Daniel and Mancini, Poulo (2004) *Comparing Media Systems.* Cambridge: Cambridge University Press.
Hamilton, James (2003) *All the News That's Fit to Sell: How the Market Transforms Information into News.* Princeton: Princeton University Press.
Hargreaves, Ian (2003) *Journalism: Truth or Dare.* Oxford: Oxford University Press.
Hargreaves, Ian and Thomas, James (2002) *New News, Old News.* London: Independent Television Commission and Broadcasting Standards Commission.
Hart, Peter and Naureckas, Jim (2002) Fox at the Front: Will Geraldo Set the Tone for Future War Coverage? *Extra!* January/February.
Hartley, John (1999) *Uses of Television.* London: Routledge.
Harvey, David (2003) *The New Imperialism.* Oxford: Oxford University Press.
Harvey, David (2007) Neoliberalism as Creative Destruction, *The Annals of the American Academy of Political and Social Science,* 610(1): 21–44.
Hendershot, Heather (2004) *Shaking the World for Jesus: Media and Conservative Evangelical Culture.* Chicago: University of Chicago Press.
Herman, Edward and McChesney, Robert (1997) *The Global Media: The New Missionaries of Corporate Capitalism.* London: Cassell.
Hickey, Neil (2002) Access Denied: The Pentagon's War Reporting Rules are the Toughest Ever, *Columbia Journalism Review,* January/February, http://www.cjr.org/year/02/1/index.asp
Hickman, Tom (1995) *What Did you do in the War, Auntie?: The BBC at war 1939–45.* London: BBC Books.
Hill, Annette (2005) *Reality TV: Audience and Popular Factual Television.* London: Routledge.
Hobsbawm, Eric (1968) *Industry and Empire: From 1750 to the Present Day.* Harmondsworth: Penguin.
Hodgson, Martin (2007) Iran Captives Disagree Over Cashing in on their Stories, the *Guardian,* April 9.
Hoffman, David (2002) Beyond Public Diplomacy, *Foreign Affairs,* 81(2).
Hoffmann, Hilmar (1996) *The Triumph of Propaganda: Film and National Socialism 1933–1945.* Oxford: Berghahm Books.
Hogarth, David (2006) *Realer Than Reel: Global Directions in Documentary.* Austin: University of Texas Press.
Hoggart, Richard (2004) *Mass Media in a Mass Society: Myth and Reality.* London: Continuum.
Holland, Patricia (2006) *The Angry Buzz: This Week and Current Affairs Television.* London: I.B. Tauris.
Holtz-Bacha, Christina and Norris, Pippa (2001) To Entertain, Inform, and Educate: Still the Role of Public Television, *Political Communication,* 18(2): 123–140.
Horrie, Chris and Nathan, Adam (1999) *Live TV: Telly Brats and Topless Darts.* London: Simon and Schuster.
Hoskins, Colin; McFyden, Stuart and Finn, Adam (2004) *Media Economics: Applying Economics to New and Traditional Media.* London: Sage.
Hoynes, William (2003) Branding Public Service: The 'New PBS' and the Privatization of Public Television, *Television & New Media,* 4(2): 117–130.
Hozic, Aida (1999) Uncle Sam goes to Siliwood: of Landscapes, Spielberg and Hegemony, *Review of International Political Economy,* 6(3): 289–312.

Hozic, Aida (2001) *Hollyworld: Space, Power, and Fantasy in the American Economy.* Ithaca, NY: Cornell University Press.
Humphreys, Peter (1994) *Media and Media Policy in Germany,* second edition. Oxford: Berg.
Humphrys, John (1999) *Devil's Advocate.* London: Hutchinson.
IBEF (2005) *Entertainment and Media.* New Delhi: India Brand Equity Foundation. Available at www.ibef.org
Ignatieff, Michael (2003) *Empire Lite, Nation-building in Bosnia, Kosovo and Afghanistan.* London: Vintage.
IHRC (2007) *The British Media and Muslim Representation: the Ideology of Demonisation.* London: Islamic Human Rights Commission.
Illouz, Eva (2003) *Oprah Winfrey and the Glamour of Misery: An Essay on Popular Culture.* New York: Columbia University Press.
ILO (2006) *Key Indicators of the Labour Market.* Geneva: International Labour Organization.
Indiantelevision.com (2006) China's Hu remains Who for Indian TV News Channels, December.
ITU (1999) *Trends in Telecommunication Reform.* Geneva: International Telecommunication Union.
James, Harold (2006) *The Roman Predicament: How the Rules of International Order Create the Politics of Empire.* Princeton: Princeton University Press.
Jameson, Fredric (1991) *Postmodernism, or, The Cultural Logic of Late Capitalism.* London: Verso.
Jamieson, Kathleen Hall (1992) *Dirty Politics,* Oxford: Oxford University Press.
Jeanneney, Jean-Noël (2006) *Google and the Myth of Universal Knowledge: A View from Europe.* Chicago: University of Chicago Press.
Jenkins, Henry and Thorburn, David (eds) (2003) *Democracy and New Media.* New Haven: Yale University Press.
Jensen, Klaus Bruhn (1987) News as Ideology: Economic Statistics and Political Ritual in Television Network News, *Journal of Communication,* 37(1): 8–27.
Jensen, Robert (2004) September 11 and the Failures of American Intellectuals, *Communication and Critical/Cultural Studies,* 1(1): 80–88.
Johnson, Chalmers (2004) *The Sorrows of Empire: Militarism, Secrecy, and the End of the Republic.* New York: Metropolitan Books.
Jones, John (ed.) (1999) *The Advertising Business: Operations, Creativity, Media Planning, Integrated Communications.* Thousand Oaks, CA: Sage.
Jones, Jeffrey (2004) *Entertaining Politics: New Political Television and Civic Culture.* Lanham: Rowman & Littlefield.
Joshel, Sandra, Malamud, Margaret and McGuire, Donald (eds) (2005) *Imperial Projections: Ancient Rome in Modern Popular Culture.* Baltimore MD: Johns Hopkins University Press.
Jowett, Garth and O'Donnell, Victoria (1999) *Propaganda and Persuasion,* third edition. Thousand Oaks, CA: Sage.
Kala, Arvind (2007) Reforms Reduce Crime, *The Times of India,* March 15.
Kaufman, Edward (2003) A Broadcasting Strategy to Win Media Wars, in Alexander Lennon, (ed.) *The Battle for Hearts and Minds: Using Soft Power to Undermine Terrorist Networks,* Cambridge MA: MIT Press.
Kaul, Inge, Grunberg, Isabelle and Stern, Marc (eds) (1999) *Global Public Goods: International Cooperation in the 21st Century.* New York: Oxford University Press.

Kellner, Douglas (2003) *Media Spectacle.* New York: Routledge.
Kerbel, Matthew (2000) *If it Bleeds, it Leads: An Anatomy of Television News.* Boulder, CO: Westview Press.
Kerbel, Matthew and Bloom, Joel David (2005) Blog for America and Civic Involvement, *International Journal of Press/Politics,* 10(4):3–27.
Keren, Michael (2006) *Blogosphere: The New Political Arena.* Lanham, MD: Lexington Books.
Khalaf, Roula and Ostrovsky, Arkady (2006) Russia Targets Middle East with Arabic TV Channel, *Financial Times,* June 15.
Khalidi, Rashid (2004) *Resurrecting Empire: Western Footprints and America's Perilous Path in the Middle East.* New York: Beacon Press.
Kilborn, Richard (2003) *Staging the Real: Factual TV Programming in the Age of Big Brother.* Manchester: Manchester University Press.
Kim, Eun-Gyoo and Hamilton, James (2006) Capitulation to Capital? OhmyNews as Alternative Media, *Media, Culture & Society,* 28(4): 541–560.
Kimmel, Daniel (2004) *The Fourth Network: How FOX Broke the Rules and Reinvented Television.* Chicago, IL: Ivan R. Dee.
Klvana, Tomás (2004) New Europe's Civil Society, Democracy and the Media Thirteen Years After: The Story of the Czech Republic, *Harvard Journal of Press/Politics,* 9(3):40–55.
Kohli, Vanita (2003a) *The Indian Media Business.* New Delhi: Sage.
Kohli, Vanita (2003b) The Making of India's Biggest Media House, *BusinessWorld,* June 2.
Kohli-Khandekar, Vanita (2006a) Beyond News, *BusinessWorld,* December 11.
Kohli-Khandekar, Vanita (2006b) Star India: Life Beyond Television, *BusinessWorld,* May 8.
Kohut, Andrew and Stokes, Bruce (2006) *America Against the World: How We Are Different and Why We Are Disliked.* New York: Henry Holt and Co.
Koppes, Clayton and Black, Gregory (1987) *Hollywood Goes to War: How Politics, Profits and Propaganda Shaped World War II Movies.* Berkeley: University of California Press.
Kovach, Bill and Rosenstiel, Tom (1999) *Warp Speed: America in the Age of Mixed Media.* New York: The Century Foundation Press.
Kristol, William and Kagan, Robert (2000) *Present Dangers: Crisis and Opportunity in American Foreign and Defense Policy.* San Francisco: Encounter Books.
Krugman, Paul (2003) Man on Horseback, *The New York Times,* May 6, P.31.
Kumar, Deepa (2004) War Propaganda and the (AB)uses of Women: Media Constructions of the Jessica Lynch Story, *Feminist Media Studies,* 4(3): 297–313.
Kung-Shankleman, Lucy (2000) *Inside the BBC and CNN: Managing Media Organizations.* London: Routledge.
Kunz, William (2006) *Culture Conglomerates: Consolidation in the Motion Picture and Television Industries.* Lanham, MA: Rowman & Littlefield.
Lal, Deepak (2006) *Reviving the Invisible Hand: The Case for Classical Liberalism in the Twenty-first Century.* Princeton, NJ: Princeton University Press.
Lal, Vinay (2002) *Empire of Knowledge: Culture and Plurality in the Global Economy.* London: Pluto.
Lall, Rashmee Roshan (2007) Shilpa Shetty Becomes Brand Ambassador for India, *The Times of India,* January 4.
Lash, Scott and Lury, Celia (2007) *Global Culture Industry.* Oxford: Polity.
Lasswell, Harold (1927) *Propaganda Technique in the World War.* New York: Knopf.

Lazarsfeld, Paul and Merton, Robert (1948) Mass communication, popular taste and organized social action, in L. Bryson (ed.) *The Communication of Ideas.* New York: Harper.
Lee, Chin-Chuan (2005) The Conception of Chinese Journalists – Ideological Convergence and Contestation, in Hugo de Burgh (ed.) *Making Journalists.* London: Routledge. pp. 107–126.
Lee, Chin-Chuan, He, Zhou and Huang, Yu (2006) 'Chinese Party Publicity Inc.' conglomerated: the case of the Shenzhen Press Group, *Media, Culture & Society,* 28(4): 581–602.
Lee, Paul (2005) Democracy, the Press and Civil Society in Hong Kong, in Angela Romano and Michael Bromley (eds) *Journalism and Democracy in Asia,* London: Routledge.
Lennon, Alexander (ed.) (2003) *The Battle for Hearts and Minds: Using Soft Power to Undermine Terrorist Networks.* New Haven, CT: MIT Press.
Lentini, Pete and Bakashmar, Muhammad (2007) Jihadist Beheading: A Convergence of Technology, Theology, and Teleology?, *Studies in Conflict and Terrorism,* 30(4): 303–325.
Lessig, Lawrence (2004) *Free Culture: How Big Media Uses Technology and the Law to Lock Down Culture and Control Creativity.* London: Penguin.
Lewis, Justin and Brookes, Rod (2004) How British Television News Represented the Case for War, in Stuart Allan and Barbie Zelizer (eds) *Reporting War.* London: Routledge.
Leys, Colin (2001) *Market-driven Politics: Neoliberal Democracy and the Public Interest.* London: Verso.
Li, X. (2002) 'Focus' *(Jiaodian Fangtan)* and the Changes in the Chinese Television Industry, *Journal of Contemporary China,*11(30): 17–34.
Lilleker, Darren (2006) *Key Concepts in Political Communication.* London: Sage.
Lindley, Richard (2002) *Panorama: 50 Years of Pride and Paranoia.* London: Politicos.
Lloyd, John (2004) *What the Media are Doing to Our Politics.* London: Constable.
Louw, Eric (2005) *The Media and Political Process.* London: Sage.
Lowe, Gregory and Per, Jauert (eds) (2005) *Cultural Dilemmas in Public Service Broadcasting.* Goteborg: Nordicom.
Luhmann, Niklas (2000) *The Reality of the Mass Media.* Cambridge: Polity.
Lumby, Catharine (2002) The Future of Journalism, in Stuart Cunningham and Graeme Turner (eds) *The Media and Communications in Australia.* Crows Nest, NSW: Allen & Unwin.
Lynch, Marc (2006) *Voices of the New Arab Public: Iraq, al-Jazeera, and Middle East Politics Today.* New York: Columbia University Press.
MacGregor, Brent (1997) *Live, Direct and Biased? Making Television News in the Satellite Age.* London: Arnold.
Machill, Marcel; Beiler, Markus and Fischer, Corinna (2006) Europe-Topics in Europe's Media: The Debate about the European Public Sphere: A Meta-Analysis of Media Content Analyses, *European Journal of Communication* 21(1): 57–88.
Majumdar, Boria (2006) Cricket as Entertainment, *The Times of India,* October 23.
Makri-Tsilipakou Marianthi (2004) The Reinforcement of Tellability in Greek Television Eyewitnessing, *Media, Culture & Society,* 26 (6): 841–859.
Mamdani, Mahmood (2004) *Good Muslim, Bad Muslim: America, the Cold War, and the Roots of Terror.* New York: Pantheon.
Mandelbaum, Michael (2006) *The Case for Goliath: How America Acts as the World's Government in the Twenty-First Century.* New York: PublicAffairs.

Marc, David and Thompson, Robert (2005) *Television in the Antenna Age: A Concise History.* Oxford: Blackwell.
Markovits, Andrei (2007) *Uncouth Nation: Why Europe Dislikes America.* Princeton, NJ: Princeton University Press.
Marr, Andrew (2004) *My Trade: A Short History of British Journalism.* London: Macmillan.
Marshall, Will (ed.) (2006) *With All Our Might: A Progressive Strategy for Defeating Jihadism and Defending Liberty.* Lahman, MA: Rowman & Littlefield.
Martin, Randy (2007) *An Empire of Indifference: American War and the Financial Logic of Risk Management.* Durham, NC: Duke University Press.
Marx, Karl (1970) *Selected Writings in Sociology and Social Philosophy.* Harmondsworth: Penguin.
Mathjis, Ernest, Jones, Janet, Hessells, Wouter and Verriest, Lara (eds) (2004) *Big Brother International: Critics, Format and Publics.* London: Wallflower Press.
Mattelart, Armand (1991) *Advertising International: The Privatisation of Public Space.* London: Routledge.
Mazzoleni, Gianpietro and Schulz, Winfried (1999) Mediatization of Politics: A Challenge for Democracy?, *Political Communication,* 16(3): 247–261.
Mccargo, Duncan (2002) *Media and Politics in Pacific Asia.* London: Routledge.
McCarthy, Anna (2001) *Ambient Television: Visual Culture and Public Space.* Durham, NC: Duke University Press.
McChesney, Robert (1993) *Telecommunications, Mass Media and Democracy: The Battle for the Control of US Broadcasting, 1928–1935.* New York: Oxford University Press.
McChesney, Robert (1999) *Rich Media, Poor Democracy: Communication Politics in Dubious Times.* Champaign, IL: University of Illinois Press.
McChesney, Robert (2004) *The Problem of the Media.* New York: Monthly Review Press.
McCormick, Barrett L. and Liu, Qing (2003) Globalization and the Chinese Media: Technologies, Content, Commerce and the Prospects for the Public Sphere, in Chin-Chuan Lee (ed.) *Chinese Media, Global Contexts.* New York: Routledge.
McKernan, Luke (2002) *Yesterday's News: the British Cinema Newsreel Reader.* London: British Universities' Film and Video Council.
McNair, Brian (2006) *Cultural Chaos: Journalism, News and Power in a Globalized World.* London: Routledge.
McPhail, Thomas (2006) *Global Communication: Theories, Stakeholders, and Trends,* second edition. Oxford: Blackwell.
Meehan, Eileen (2005) *Why TV is not our Fault: Television Programming, Viewers, and Who's Really in Control.* Lanham, MD: Rowman & Littlefield.
Mehta, Nalin (2006) Modi and the Camera: The Politics of Television in the 2002 Gujarat Riots, *South Asia: Journal of South Asian Studies,* 29(3): 395–414.
Meyer, Thomas and Hinchman, Lew (2002) *Media Democracy: How the Media Colonize Politics.* Oxford: Polity.
Mickiewicz, Ellen (2005) Excavating Concealed Tradeoffs: How Russians Watch the News, *Political Communication,* 22, 355–380.
Mindich, David (2005) *Tuned Out: Why Americans Under 40 Don't Follow the News.* New York: Oxford University Press.
Mishkin, Frederic (2006) *The Next Great Globalization: How Disadvantaged Nations Can Harness Their Financial Systems to Get Rich.* Princeton, NJ: Princeton University Press.

Moeller, Susan (2004) Media Coverage of Weapons of Mass Destruction. Report of the Center for International and Security Studies at Maryland. Available at http://www.cissm.umd.edu

Mooij, Marieke (1998) *Global Marketing and Advertising. Understanding Cultural Paradoxes.* London: Sage.

Moran, Albert (1998) *Copycat TV: Globalisation, Program Formats and Cultural Identity.* Luton: University of Luton Press.

Morris, Jonathan (2005) The Fox News Factor, *Harvard International Journal of Press/Politics,* 10(3):56–79.

Mott, Frank Luther (1962) *American Journalism: A History: 1690–1960,* third edition. New York: Macmillan.

Moy, Patricia, Xenos, Michael A. and Hess, Verena K. (2005) Communication and Citizenship: Mapping the Political Effects of Infotainment, *Mass Communication & Society,* 8(2): 111–31.

Naím, Moisés (2007) The YouTube Effect, *Foreign Policy,* January/February.

National Research Council (1996) *Modeling and Simulation: Linking Entertainment and Defense.* US National Research Council. Available at http://bob.nap.edu/html/modeling

Nederveen Pieterse, Jan (2004) *Globalization or Empire?* London: Routledge.

News Corporation (2007) *Imagining the Future...Today.* Annual Report 2006: New York: News Corporation.

Ninan, Sevanti (2004) When a Soldier Returns.... *The Hindu,* September 26.

Ninan, Sevanti (2005) Reality Unplugged, *The Hindu,* February 27.

Ninan, Sevanti (2006a) A Problem of Plenty, *The Hindu,* August 13.

Ninan, Sevanti (2006b) Changing News, *The Hindu,* October 29.

Ninan, Sevanti (2007) Battles Ahead, *The Hindu,* January 7.

Noam, Eli (2004) Will Internet TV be American, in Darcy Gerbarg, Jo Groebel, and Eli Noam (eds) *Internet Television.* Mahwah, NJ: Lawrence Erlbaum.

Norris, Pippa (2000) *A Virtuous Circle: Political Communications in Post-industrial Democracies.* Cambridge: Cambridge University Press.

Nye, Joseph (2004) *Power in the Global Information Age: From Realism to Globalization.* New York: Routledge.

Nye, Joseph (2007) Softly, Softly... in *Global Voice: Britain's Future in International Broadcasting.* London: Premium Publishing.

Odhiambo, Tom (2006) Inventing Africa in the Twentieth Century: Cultural Imagination, Politics and Transnationalism in *Drum Magazine, African Studies,* 65(2): 157–74.

Ofcom (2005) *Ofcom Review of Public Service Television Broadcasting Phase 3: Competition for Quality.* London: Office of Communications.

Ofcom (2006) *Ofcom Review of Media Ownership Rules 2006.* London: Office of Communications.

Ofcom (2007) *Public Service Broadcasting: Annual Report 2007.* London: Office of Communications.

Open Society Institute (2005) *Television across Europe: Regulation, Policy and Independence.* Budapest: Open Society Institute.

Oslund, Robert and Pelton, Joseph (eds) (2004) *Communications Satellites: Global Change Agents.* Mahwah, NJ: Lawrence Erlbaum.

Ó Tuathail, Gearóid (2005) The Frustrations of Geopolitics and the Pleasures of War: *Behind Enemy Lines* and American Geopolitical Culture, *Geopolitics,* 10(2): 356–77.

Outfoxed: Rupert Murdoch's War on Journalism (2004) directed and produced by Robert Greenwald. 77 minutes. Distributed by Robert Greenwald Productions. Contact: info@outfoxed.org

Padovani, Cinzia (2004) *A Fatal Attraction: Public Television and Politics in Italy.* Lanham, MA: Rowman & Littlefield.

Padovani, Cinzia and Tracey, Michael (2003) Report on the Conditions of Public Service Broadcasting, *Television & New Media,* 4(2): 131–153.

Page, Bruce (2003) *The Murdoch Archipelago.* New York: Simon & Schuster.

Page, David and Crawley, William (2001) *Satellites Over South Asia: Broadcasting, Culture and the Public Interest.* New Delhi: Sage.

Painter, James (2007) *The Boom in Counter-hegemonic News Channels: A Case Study of Telesur,* unpublished research paper. Oxford: Reuters Institute for the Study of Journalism.

Parks, Lisa (2005) *Cultures in Orbit: Satellites and the Televisual.* Durham, NC: Duke University Press.

Pasti, Svetlana (2005) Two Generations of Contemporary Russian Journalists, *European Journal of Communication,* 20(1): 89–115.

Patterson, Thomas (2000) *Doing Well and Doing good: How Soft News and Critical Journalism are Shrinking the News Audience and Weakening Democracy – and What News Outlets Can Do About It,* 1–28, Cambridge, MA: Joan Shorenstein Center on the Press, Politics, & Public Policy.

Patterson, Thomas (2002) *The Vanishing Voter: Public Involvement in an Age of Uncertainty.* New York: Knopf.

Perlmutter, David and Golan, Guy (2005) Counter-imaging: Myth-making and Americanization in Israeli Labor Party Campaign Ads, 2003, *Visual Communication,* 4, (3): 304–332.

Peter, Jochen and de Vreese, Claes (2004) In Search of Europe: A Cross-National Comparative Study of the European Union In National Television News, *The Harvard International Journal of Press/Politics,* 9(4): 3–24.

Peters, John Durham (2003) The Subtlety of Horkheimer and Adorno: Reading 'Culture Industry', in Elihu Katz, John Durham Peters, Tamar Liebes and Avril Orlof (eds) *Canonic Texts in Media Research.* Oxford: Polity.

Petersen, Neville (1993) *News not Views: The ABC, the Press and Politics, 1932–1947.* Sydney: Hale and Iremonger.

Peterson, Peter (2002) Public Diplomacy and the War on Terrorism, *Foreign Affairs,* September/October.

Peyser, Marc (2005) Fighting the Good Fight, *Newsweek,* July 25.

Pew Research Center (2005) *US Image Up Slightly, But Still Negative: American Character Gets Mixed Reviews.* Pew Global Attitudes Project, Washington: Pew Research Center for the People and the Press. Released 23 June 2005. Available at: http://pewglobal.org/reports/display.php?ReportID=247

Pew Research Center (2006) *Conflicting Views in a Divided World 2006: How Global Publics View: Muslim-Western Relations, Global Issues, US Role in the World, Asian Rivalries.* Washington: Pew Research Center for the People and the Press.

Pfetsch, Barbara (1996) Convergence Through Privatization? Changing Media Environments and Televised Politics in Germany, *European Journal of Communication,* 11(4): 427–451.

Phoenix Experience (2006) Phoenix Corporation in-house publication, Hong Kong.

Phoenix website: http: //www.phoenixtv.com

Picard, Robert (1989) *Media Economics.* Newbury Park, CA: Sage.

Pickard, Victor (2006) United yet Autonomous: Indymedia and the Struggle to Sustain a Radical Democratic Network, *Media, Culture & Society,* 28(3): 315–336.

Plasser, Fritz (2005) From Hard to Soft News Standards? How Political Journalists in Different Media Systems Evaluate the Shifting Quality of News, *Harvard International Journal of Press/Politics* 10(2): 47–68.

Plunkett, John (2003) *Queen Victoria, First Media Monarch.* Oxford: Oxford University Press.

Poniewozik, James and Cagle, Jess (2002) That's Militainment!, *Time,* March 4.

Posen, Barry (2003) Command of the Commons: The Military Foundation of US Hegemony, *International Security,* 28(1): 5–46.

Postman, Neil (1985) *Amusing Ourselves to Death: Public Discourse in the Age of Show Business.* New York: Viking.

Price, Monroe (1999) Satellite Broadcasting as Trade Routes in the Sky, *Public Culture,* 11(2): 69–85.

Price, Monroe and Raboy, Marc (eds) (2001) *Public Service Broadcasting in Transition: A Documentary Reader.* Brussels: European Institute for the Media.

Price, Monroe and Verhulst, Stefaan (eds) (1998) *Broadcasting Reform in India: A Case Study in the Uses of Comparative Media Law.* Oxford: Oxford University Press.

PricewaterhouseCoopers (2005) *Global Entertainment and Media Outlook: 2005–2009.* London: PricewaterhouseCoopers.

Priest, Dana (2003) *The Mission: Waging War and Keeping Peace with America's Military.* New York: W.W. Norton.

Prior, Markus (2003) Any Good News in Soft News? The Impact of Soft News Preference on Political Knowledge, *Political Communication,* 20(2): 149–171.

Project for Excellence in Journalism (1998) *Changing Definitions of News,* March 6. Available at: http://www.journalism.org/resources/research/reports/

Project for Excellence in Journalism (2003) 'Jessica Lynch: Media Myth-Making in the Iraq War'. Available at: http://www.journalism.org/resources/research/reports/war/postwar/lynch.asp

Project for Excellence in Journalism (2005) *The State of the News Media 2004: An Annual Report on American Journalism.* Available at: http://www.stateofthenews-media.org/narrative_overview_intro.asp?media

Project for Excellence in Journalism (2006) *The State of the News Media: An Annual Report on American Journalism, 2006.* Available at http://stateofthemedia.org/2006

Rai, Mugdha and Cottle, Simon (2007) Global Mediations: On the Changing Ecology of Satellite Television News, *Global Media and Communication,* 3(1): 51–78.

Rajan, Nalini (ed.) (2005) *Practising Journalism: Values, Constraints, Implications.* New Delhi: Sage.

Ram, Narasimha (1990) An Independent Press and Anti-Hunger Strategies: The Indian Experience, in Jean Dreze and Amartya Sen (eds) *The Political Economy of Hunger,* Vol. I. Oxford: Clarendon Press.

Ramesh, Randeep and Jha, Sanjay (2007) India's Newspaper War Hots Up With New Tabloid Hitting Capital's Streets, the *Guardian,* February 5, p. 24.

Rampton, Sheldon and Stauber, John (2004) *Weapons of Mass Deception.* New York: Penguin.

Rantanen, Terhi (2002) *The Global and the National: Media and Communication in Post-Communist Russia.* Lanham, MA: Rowman & Littlefield.
Raslan, Karim (2000) Celebrity Government: Entertainment and Free Media will Decide our Leaders, *Asiaweek*, 26(27), July 14.
Reith, John (1924) *Broadcast Over Britain.* London: Hodder and Stoughton.
Rendall, Steve and Broughel, Tara (2003) Amplifying Officials, Squelching Dissent. *Extra*! Available at www.fair.org/extra/0305/warstudy.html
Renou, Xavier (2005) Private Military Companies Against Development, *Oxford Development Studies,* 33(1):107–15.
Reuters TV website (2007) http://about.reuters.com/tv/tv/wns.htm
Reyntjens, Filip (2005) The Privatisation and Criminalisation of Public Space in the Geopolitics of the Great Lakes Region, *The Journal of Modern African Studies,* 43(4): 587–607.
Rieff, David (2005) *At the Point of a Gun: Democratic Dreams and Armed Intervention.* New York: Simon and Schuster.
Robb, David (2004) *Operation Hollywood: How the Pentagon Shapes and Censors the Movies.* Amherst, NY: Prometheus Books.
Robinson, Piers (2002) *The CNN Effect: The Myth of News, Foreign Policy and Intervention.* London: Routledge.
Robson, Mark (2004) The Baby Bomber, *Journal of Visual Culture,* 3(1): 63–76.
Rosen, Jay (2001) *What are Journalists for?* New Haven, CT: Yale University Press.
Rowe, David (1999) *Sports, Culture and the Media.* Buckingham: Open University Press.
Rydell, Robert and Kroes, Rob (2005) *Buffalo Bill in Bologna: The Americanization of the World, 1869–1922.* Chicago: University of Chicago Press.
Sabato, Larry, Stencel, Mark and Lichter, Robert (2001) *Peepshow: Media and Politics in an Age of Scandal.* Lanham, MA: Rowman & Littlefield.
Said, Edward (1993) *Culture and Imperialism.* London: Chatto and Windus.
Said, Edward (1997) *Covering Islam: How the Media and the Experts Determine How We See the Rest of the World,* second edition. New York: Vintage.
Sakr, Naomi (2001) *Satellite Realms: Transnational Television, Globalization and the Middle East.* London: I. B. Tauris.
Scheuer, Jeffrey (2001) *The Sound Bite Society: How Television Helps the Right and Hurts the Left.* New York: Routledge.
Schiller, Dan (1999) *Digital Capitalism: Networking the Global Market System.* Cambridge, MA: MIT Press.
Schiller, Herbert (1969) *Mass Communications and American Empire.* New York: Augustus M. Kelley.
Schiller, Herbert (1976) *Communication and Cultural Domination.* New York: International Arts and Sciences Press.
Schiller, Herbert (1996) *Information Inequality: The Deepening Social Crisis in America.* London: Routledge.
Schudson, Michael (1978) *Discovering the News: A Social History of American Newspapers.* New York: Harper.
Schudson, Michael (1996) *The Power of News.* Cambridge, MA: Harvard University Press.
Schulz, Winfried, Zeh, Reimar and Quiring, Oliver (2005) Voters in a Changing Media Environment: A Data-Based Retrospective on Consequences of Media Change in Germany, *European Journal of Communication,* 20(1): 55–88.
Satellite & Cable TV (2005) National News, *Satellite & Cable TV,* September. http://www.scatmag.com/

Scruton, Roger (2000) *England: an Elegy*. London: Chatto and Windus.
Seaton, Jean (2005) *Carnage and the Media: The Making and Breaking of News About Violence*. London: Allen Lane.
Seib, Philip (2004) *Beyond the Front Lines: How the News Media Cover a World Shaped by War*. London: Palgrave.
Sen, Amartya (2005) *The Argumentative Indian: Writings on Indian Culture, History and Identity*. London: Penguin.
Seymour, Emily and Barnett, Steven (2006) *Bringing the World to the UK: Factual International Programming on UK Public Service TV, 2005*. London: 3WE.
Shepard, Leslie (1973) *The History of Street Literature*. Newton Abbott: David and Charles.
Shoemaker, Pamela and Cohen, Akiba (2005) *News Around the World: Content, Practitioners, and the Public*. London: Routledge.
Silverstone, Roger (2007) *Media and Morality: On the Rise of the Mediapolis*. Cambridge: Polity.
Simpson, John (2002) *News From No Man's Land: Reporting the World*. London: Macmillan.
Singer, Peter (2003) *Corporate Warriors: The Rise of the Privatized Military Industry*. Ithaca, NY: Cornell University Press.
Singer, Peter (2005) Outsourcing War, *Foreign Affairs*, 84(2): 119–32.
Singhal, Arvind and Rogers, Everett (2004) The Status of Entertainment-Education Worldwide, in Arvind Singhal, Michael Cody, Everett Rogers and Miguel Sabido (eds) *Entertainment-Education and Social Change*. Mahwah, NJ: Lawrence Erlbaum.
Sinha, Meenakshi (2005) News Goes Crazy, *Times of India*, December 4.
SIPRI (2006) *SIPRI Yearbook 2006: Armaments, Disarmament and International Security*. Oxford: Oxford University Press.
Siwek, Stephen (2005) *Engines of growth: Economic contributions of the US intellectual property industries*, produced by Economists Incorporated and Commissioned by NBC Universal. http://www.nbcumv.com/corporate/Engines_of_Growth.pdf.
Sklair, Leslie (2002) *Globalization: Capitalism and its Alternatives*. Oxford: Oxford University Press.
Smith, Anthony (ed.) (1998) *Television: An International History*, second edition. Oxford: Oxford University Press.
Snow, Jon (2004) *Shooting History*. London: HarperCollins.
Soriano, César and Oldenburg, Ann (2005) With America at War, Hollywood Follows, *USA Today*, February 7.
Sparks, Colin (1998) Is There a Global Public Sphere?, in Daya Kishan Thussu (ed.) *Electronic Empires: Global Media and Local Resistance*. London: Arnold.
Sparks, Colin (2000) Introduction: The Panic over Tabloid News, in Colin Sparks and John Tulloch (eds) *Tabloid Tales: Global Debates over Media Standards*. Lahman, MA: Rowman & Littlefield.
Sparks, Colin (2001) The Internet and the Global Public Sphere, in Lance Bennett and Robert Entman (eds) *Mediated Politics: Communication in the Future of Democracy*. Cambridge: Cambridge University Press.
Spigel, Lynn and Olsson, Jan (eds) (2004) *Television After TV: Essays on a Medium in Transition*. Durham: Duke University Press.
Splichal, Slavko (2006) In Search of a Strong European Public Sphere: Some Critical Observations on Conceptualizations of Publicness and the (European) Public Sphere, *Media, Culture & Society*, 28(5): 695–714.

Sreedharan, Sujatha (2007) News channels go the whole 22 yards, Indiantelevision.com, Special Report. Available at: http://us.indiantelevision.com/special/y2k7/specialreport_news%20channels%20cricket.php

Stahl, Roger (2006) Have You Played the War on Terror?, *Critical Studies in Media Communication*, 23(2): 112–130.

Star website (2007) www.Startv.com

Steemers, Janet (2004) *Selling Television: British Television in the Global Marketplace*. London: BFI.

Stengrim, Laura (2005) Negotiating Postmodern Democracy, Political Activism, and Knowledge Production: Indymedia's Grassroots and e-Savvy Answer to Media Oligopoly, *Communication and Critical/Cultural Studies*, 2(4): 281–304.

Stephens, Mitchell (1998) *The Rise of the Image the Fall of the Word*. Oxford: Oxford University Press.

Stiglitz, Joseph (2002) *Globalization and its Discontents*. London: Penguin.

Subramanian, Nirupama (2006) Stirring the *Hudood* pot, *The Hindu*, June 27.

Sunstein, Cass (2002) *Republic.Com*, second edition. Princeton, NJ: Princeton University Press.

Sussman, Gerald (2005) *Global Electioneering: Campaign Consulting, Communications, and Corporate Financing*. Lanham, MA: Rowman & Littlefield.

Sussman, Gerald and Galizio, Lawrence (2003) The Global Reproduction of American Politics, *Political Communication*, 20: 309–328.

Syvertsen, Trine (2003) Challenges to Public Television in the Era of Convergence and Commercialization, *Television & New Media*, 4(2): 155–175.

Taylor, Philip (2003) *Munitions of the Mind: A History of Propaganda From the Ancient World to the Present Era*, third edition. Manchester: Manchester University Press.

Television Business International (2006) Getting the AFP Mix Right, October 1.

Thaler, Paul (1997) *The Spectacle: Media and the Making of the O.J. Simpson Story*. Westport, CT: Praeger.

The Economist (1998) Wheel of Fortune: A Survey of Technology and Entertainment, November 21.

The *Guardian* (2003) Television Agendas Shape Images of War. March 27.

The Hindu (2007) The Manufacture of Dissent, *The Hindu*, editorial, January 30.

The History Channel (2004) Hollywood and the Pentagon, *The History Channel*, June 19.

Thomas, Amos Owen (2005) *Imagi-nations and Borderless Television: Media, Culture and Politics Across Asia*. New Delhi: Sage.

Thornton, Bridget, Walters, Brit and Rouse, Lori, (2005) *Corporate Media is Corporate America: Big Media Interlocks with Corporate America and Broadcast News Media Ownership Empires*. Project Censored Report.

Thussu, Daya Kishan (ed.) (1998) *Electronic Empires: Global Media and Local Resistance*. London: Arnold.

Thussu, Daya Kishan (2000a) Legitimizing 'Humanitarian Intervention'? CNN, NATO and the Kosovo Crisis, *European Journal of Communication*, 15(3): 345–361.

Thussu, Daya Kishan (2000b) Development News vs. Globalised Infotainment, in Anandam Kavoori and Abbas Malek (eds) *The Global Dynamics of News: Studies in International News Coverage and News Agendas*. Toronto: Ablex.

Thussu, Daya Kishan (2002) Privatizing Intelsat: Implications for the Global South, in Marc Raboy (ed.) *Global Media Policy in the New Millennium*. Luton: University of Luton Press.

Thussu, Daya Kishan (2003) Live TV and Bloodless Deaths: War, Infotainment and 24/7 news, in Daya Kishan Thussu and Des Freedman (eds) *War and the Media: Reporting Conflict 24/7*. London: Sage.
Thussu, Daya Kishan (2004) Media Plenty and the Poverty of News, in Annabelle Sreberny and Chris Paterson (eds) *International News in the Twenty-first Century*. Luton: University of Luton Press.
Thussu, Daya Kishan (2005a) The Transnationalization of Television: The Indian Experience, in Jean Chalaby (ed.) *Transnational Television Worldwide: Towards a New Media Order*. London: I. B. Tauris.
Thussu, Daya Kishan (2005b) Selling Neo-imperialism, Television and US Public Diplomacy, in James Curran and Michael Gurevitch (eds) *Mass Media and Society*, fourth edition. London: Arnold.
Thussu, Daya Kishan (2006a) *International Communication: Continuity and Change*, second edition, London: Hodder Arnold.
Thussu, Daya Kishan (2006b) Televising the 'War on Terrorism': The Myths of Morality, in Anandam Kavoori and Todd Fraley (eds) *Media, Terrorism, Theory: A Reader*. Lanham, MA: Rowman & Littlefield.
Thussu, Daya Kishan (2007a) Mapping Global Media Flow and Contra-Flow, in Daya Kishan Thussu (ed.) *Media on the Move: Global Flow and Contra-Flow*. London: Routledge.
Thussu, Daya Kishan (2007b) The 'Murdochization' of News? The Case of Star TV in India, *Media, Culture & Society*, 29(3): 593–611.
Torcal, Mariano and Montero, José Ramón (eds) (2006) *Political Disaffection in Contemporary Democracies: Social Capital, Institutions, and Politics*. New York: Routledge.
Townsend, Mark (2005) Fury at Security Firm's 'Shoot for Fun' memo, *Observer*, April 3.
Tracey, Michael (1998) *The Decline and Fall of Public Service Broadcasting*. Oxford: Oxford University Press.
Tremlett, Giles (2002) Pop Idol Mania Grips Spanish Politicians, the *Guardian*, February 14, p. 15.
Tunstall, Jeremy and Machin, David (1999) *The Anglo-American Media Connection*. Oxford: Oxford University Press.
Turner, Graeme (2005) *Ending the Affair: The Decline of Television Current Affairs in Australia*. Sydney: University of New South Wales Press.
Turner, Graeme (2006) 'Celetoids', Reality TV and the 'Demotic Turn', *International Journal of Cultural Studies*, 9(2): 153–65.
UNCTAD (2005) *Information Economy Report 2005: E-commerce and Development*. Geneva: United Nations Conference on Trade and Development.
UNDP (1999) *Human Development Report 1999: Globalization with a Human Face*. United Nations Development Programme, Oxford: Oxford University Press.
UNDP (2003) *Human Development Report 2003: Millennium Development Goals: A Compact Among Nations to End Human Poverty*. United Nations Development Programme. Oxford: Oxford University Press.
UNDP (2006) *Human Development Report 2006: Beyond Scarcity: Power, Poverty and the Global Water Crisis*. United Nations Development Programme. New York: Palgrave Macmillan.
UNESCO (1995) *Our Creative Diversity: Report of the World Commission on Culture* and *Development*. Paris: United Nations Educational, Scientific and Cultural Organization.

UNESCO (2005) *International Flows of Selected Cultural Goods and Services 1994–2003.* UNESCO Institute for Statistics, Paris: United Nations Educational, Scientific and Cultural Organization.
UNESCO (2006a) *What is Public Service Broadcasting?* Paris: United Nations Educational, Scientific and Cultural Organization. http://portal.unesco.org/ci/en/ev.php
UNESCO (2006b) *Education for All – Global Monitoring Report 2006.* Paris: United Nations Educational, Scientific and Cultural Organization.
Ungar, Sanford (2005) Pitch Imperfect, *Foreign Affairs,* May/June.
US Government (2002a) *Marrying the Mission to the Market. Strategic Plan, 2002–2007.* Broadcasting Board of Governors. Available at: http://www.bbg.gov/bbg_plan.cfm
US Government (2002b) Annual Report to the President and the Congress by Donald H. Rumsfeld, Secretary of Defence. Available at: http://www.defenselink.mil/execsec/adr2002/index.htm
US Government (2003) US Secretary of State Colin Powell addresses the UN Security Council, 6 February. Available at: www.whitehouse.gov/news/releases/2003/02/20030205-1.html
US Government (2004a) The 9/11 Commission Recommendations on Public Diplomacy: Defending Ideals and Defining the Message. Patricia S. Harrison, Assistant Secretary of State for Educational and Cultural Affairs. Statement Before the House Committee on Government Reform: Subcommittee on National Security, Emerging Threats, and International Relations, Washington, DC August 23, 2004. Available at: http://exchanges.state.gov/news/2004/082304.htm
US Government (2004b) *The 9/11 Commission Report: Final Report of the National Commission on Terrorist Attacks Upon United States.* Available at http://www.9-11commission.gov/report/911Report.pdf
US Government (2005a) *US International Services: Cross-border Trade in 2004.* Washington: US Bureau of Economic Analysis.
US Government (2005b) President Sworn-in to Second Term. Washington: the White House. Available at: http://www.whitehouse.gov/news/releases/2005/01/20050120-1.html
US Government (2007a) *Supporting Human Rights and Democracy: The US Record 2006.* Washington: Department of State. Available at: http://www.state.gov/g/drl/rls/77771.htm
US Government (2007b) *Public Diplomacy and Public Affairs Strategic Goal 11: Public Diplomacy and Public Affairs Increase Understanding For American Values, Policies, and Initiatives to Create a Receptive International Environment.* Department of State and US Agency for International Development FY 2007 Joint Performance Summary. Available at: http://www.state.gov/documents/organization/59181.pdf.
US Government (2007c) *Executives develop eleven ways that business can help with US Public Diplomacy,* US Department of State, Office of Public Diplomacy and Public Affairs. February. Available at: http://www.state.gov/documents/organization/80924.pdf
Utley, Garrick (1997) The Shrinking of Foreign News: From Broadcast to Narrowcast, *Foreign Affairs,* 76(2): 2–10.
Utley, Garrick (2000) *You Should Have Been Here Yesterday: A Life in Television News.* New York: Public Affairs.

Valladão, Alfredo G.A. (2006) Democratic Hegemony and American Hegemony, *Cambridge Review of International Affairs*, 19(2).
van Zoonen, Liesbet (2004) *Entertaining the Citizen: When Politics and Popular Culture Converge*. Lanham, MA: Rowman & Littlefield.
Vasudev, Shefalee (2005) Idiot Sheets? *Outlook*, October 17.
Verghese, George (ed.) (2003) *Breaking the Big Story: Great Moments in Indian Journalism*. New Delhi: Penguin.
Vernini, James (2005) War Games, the *Guardian*. April 19, p. 6.
Vettehen, Paul Hendriks; Nuijten, Koos and Beentjes, Johannes W.J. (2006) Sensationalism in Dutch Current Affairs Programmes 1992–2001, *European Journal of Communication*, 21(2): 227–37.
Vogel, Harold (2004) *Entertainment Industry Economics: a Guide for Financial Analysis*, sixth edition. Cambridge: Cambridge University Press.
Volkmer, Ingrid (1999) *News in the Global Sphere: A Study of CNN and its Impact on Global Communications*. Luton: University of Luton Press.
Volkmer, Ingrid (2003) The Global Network Society and the Global Public Sphere, *Development*, 46(1): 9–16.
Watts, Jonathan (2004) Taiwan Voters Demand Proof of Shooting, the *Guardian*. March 22.
Weber, Cynthia (2006) *Imagining America at War: Morality, Politics, and Film*. London: Routledge.
Wiener, Joel (ed.) (1988) *Papers for the Millions: The New Journalism in Britain 1850–1914*. New York: Greenwood.
Wolff, Michael (2003) You Know Less than When You Arrived, the *Guardian*, March 31, Media section, pp. 1–3.
Woodward, Gary (2006) *Center Stage: Media and the Performance of American Politics*. Lanham, MA: Rowman & Littlefield.
World Bank (1998) *Knowledge for Development: World Development Report 1998–1999*. Washington, DC: World Bank Publications.
Wright, Bradford (2001) *Comic Book Nation: The Transformation of Youth Culture in America*. Baltimore, MD: Johns Hopkins University Press.
WTO (1998) *Annual Report 1998*. Geneva: World Trade Organization.
York, Geoffrey (2000) It's the Truth: Nude News Heat up Moscow TV, *The Globe and Mail*, October 2.
Zaller, John (2003) A New Standard of News Quality: Burglar Alarms for the Monitorial Citizen, *Political Communication*, 20(2): 109–30.
Zassoursky, Ivan (2005) *Media and Power in Post-Soviet Russia*. Armonk, NY: M.E. Sharpe.

INDEX